HUMAN ORGANIZATIONS
AND SOCIAL THEORY

Human Organizations and Social Theory

Pragmatism, Pluralism, and Adaptation

MURRAY J. LEAF

UNIVERSITY OF ILLINOIS PRESS

URBANA AND CHICAGO

Library of Congress Cataloging-in-Publication Data

Leaf, Murray J.
Human organizations and social theory : pragmatism, pluralism, and
adaptation / Murray J. Leaf. — Cloth ed.
p.   cm.
Includes bibliographical references and index.
ISBN 978-0-252-03424-4 (cloth : alk. paper)
1. Social structure.   2. Organization.   I. Title.
HM706.L43   2009
302.3'5—dc22   2008045153

Physical Processing

Order Type: **NTAS**

Sel ID/Seq No:

222985

/72

Cust/Add: 240950003/02   **TGHR-T**   **UNIVERSITY OF GUELPH**

Cust PO No.   **91420**   Cust Ord Date: **23-Dec-2009**

BBS Order No: **C1201980**   Ln: **21**   Del: **1**   BBS Ord Date: **23-Dec-2009**

0252034244-40918427   Sales Qty: **1**   #Vols: **001**

(9780252034244)

Human organizations and social theory

Subtitle: **pragmatism, pluralism, and adaptation**   Stmt of Resp: **Murray J. Leaf.**

HARDBACK   Pub Year: **2009**   Vol No.:   Edition:

Leaf, Murray J.   Ser. Title:

University of Illinois Press

Acc Mat:

Profiled   **Barcode Label Applicati**   **Affix Security Device US**   **Spine Label Protector U!**

Tech   **Base Charge Processing**   **Security Device US**

Services: **Circulation (Author/Titl**   **Affix Spine Label US**

       Property Stamp US   **Spine Label BBS US**

                                 Location: **BLKW-1609**

                                 Department: **BLKW-1609**

Fund: **BLKW-1609**

Stock Category: Collection:

Class #:   Cutter:

Order Line Notes:

Notes to Vendor:

351208

Blackwell Book Services

CONTENTS

Preface   vii

Acknowledgments   ix

Note on Orthography   xi

Figures   xiii

Tables   xiv

Introduction   1

1. Empirical Starting Points   15

2. Skepticism, Pragmatism, and Kant   39

3. New Tools   67

4. Social Idea Systems   82

5. Technical Information Systems   134

6. Organizations   140

7. Groups and Institutions   175

8. Adaptation   195

9. Conclusion   211

Notes   221

Bibliography   225

Index   237

PREFACE

My purpose is to present a new kind of social theory. The center of the theory is a new view of social organization: what its parts are, how they are combined, and how it all is related to behavior. With it, our previous preoccupation with society or culture as underlying realities that organizations merely manifest turns inside out. They are seen as projections of the organization process, not underlying causes. Phenomena and epiphenoma change places. Where everything important seemed hidden, now we see the importance of what is observed.

The analysis applies to organizations of all kinds: kinship as well as government, "ours" as well as "theirs," traditional as well as modern, face-to-face as well as global, those normally dealt with by anthropologists as well as those normally dealt with in the other social sciences. It also applies to the sciences and social sciences themselves.

During the last twenty years, self-labeled proponents of postmodernism and interpretivism have made their careers by conspicuously rejecting the very possibility of an ethnological science. Even before this, however, a far more corrosive attack originated not from these declared enemies of empiricism but rather from those who represented themselves as its friends, primarily proponents of positivistic metatheory and related views. It is in positivist pseudoscience that the postmodernist misrepresentations actually originate, and it is the confusion and misdirection that positivism has generated that lends them plausibility. What I am arguing for here is neither positivism nor postmodernism; it is radical empiricism.

There are several good general counter-critiques of the interpretivist and postmodernist arguments, including J. Tim O'Meara's article "Anthropology as Empirical Science" (1989), Paul Gross and Norman Levitt's *Higher Superstition* (1994), Lawrence Kuznar's *Reclaiming a Scientific Anthropology* (1997), James Lett's *Science, Reason, and Anthropology* (1997), and Ian Hacking's *The Social Construction of What?* (1999). Yet there is still no comparable critique of positivism and its allies. I will therefore provide one, but my main purpose is to present the theory that positivism has heretofore prevented us from developing.

Positivism begins with philosophical dogma. Empirical theory begins and ends with observables. In human social organizations around the world, three observations stand out uniformly and stubbornly. First, no society ever has just one organization or structure. The innumerable efforts to justify the idea of a unitary social organization, social structure, or culture that occupied the better part of the last century consistently failed. All societies, regardless of scale, are pluralistic. The real problem is not to show how everything is really unified but rather to show how the evident pluralism is maintained.

The second recurrent observation is that such organizations do not control us. We use them to try to control each other, with varying success. Nor do organizations or societies simply evolve as though on their own. People use them to accomplish common purposes, also with varying success, and the outcome is a societal adaptation, which also may be variably successful. The archaeological record is paved with the bones of organizational failures.

The third recurrent observation is that organizations are purposive constructions of their members. They consist of an orderly set of indigenous ideas and resources in use, and the use is future-oriented. The fact that the concept of purpose has proved to be so troublesome up to now should not deter us. There is a way to handle it, and it rests on recognizing that it is not we as analysts but rather those who actually construct the organizations who have to say what these organizational purposes are. What we need to do is elicit them without prejudging them.

Rigorous empiricism, relativism, and pluralism are hallmarks of the line of social theory associated with Kantian skepticism in Europe and pragmatism in America, not exclusively but importantly. Both of these traditions are constructivist. They include analyses of the social construction of the self, of interaction, of language acquisition, of cognitive development, of government, and of law and legal processes, inter alia. They have also been enormously successful in the area of public policy. What has been lacking is a consistent and comprehensive constructionist analysis of organization as such, and without this there is no center to pull the rest together. We will fill this gap.

ACKNOWLEDGMENTS

I first thank the villagers of Sidhpur Kalan, Punjab, India. I especially thank Netar Singh and the other members of the family of Inder Singh as well as Naranjan Singh and the family of Bhaktavar Singh. Also in India, I continue to be indebted to M. S. Gill, who was the district commissioner of Ambala when I first began fieldwork and who has continued to be a friend and adviser. S. S. Sodhi, former justice of the Punjab High Court and chief justice of the Allahabad High Court, has provided influential guidance in Indian law, the common law tradition generally, and the need to recognize legal theory as social theory.

Two other crucial debts are to Dwight Read and Michael Fischer. My ongoing conversations and collaboration with Read for the last thirty-five years and Fischer for the last fifteen or so years are reflected in the overall structure of the theory, the central place given to the notion of instantiation, and the basic parallelism that I am arguing for regarding formal analysis, computer simulation, and experimental demonstration. This is exemplified by my incorporation of Read and Fischer's computerization of Read's algebraic analysis of kinship terminologies but is by no means limited to it.

Other colleagues whose ideas and conversations are reflected in these pages in ways beyond what I can acknowledge in endnotes include John Adams, Nathan Berg, Anthony Champagne, David Channell, Ted Harpham, Alfonso Morales, David French, Harold Garfinkel, Nicholas S. Hopkins, David Kronenfeld, Kris Lehman, Anne Mayhew, Fred Plog, Walter C. Neale, Kim Romney, David Schneider, Milton Singer, Roy Wagner, and Douglas White.

Figure 10 has been previously published in "The Message Is the Medium: Language, Culture and Informatics," in *Mathematical Modeling and Anthropology: Its Rationale, Past Successes and Future Directions,* published as a special issue of *Cybernetics and Systems: An International Journal* 36(8) (2005): 903–17, edited by Dwight Read and published by Taylor and Francis. Figure 21, the general model of social process, was first presented in "Cultural Systems and Organizational Processes: Observations on the Conference Papers" in the same volume.

Alfonso Morales and Nathan Berg have read and commented extensively on earlier versions of the manuscript, as have Lawrence Kuznar and Martin

Ottenheimer on the penultimate version. Michelina Leaf, my wife, has provided patient editorial attention. And finally, I gratefully acknowledge support from the Cecil H. Green Distinguished Chair in Academic Leadership, at the University of Texas, Dallas.

NOTE ON ORTHOGRAPHY

For South Asian Indo-European languages transliterated into Roman characters, the letters generally have the values they do in English with the following exceptions.

Consonants

The letter "c" is always pronounced as the "tch" in pitcher.

The letter "z" may be pronounced either as the initial continuant in "zero" or "jeer." The difference is not phonemic.

Stops with a following "h" are aspirated. These may occur in initial as well as other positions. The combination "ch" is phonemically different from "c" and is pronounced as the "ch" in "check."

Capitalization of "R," "T," "Th," "D," and "Dh" is used to indicate retroflex continuants and stops. Retroflex continuants and stops are made with the underside of the tip of the tongue against the alveolar ridge. The initial stop in *Taia* (father's elder brother) contrasts with that in *tawa* (a skillet).

Vowels

The letter "a" is as the vowel in "but."

The letter "ā" is as the vowel in "ball."

The letter "i" is as the vowel in "bit."

The letter "ī" is as the "ee" in "beet."

The letter "u" is as the vowel in "pull."

The letter "ū" is as the "ui" in "juice."

South Asian writing systems lack the difference between uppercase and lowercase. Therefore, there are no conventions concerning capitalization. I have capitalized South Asian personal names and a few proper nouns such as Guru Granth Sahib when this usage is established in South Asian English but have otherwise transliterated the indigenous orthography letter for letter. South Asian letters represent syllables. Syllables are understood to consist of a stop or continuant plus an "a" unless the "a" is replaced by another vowel. Therefore, words that end in stops (rather than vowels) are commonly transliterated with a final "a," as in *vedanta*. This final "a" is not pronounced. Other vowels in final position are pronounced.

FIGURES

Figure 1.   Core kinship positions   92
Figure 2.   American kinship positions   93
Figure 3.   Punjabi kinship positions   94
Figure 4.   Fully simplified American kinship   97
Figure 5.   American kinship map regenerated by KAES   98
Figure 6.   KAES structural simplification of English   99
Figure 7.   KAES structural simplification of Punjabi   100
Figure 8.   Farmer's cost record, India   119
Figure 9.   The faction idea system   126
Figure 10.   The communication cycle   132
Figure 11.   The logic of occupational choice   165
Figure 12.   *Meli* networks, three families   169
Figure 13.   Pajek party network   170
Figure 14.   Village party network by cases   171
Figure 15.   Bride and groom before the Guru Granth Sahib   181
Figure 16.   Circumambulating the Guru Granth Sahib   183
Figure 17.   Display of the gifts to the bride   184
Figure 18.   Arrival of bride's *nana*   186
Figure 19.   Arrival of the groom's *brāt*   188
Figure 20.   Inverse *fahu* and warfare (Small 1999)   209
Figure 21.   The social process   211

TABLES

Table 1.   Cayley table for simplified Punjabi base algebra   101
Table 2.   Cayley table with siblings and reciprocals   102
Table 3.   Market prices, Eastern Maharashtra, 1987–88   122
Table 4.   Medium-scale farm, Pus Project, India   151
Table 5.   Diet Budget Projection for Bojala Village, Maharashtra, 1987   159
Table 6.   Pus income projection, 1987   161

HUMAN ORGANIZATIONS AND SOCIAL THEORY

Introduction

A new kind of social theory is emerging in anthropology. It is in every respect a new paradigm in Thomas Kuhn's sense, comparable to the Copernican revolution in physics (1962, 43). Leaving behind empirically ungrounded divisions, this social theory is cultural as well as social, cognitive as well as structural, theoretical as well as applied. It is focused on values as well as rules, cosmology and folklore as well as material culture and ecology, formal analysis of cultural ideas as well as the dynamics of human evolution. It recognizes the social construction of reality, but it also recognizes that such constructions are intellectually compelling and adaptively efficacious, as real as you and me, life and death. What allows all these threads to be brought together is its method. It is radically empirical. To those who say that this cannot be done and it will not work, we say it has been done and it does work.

There has been a long debate between those who think that empirical theory must arise from fact and those who think that there is no fact unless we first have a metatheory and a theory that say what a fact can be. Sometime in the early 1950s, positivistic and allied versions of the theory-first view became a kind of orthodoxy.

There is much confusion about positivism in anthropology. Murray Wax's (1997) article exemplifies it; Paul Roscoe's (1995) survey of criticisms documents it. Wax contrasts positivism to dialectic as opposed views of historical causality within a stream of Hegelian thought primarily concerned with religion and says that within this argument the positivists claimed to draw their ideas of causality from the natural sciences. All this is true and certainly relevant to understanding their original orientation and motivation. But he fails to describe the ways in which their view of the natural sciences was fundamentally wrong, factually and epistemologically, and this is where the influence of positivism has been strongest.

Similarly, Roscoe describes the many contradictory ways that positivism has been represented in order to suggest that it is nothing more than a kind of all-purpose boogeyman, a name with no particular meaning. To some extent it has now become so. But we have to ask where the fogginess comes from, and the answer is that it comes from positivism itself.

Positivism is not an anthropological fiction but a philosophical movement. Its philosophical identity and character are clear, and it is this clear sense that I am concerned with. Positivism began with August Comte; he named it and defined it. It was a comprehensive scheme for reordering society as a new version of what he believed medieval Catholicism had been (1851, 1854). Its aim was to produce a new universal Western empire with France as its natural center, sociology (another term he coined) as its theory of government, a positivist council as its ruling body to which all heads of industry would be subordinated, and the Religion of Humanity as its state religion.

Comte was self-consciously within the socialist tradition initiated by St. Simon. Comte's aim was to provide a totalitarian solution to the social disorder he saw as arising from the industrial revolution and the rising tide of republicanism. John Stuart Mill (1865) treated positivism as a movement that Comte was only taking part in, sanitized it, and anglicized it. Herbert Spencer joined it with his version (1862). None of these were experimental scientists, and none understood experimental science; their arguments were popular politics and pseudoscience.

Comte, Mill, and Spencer differ in details but agree on certain simple fundamentals. The first is that they assume that there is one encompassing answer for all questions, and that answer is deterministic. The second is their imagery. Order is represented by hierarchy: the ideal state is singular and ruled by an elite, religion and science are deductive, and their own schemes similarly purport to follow from first principles. Justifying this imagery is a cluster of supposedly a priori and universal dichotomies revolving around the distinction between subjective and objective: subjective versus objective truths; subjectivity versus objectivity as forces, things, or processes; subjectivity as mental versus objective as physical; and theory (mental constructs) versus fact (physical realities). Another cluster involves the difference between appearance and reality. Appearances are pluralistic and many-sided; reality must be consistent and follow from first principles. Appearances are that freedom is desirable; in reality without central control there are disorder and danger. Appearance is that science is built on facts; in reality there are no facts except when theory lets us recognize them. Finally, and supporting this, one of the central theses of both Comte and Mill was that what science shows is that there is actually no inherent order in nature. Ideas such as cause are metaphysical, and metaphysics is an obsolete kind of thinking left over from the previous stage of society. In the new age of positivism, we know that there are only laws, defined by Comte as "invariable relations of succession and resemblance" (1896, 28) and by Mill as associations among sensations. Order only comes about by the imposition of subjectivity, quite literally mind over matter in deliberate opposition to Marx's matter over mind.

After Comte and Mill, positivism acquired academic proponents and apologists in two main forms. One concentrated on the analysis and reform of society: French and German sociology as represented by Durkheim and Weber, respectively. The other concentrated on the reconstruction of science: the Vienna Circle positivists and subsequent unity of science movement. Spencer's social Darwinism was separate, although the two sets of arguments seem to have often resonated with the same people. All quickly gave rise to schools of opponents who were in fact imitators and acolytes offering arguments of the same sort but different in the details of their premises.

Roscoe points out that there was virtually no use of the term "positivism" in anthropology until 1971 and infers from this that positivistic influence cannot go back before then. This is not so. The influence began much earlier, but its proponents recognized that the leading scientific thinkers of their time rejected positivism as pseudoscience and would have none of it. Real scientists were experimentalists. Early anthropologists with backgrounds in the physical sciences, such as Franz Boas and Bronislaw Malinowksi, understood what this meant even though they ultimately were not successful in applying this understanding in a way that could make it stick. This is an understanding we need to restore.

Positivism was first connected to the idea of culture in Edward Tylor's *Primitive Culture* (1889). Tylor does not identify himself as a positivist or use the term "positivism," but he explicitly accepts Comte's conception of history as explanation (1889, i, 19) and describes Comte's "fetishism" as the forerunner of his own "animism" (1889, i, 144). Tylor's definition of culture as that "whole which includes knowledge, belief, art, morals, law, custom, and any other capabilities and habits acquired by man as a member of society" (1889, i, 1) is Comte's totalistic, deterministic conception of society with the hierarchy flattened, consistent with Comte's own view of social evolution. Tylor's equation of scientific explanation with rejecting "the popular notion of human free will" (1889, 3) corresponds to Comte's social determinism, and Tylor's argument that objectivity requires imposing his own interpretations of cultural ideas in place of the interpretations of those whose ideas they are corresponds to Comte's argument for science as the imposition of subjectivity.

Tylor was popularized in America by Alfred Kroeber, Robert Lowie, and others who joined Clark Wissler at the American Museum of Natural History in the 1920s in arguing for diffusionism. Lowie's *The History of Ethnological Theory* (1937) made Tylor a founding figure of ethnology as a whole, offered his definition as *the* definition of culture, celebrated his social determinism, and included a paean to Ernst Mach, the recognized icon of the logical positivists of the Vienna Circle, all still without actually using the term "positivism." Kroeber's description of culture as the superorganic added the imagery of Emile Durkheim and Spencer.

In Britain (Tylor notwithstanding) and France, the more usual focus of positivist theory and metatheory was not culture but society, drawing on French sociology. This was the thrust of Radcliffe-Brown's (1952) argument for anthropology as comparative sociology in contrast to Bronislaw Malinowski's functionalism whose roots were in Wundt's experimental psychology. Others drew on Marcel Mauss, Lucien Lévy-Bruhl, Max Weber, Georg Simmel, and the Logical Positivists.

The positivism that shaped the social science of the 1950s was a hodgepodge from all these sources. The central claim was that we could develop a science if we would agree on (the positivist view of) what theory was, develop a theory on this basis, and then apply and test it. Many such theories were proposed.

But this is not actually the way science develops, and the result was that by the 1980s anthropology was in crisis, in Kuhn's sense. The postmodernist critiques recognized it but also perpetuated it. Agreeing with the positivists that science requires imposing conceptions of objectivity and that such conceptions are inherently arbitrary and further agreeing that the opposite of objectivity is subjectivity, the postmodernist counterargument has been that positivist theory is subjectivity in disguise. What we are really about is imposing alternative subjectivities, usually construed as part of a Western or imperialistic hegemonic enterprise of one kind or another (Comaroff and Comaroff 1991; reviewed by Switzer 1998).

The new paradigm I am speaking for is empiricism first of all. It is a return to experimentalism, only this time we actually follow where it leads us. It leads to a new and much more differentiated view of the social and cultural phenomena and processes that have been blurred together and distorted by the positivist impositions, which in turn leads to a new view of the relations among all the social and behavioral sciences.

My central focus is on the way organizations are constructed by their participants conceptually and in action. In addition, however, I want to describe the power of computer simulations to make the inner order of this constructive process demonstrable outside of the field situation in which it is initially encountered and delineated. This is a new possibility, just taking shape, and it greatly increases our ability to distinguish theory that is firmly grounded in observation from theory that is not.

Participant Observation

The primary method of scientific ethnology is participant observation in the sense first developed by Malinowski (1922, 1926). Although this is now a commonly used phrase with many meanings, Malinowski's version had a specific theoretical basis in Wundt's philosophically informed psychological experimentalism and *Volkerpsychologie* and William James's related functional psychology in which experiment and introspection were mutually supportive rather than mutually exclusive (Boring 1950, 322ff.; Leaf 1979, 128–30).

The usual view of the field situation in Malinowski's time was as a place where observations and materials were collected for later analysis in the laboratory back home, at the university or museum. For Malinowski, however, it is where the primary analysis is carried out. The field is the laboratory. This primary analysis involves devising a series of experimental methods that let the analyst observe the social process of interest by reproducing it around them. The first experiments provide initial understandings that we test by further experiments until we are able to construct the same social relations or positions for ourselves and achieve de facto recognition from those in the community[1] that we have done so. In my own view, the aim is to "go native" but to do so consciously and self-consciously so that we understand and can describe the process.

Of course I am not saying that this is what all anthropologists mean by participant observation. My own first field study, in Punjab, had been explicitly planned to last twenty-four months. I arrived in India in May 1964. The research proposal called for drafting my dissertation in the field and going over it with the villagers. The aim was to be sure that the analysis was in their terms, not in alien terms. My prediction was that their response would be that it was "what everybody knows" but that they would also regard it as complete and accurate. It would not be offensive, odd, alien, or even particularly interesting.

At the end of about twenty months I received an urgent-sounding letter from David Schneider, my dissertation chair, saying that I should return to the United States immediately. Since there had just been a brief war between India and Pakistan, it seemed possible that he knew of some danger from sources unavailable to me that he did not want to describe. But I was not finished. Although all the component analyses had been done publicly and checked openly, the final synthesis had not. So I rushed to finish the draft, reading out only the key parts and what I thought might be questionable to two different groups, and was able to come back about two months earlier than planned.

Upon my return, I immediately handed Schneider the draft, which was in three bound copies. He seemed surprised but did not explain why he had told me to come back so urgently. So I asked. His response was, "We thought you were going native." Evidently, the overriding assumption was that I was either one of them or one of us, and *they are not* anthropologists. The fact that I had plainly said in advance what I would do by way of experimentally testing the conclusions of my analysis and was actually doing what I had said was evidently not salient by comparison.

Schneider's assumption persists. James Clifford, for example, describes participant observation this way:

> Participant observation obliges its practitioners to experience, at a bodily as well as an intellectual level, the vicissitudes of translation. It requires arduous language learning, some degree of direct involvement and conversation, and

often a derangement of personal and cultural expectations. There is, of course, a myth of fieldwork. The actual experience, hedged around with contingencies, rarely lives up to the ideal—but as a means for producing knowledge from an intense, intersubjective engagement, the practice of ethnography retains a certain exemplary status. Moreover, if fieldwork has for a time been identified with a uniquely Western discipline and a totalizing science of anthropology these associations are not necessarily permanent. Current styles of cultural description are historically limited and are undergoing important metamorphoses. (Clifford 1988, 24)

Note how the wording separates the fieldwork from the subsequent analysis. Fieldwork is an emotion-laden experience of being out of place. Analysis is how fieldwork is identified and is also the "styles" of "cultural description" used in writing about it later. Since the latter can, by implication, be switched without regard to the former, they must be logically unconnected. This is the opposite of what I am urging.

Clifford has not done fieldwork eventuating in an ethnography. He speaks only on the basis of the documents and publications of others, mainly of the French Melanesianist-missionary Maurice Leenhardt (Clifford 1982). Leenhardt spent many years in the field but was no exemplar of participant observation in the present sense. Being a missionary does not bespeak the kind of willingness to learn how to attain and demonstrate competence with indigenous idea systems that I am talking about. At best it involves a stubborn commitment not to. More often, it implies a firm intent to impose one's own ideas on the presumption that they are unquestionably superior. Leenhardt's intellectual affiliations were with the French positivist sociology of Mauss and Lévy-Bruhl, the antithesis of Malinowski's pragmatism and experimentalism.

Using similar imagery, Renato Rosaldo describes fieldwork in terms of a series of dichotomous contrasts including retaining or losing one's "detachment," adopting a "heroic" masculine discipline as represented by Weber or a more responsive and feminine one, and striking a balance between objectivity and subjectivity. What he recommends is "dismantling objectivism," which then "creates a space for ethical concerns in a territory once regarded as value-free. It enables the social analyst to become a social critic" (Rosaldo 1989, 179–81).

Rosaldo and I agree in part. In *Man, Mind, and Science* I argued that empirical, pragmatic field methods "involved a concern with the fundamental equality and relativity of all perspectives" (Leaf 1979, 298). For Robert Manners, a conscientious positivist, this was "inviting us to abandon the anthropological enterprise altogether. . . . If all perspectives are equal then not only the anthropologist's comparative method must collapse but *all* knowledge outside of individual experience is threatened. That sort of relativism is not the handmaiden of anthropology but its executioner" (Manners 1980, 379). The privileged perspective that Manners is arguing for is what Rosaldo and I argue against. But

Rosaldo agrees with Manners that objectivity depends on such a perspective, on imposition from above. My argument is that it does not. We (whoever "we" is) have no monopoly on objectivity, nor does understanding require alienation. The purpose of any experiment is to make observations definite and repeatable. In ethnographic experiments, this definiteness cannot be only for the anthropological stranger and the audience back home; it must include the people in the community being described. The chain of evidence has to run from what is made observable in the community to the conclusion, not just from the inner thoughts of the ethnographer to the conclusion.

The same methodological divide that we have to overcome in anthropology recurs in the other social and behavioral sciences as well as in philosophy and law. In most there is at least some tradition of fieldwork of the present sort, but there are also traditions of fieldwork and of experiment framed in quite different terms as well as traditions of analysis that are not focused on fieldwork or experimentation in any sense. The theory developed here draws on—and draws together—empirically grounded results and assumptions from the physical sciences, anthropology, geography, sociology, economics, political science, linguistics, psychology, jurisprudence, and philosophy.

Empiricism, Skepticism, and Experimentalism

By an empirical theory, I mean something we can verify or falsify on the basis of shared experience. It also explains,[2] and it does so in a very specific way. It does not work in the manner of a just-so story or an ideology. Explaining the evident fit between the outlines of Earth's continents by supposing that the planet had expanded since its first formation turned out to be a just-so story; continental drift did not. Ideologies are logically circular systems of claims and definitions designed to be held true no matter what, usually by including some claim to the effect that they do not describe mere appearances or mere individual experiences but something we cannot observe directly that lies behind them and produces them. Many social theories are of these sorts. Such explanations can be shared but cannot be verified on the basis of shared experience.

Nor does empirical theory explain by inventing laws or lawlike statements from which the observation may be deduced, as logical positivists and similar writers such as Hans Reichenbach, Karl Hempel, Wesley Salmon, and Karl Popper have urged.[3] Explanation cannot be equated with prediction (Rescher 1958).

To see what science is, you have to be an ethnographer of science. Watch scientists in their laboratories, and read what they write. Read Newton, Galileo, *Science* magazine, or popular but still authentic works such as Stephen Hawking's *A Brief History of Time* (1988). Or read some of the studies in the modern descriptive tradition of the history of science that has developed in large part as a rebuttal to the philosophical misrepresentations. Exemplary collections are

E. McMullin's *Galileo: Man of Science* (1967) and Myles Burnyeat's *The Skeptical Tradition* (1983). For more monographic accounts, there are Shapin and Schaffer's *Leviathan and the Air-Pump* (1985), which contrasts Robert Boyle's experimental method and consensual view of governmental authority with Thomas Hobbes's deductive method and authoritarian conception of governmental authority, and Peter Galison's history of the beginnings of microphysics in *Image and Logic* (1997). Whereas the logical positivists, Popper, and Hempel are strikingly data-poor, these are data-rich, and while the historians do not provide simple prescriptive formulas, they are richly instructive in the way good ethnographies are. They re-create the situations in which the research was done and let you imagine yourself in the researchers' places.

The building blocks of empirical theory are experiments or demonstrations. The core idea of a demonstration is that we test our explanations by constructing a situation in which that explanation rather than others will be shown to be true or false, right or wrong. It does not matter if the construction is largely physical, such as a trial between two varieties of wheat in side-by-side plots, or a largely conceptual simulation leading only eventually to a predicted observation, such as the calculation of an astronomical orbit. It does not matter if we are dealing with the relations between things, processes, or ideas. All that matters is that our analysis begins and ends in observations, does not depart from observation in its reasoning, and allows us to control the process of observation insofar as necessary to answer our questions. As Bacon said, experiments are ways to observe "nature under constraint and vexed." The phrase was from law, referring to a trial by torture. But we should notice that in putting nature under constraint by limiting the alternative outcomes that might appear for observation, we are also putting ourselves under constraint by limiting what we might experience. Experiment is not just a way of observing nature; it is a way of interacting with it.

Although the experimental method is inherently open, it often reveals closed systems. Indeed, the openness is precisely what allows the closed systems to be exposed. When Galileo discovered the law of acceleration, which integrates a quite tight little bundle of physical conceptions, he did not begin with a deduction of what that law might be or even with any idea from which such a deduction would be made. He was not thinking about acceleration at all. His aim had been to test ideas regarding impressed force acting to suspend bodies in a medium. He lived in a mercantile city, and the concept had an obvious bearing on the problem of loading ships with cargo without having them sink. This seemed to involve a kind of force and counterforce. As more force pushed down, more force seemed to push back until equilibrium was reached. This was what he started to try to measure. What he found, however, was that he could not set up experiments in such a way as to isolate such a process. One attempt led to another in a way that forced him, in successive trials, to strip away not only the alternative original theories but also the entire original concept. Acceleration, in free fall and under various constraints, which *could* be examined experimentally without unwarranted assumptions or imputations, is what replaced it (Settle 1967).

Similarly, when Galileo argued for the Copernican system in the *Dialogue concerning the Two Chief World Systems* (Galilei 1953), the bulk of his argument was devoted to stripping away the gratuitous assumptions that had led previous thinkers to offer unconnected explanations for a wide range of phenomena that were actually interconnected. These were not limited to calculating the apparent movements of the planets and other heavenly bodies. They also included the rate of acceleration of falling bodies, relative motion of projectiles fired from weapons on moving vehicles, relative motion of objects dropped on and from moving vehicles, estimates of the distance to the new star (nova) of 1572 compared to the distance to the moon, the presence of landmarks on the surface of the moon, the phases of the moon, the constant face of the moon, the phases of Mercury and Venus, the lack of phases of Jupiter and Saturn, the changing shapes and motions of sunspots, the orbiting of the moons of Jupiter and Saturn, the difference between the relative sizes of stars and planets when seen through telescopes, the relation between brightness and apparent size of stars and planets when seen through a telescope, the nature of reflectivity, the relation between a body's reflectivity and its luminescence, and the procession and recession of the tides. What was rejected was not just Ptolemy's crystalline spheres around a stationary earth but, more basically, the Aristotelian a priori reasoning upon which both the Aristotelian and Ptolemaic systems were based, using a host of supposedly universal and necessary dichotomies including essential versus inessential properties, perfect versus imperfect shapes, internal versus external or impressed motion, straight versus circular motion, terrestrial versus celestial bodies, corruptibility versus incorruptibility, and perfection versus imperfection.

Since about 200 CE, the philosophical tradition most closely associated with experimentalism has been skepticism. In a strict sense the term "empiricism" is simply an alternate name. The term is taken from the Greek term for demonstrative knowledge as well as the name of the medical skeptic Sextus Empiricus, whose encyclopedic *Against the Dogmatists* was a standard work of the tradition from the second century to the nineteenth (Goold 1976). Although Galileo did not describe his position as skeptical in the *Dialogue concerning the Two Chief World Systems,* the affinity between experimentalism and skepticism was unanimously reaffirmed by his three immediate successors—Robert Boyle, William Harvey, and Robert Hooke—and has been continuously recognized ever since.

Since Galileo, the most important development in the skeptical tradition has been its transformation by Immanuel Kant into what he called a "formal science," as described in chapter 2. Kant's formulations, in turn, provided the conceptual foundations for a tremendous expansion of experimentally grounded research into most of the topics that occupy the social and behavioral sciences as we now recognize them: linguistics, human geography, experimental psychology, and ethnology in addition to the previously established areas of law, jurisprudence, politics, history, and religion, all of which eventually were drawn on in framing American pragmatism.

Since American pragmatism is simply a particularly cohesive—and particularly American—version of the larger skeptical tradition, it should not be surprising that William James's definition of radical empiricism is a succinct statement of the common methodological aim of pragmatism itself, experimentalism, and Kantian skepticism. James was contrasting radical empiricism with the ordinary empiricism of David Hume: "To be radical, an empiricism must neither admit into its constructions any element that is not directly experienced, nor exclude from them any element that is directly experienced. For such a philosophy, the relations that connect experiences must themselves be experienced relations, and any kind of relation experienced must be accounted as 'real' as anything else in the system" (1904, 534).

The most pertinent and clear contemporary account of the way such reasoning works in the physical sciences is Galison's *Image and Logic* (1997). "Image" in the title is the experimenters' understanding of the experiment, revolving around the development and use of the cloud chamber. It is not just *any* image, of course, but the one that actually captures what is done. One of Galison's main themes is that the logic of the field is embedded in that imagery and comes from it. What the imagery does not apply to is also what the logic does not apply to. Logic in the sciences is not some separate set of pure rules of inference provided by the mind alone, as Aristotle and Mill imagined. This reflects an important but seldom explicitly discussed difference between the skeptical and the dogmatic or dualistic traditions generally, which we will return to repeatedly.

In the dogmatic tradition there has always been a notion that logic was a system of absolute rules of reasoning, applicable to all inference and independent of any subject matter. The principal exemplar has been what is called Aristotelian or syllogistic logic. Aristotle's scheme, described in the *Organon,* was to use his method of division to cut through the false classes and false definitions and arrive at true ones. This decomposed knowledge would then be arranged by class inclusion in their true order. The result would be a complete and comprehensive system in which all knowledge would be deducible from first principles. Aristotle never finished the analytic phase, but from then to now some such scheme has remained the goal of dogmatic scholarship.

The logical positivists' aim was to expand Aristotelian logic in a way that would include the apparently different logics of the various branches of the sciences and mathematics while reducing all referents to a finite list of sensations. For a while, they got some support from Russell and Whitehead's claims to have shown in principle that mathematics could be derived from logic and from Wittgenstein's *Tractatus,* which purported to show that ordinary language was itself a closed, self-contained, logical system. But Russell and Whitehead's arguments were turned on themselves by Kurt Gödel in 1931 and Wittgenstein's by Wittgenstein himself in 1953. The effort is now generally agreed to have come, once again, to nothing.

The view of logic in the skeptical tradition is very different. It has been accepted more or less as a matter of course that different subject matters have different logics and that the only thing that all such logics have in common is self-consistency, or the avoidance of self-contradiction. In this view, the existence of different logics in the different sciences is not a problem to be overcome but an accomplishment to be extended. It is not a failure of our ability to impose our order on nature but the achievement of getting various things in nature to reveal their order to us.

Galison's notion of an image covers the same ground as Kuhn's paradigm, but Galison is much clearer and should be more difficult to misconstrue.[4]

Participant observation must be experimental to be productive, but an ethnographic field study cannot be just one experiment any more than an investigation in the physical sciences can. Although a study may focus on one overall general question, it must always involve a system of experiments setting up the question and defining its context. In ethnology it is usually many hundreds, each in itself almost microscopic: "He reacted as though I said something wrong; if I say X will it lead to a different facial expression and an indication of agreement?" "If I ask farmers why they do not grow high-yielding crops, the answer should be given in terms of cost and benefit rather than in terms of adherence to tradition." "If I ask farmers what the items of cost are, they should include all out of pocket costs and interest rates, but not an imputed cost for their time." You keep going until you can predict the outcome as consistently as a recognizably competent member of the community. But since you are also a scientist, you should also be able to explain how you make these predictions and how you gain this recognition. Knowledge of what to expect cannot be allowed to become merely habitual. This involves forming a definite conscious analysis of what idea goes with what other ideas under what circumstances and why.

Eliciting anything substantial involves far too many such small tests to recount each one in a finished monograph. For the most part, the monograph can only summarize the conclusions. Nevertheless, key experiments can be described and the rest of the account can be given in such a way that empirically minded readers can imagine for themselves what the experiments behind it should have been.

Empirical Formalism

A central part of my argument is that organizations are built up in communities by the use of shared cultural idea systems and that these idea systems are formal systems in a strict sense. By "formal system" I mean a set of ideas that have a formal structure. I also mean a structure such as that of systems of logic or mathematics, some very well-formed ideologies, and now computer languages. A formal structure has a few ideas that serve as its premises and a usually small number of operations that specify the ways these ideas can be compared and combined, such as larger than, smaller than, contained in, related to, progenitor of, equal to, and not. True inferences are those consistent with the rules; false inferences are those that violate the rules. The implications are then drawn out by concatenating the ideas of the premises consistently according to the allowed operations. By the "logic" of an idea system or a formal structure, I mean the general pattern of inferences that it gives rise to.

The empirical status of formal systems is a fundamental conceptual problem. In the physical sciences, experiments often reveal relationships that can be expressed mathematically or in other highly formalized ways, such as the conceptual models of the atom, evolutionary tree diagrams, or formulas representing chemical reactions. It is the same in the social sciences but with an added twist. In the physical sciences, the formal or formalizable relations exist in the data. The problem is to find them. This is also true in the social sciences, but in addition, as I will show, the data sometimes actually consists of formal systems. In this case, the problem is not only to find them but also to render or translate them without contaminating them with concepts that are alien to them. Locating and characterizing such systems often takes us to the absolute frontiers of knowledge, where the struggle to recognize new phenomena is inseparable from a struggle to find new ways to think.

An important part of the argument of the positivists and their allies is that systems of mathematics such as Euclidian geometry are analytic rather than synthetic. The dichotomy harks back to Mill's distinction between propositions that were real as against those that were merely emotive and then his further division of real propositions into those that were essential and those that were nonessential or accidental. An essential proposition is one that "asserts of a thing under a particular name only what is asserted of it in the fact of calling it by that name, and which, therefore, either gives no information, or gives it respecting the name, not the thing 'merely verbal' and 'either gives no information or gives it respecting the name, not the thing. . . .' Non-essential, or accidental propositions, on the contrary, may be called real propositions, in opposition to verbal. They predicate of a thing some fact not involved in the signification of the name by which the proposition speaks of it, some attribute not connoted by that name" (Mill 1950, 87–88).

Analytic systems are treated as systems of essential propositions in Mill's sense. They are purely matters of definition, owing nothing to observation. They are not in nature but must be imposed on it—mind over matter, subjective over objective—and hence might have been invented purely as an exercise of the imagination. This claim of the fundamental arbitrariness and analyticity of all logics was the justification for their scheme to integrate the sciences by providing them with a newer and still more general logic from which all present logics could be deduced. But the argument is a play on the idea of might. Might in the logical sense of not inconceivable or not a self-contradiction is very different from might in the sense of realistically likely.

Euclidian geometry is certainly a formal system, but this in itself hardly proves that it is not also genuinely empirical. Any set of distinctions, as noted, can be the basis of a formal system of deduction. There is in principle no necessity that such distinctions should make sense to us; any set of symbols will do. It follows that there is an exceedingly large number of such possible systems. But the probability that any one such scheme would actually work as a geometry, in the way Euclidian geometry does, is exceedingly small. The ratio is, in fact, whatever "exceedingly large" translates to as a number to about three—three being the most commonly recognized number of alternate geometries that are actually usable—and they are all variants of Euclidian geometry. It follows that even if creating formalizations without a descriptive target may be possible, once you have such a target this is an exceedingly inefficient way to try to hit it.

The sense of form that I argue for is neither arbitrary nor external. If this form can be expressed by mathematical or other notation, or in a computer program, it is in my view absurd to argue that the mathematics or the computer program actually creates or causes it. It is not absurd, however, to argue that both the form and the notation embody and reflect the same underlying requirements of consistency and coherence.

There is a great deal of overlap between the idea of a formal system and the idea of a structure. It is often the case in ethnology that systems of indigenous ideas used for constructing organizations, as well as organizations themselves, can be most readily captured in field elicitations in the form of diagrams. It is also the case that such diagrams can be represented, or even explained, by systems of formal rules.

Certain systems of ideas fall under the heading of the "synthetic a priori." Such systems of ideas are not simply analytic in the positivists' sense, nor are they simply synthetic. They are not merely matters of definition and not merely statements of fact but rather seem to be both, true by definition or a priori in some sense and yet also expansive of their subject matter. Kant considered the ideas of geometry to be of this sort and explained why. The explanation turned on a very specific sense of a priori that is quite different from that of the positivists: it is not true by definition or *before* experience but instead true as a necessary presupposition *in* experience. The ideas of geometry embodied fundamental presuppositions for physical experience. Other ideas were synthetic a priori for other categories of experience: moral, social, and esthetic.

Kant's analysis was what the positivistic rejection of metaphysics was intended to set aside, recognizing that it nullified the simplistic analytic-synthetic dichotomy on which their own schemes depended.

We can now see that Kant's analyses were incomplete. There are other systems of ideas that are synthetic a priori in his sense that he did not describe. These are the ideas used to construct organizations. As will be shown, these are generative systems, exactly like geometries and systems of mathematics. This means that they are much more than just a few interrelated ideas that we can represent with formalizations if we want to. They are systems that require such representation and cannot be understood otherwise. This is why it is not adequate to describe them simply as cultural beliefs, templates, or mazeways. They are, as we will see, well-formed and highly structured systems of conceptual premises that generate large numbers of possible inferences. Moreover, they are not only found here and there in culture; they are the basis of it. They are what generate and support many of the more ordinary stereotypes and beliefs, just as the premises of geometry generate and support the specific figures of geometry. They are the basis of the distinctively human expansion of communicative and organizational abilities, and they are what make cultural and organizational consensus possible.

Although the character of formal systems in culture has been obscured by theory and metatheory that made it impossible for them to be uncovered in their own terms, they are not mysterious when approached without such an intellectual overburden. This will be demonstrated.

The Argument

The first half of my argument is retrospective and synthetic. Chapter 1 pulls together important points of social theory that can be regarded as already established. Chapter 2 describes the Kantian and pragmatic articulations of the principles that tie them together and establish the direction we need to move in. Chapter 3 provides a brief overview of the new technologies associated with computers that aid us in doing so. The remaining chapters supply the analysis of human organizations as such. The resulting picture is justifiably described as a new paradigm for social analysis. It is more comprehensive than anything previous, descriptively accountable, testable in detail, and immediately applicable to pressing issues of social and economic policy.

CHAPTER 1

Empirical Starting Points

Notwithstanding the increasing murkiness in what has been regarded as general social theory associated with the rise and fall of positivism over the last seventy-odd years, there have been important pockets of illumination, new and important clarifications of complex and elusive matters of fact that a comprehensive empirical theory must incorporate.

Group and Organization

Anthropologists and sociologists often start discussions of organizational theory with a distinction between emic aggregates that are recognized as meaningful by their participants and etic aggregates based on objective criteria imposed by an outside viewer. A family might be an example of the former; a group waiting to cross at a traffic light is an example of the latter. Like all other applications of the subjective-objective dichotomy, this is more problematic than it might at first seem.

While there is a difference between a set of people arbitrarily grouped together and a group that is self-recognized, the characteristics of self-recognized groups vary enormously. It is far more important for social analysis to get a sense of this variation than of the fine line between the most minimal indigenous conception and no conception at all. Moreover, who recognizes a group is not as fixed and clear as the distinction seems to suggest. When I present a purely arbitrary idea such as social class as defined by some occupational grouping to a university class in anthropology or sociology, it is never long before the students start speaking of themselves in its terms. Has the etic concept then become emic? When Marx's term "capitalism" is used by Americans as though it did in fact describe their economic system, is it emic or etic? Either way, if this is the first step, what is the next?

A much firmer yet more inclusive starting point is with the difference between groups and organizations. Groups are aggregates of people whose members can be named but whose mutual relations cannot be. Organizations are people under some common group name and with mutually adjusted behavioral expectations. Both of these are both emic and etic. This distinction accords with ordinary usage but also makes empirical sense. People in communities everywhere have indigenous concepts for groups as distinct from organizations, and we can also recognize them objectively. We can get lists of their members. People in communities also recognize that they have organizations as distinct from the groups that form them, and we can recognize this objectively as well. We can describe the positions and their mutual relationships. The members of self-recognized groups may or may not form organizations, but an organization will always define a group. This is extremely important.

Organizations

In the most general sense, an organization exists wherever organisms engage in a mutual adjustment of behavior, meaning that what one organism does is dependent on what others are expected to do. In this sense, all sorts of natural communities are organized. But for human beings there is more. For us, an organization is not only a mutual adjustment of behavior but one that the participants are conscious of engaging in, that has a name or designation, that involves mutual recognition by the members of each other, that involves conscious commitments of the members to each other, and that the members expect to persist over a specifiable time period. More briefly, an organization in the strict sense is a mutual adjustment of behavior in a named arrangement based on conscious agreement and mutual recognition. An organization is thus inherently anticipatory. It looks ahead.

Usually this named arrangement is an association in a jurisprudential sense, but it may not be. A sale transaction involves the creation of an organization (for the moment of the transaction) but does not create an association.

In this strict sense, a named entity that involves no actual mutual adjustment of behavior is not an organization, and neither is a mutual adjustment of behavior that is not based on conscious agreement in a named arrangement. An example of the first would be what is colloquially called a dummy corporation set up to hide or transfer assets in business dealings; another example is any number of supposed social groups or classes whose members may be said by others to exist but have no actual mutually recognized behavioral expectations among themselves. Examples of the second would be people who move aside to avoid colliding when walking on the street or avoid intruding upon each other on a public beach.

This definition draws on two parallel lines of pragmatic theory, one in social psychology and the other in law and jurisprudence.

I take the phrase "mutual adjustment of behavior" from George Herbert Mead, and Mead's analysis lays out the social-psychological side of the organizational process. Building on the experimental psychology that began with Wilhelm Wundt and Wilhelm von Helmholtz, Mead's argument in *Mind, Self, and Society* was that a mutual adjustment of behavior occurred whenever communication occurred:

> Meaning is thus not to be conceived, fundamentally, as a state of consciousness, or as a set of organized relations existing or subsisting mentally outside the field of experience into which they enter; on the contrary, it should be conceived objectively, as having its existence entirely within this field itself. The response of one organism to the gesture of another in any given social act is the meaning of that gesture, and also is in a sense responsible for the appearance or coming into being of the new object or new content of an old object—to which that gesture refers through the outcome of the given social act in which it is an early phase. For, to repeat, objects are in a genuine sense constituted within the social process of experience, by the communication and mutual adjustment of behavior among the individual organisms, which are involved in that process and which carry it on. Just as in fencing the parry is an interpretation of the thrust, so, in the social act, the adjustive response of one organism to the gesture of another is the interpretation of that gesture by that organism—it is the meaning of that gesture. (Mead 1934, 78)

And since linguistic and other symbols among humans are an extension of gestures, so too among humans there is a mutual adjustment of behavior whenever there is an exchange of symbols. "At the level of self-consciousness such a gesture becomes a symbol, a significant symbol. But the interpretation of gestures is not a process going on in the mind as such, or one necessarily involving a mind; it is an external, overt, physical or physiological process going on in the actual field of social experience" (Mead 1934, 78).

There is also a mutual adjustment of behavior in the definitions of self and other built up through communication and hence in the assignment of roles to the selves and others thus created.

An important question concerning the social construction of the self is whether we have one or many. The argument here is that we have both one and many, but they have very different epistemological statuses and operational saliency. We have selves defined in relation to others in organizational contexts, as part of creating those organizational contexts. And we also have a more personal kind of self that we construct as the locus of these organizational selves. This formulation draws on a large literature and will make more sense after the discussion of Kant in chapter 2. For the moment the key point is that for human beings the process of creating the organizational selves involves setting up mutual adjustments of behavior with various recognized others, in Mead's sense, and since these others are people, this necessarily presents the problem of making and keeping agreements. Mutual adjustments of behavior based on agreements, in turn, are the same things as mutual systems of obligations and privileges or rights and duties. This inevitably involves the creation of sanctions.

At the present time, the most penetrating empirical analyses of how organizations work and the role of sanctions in the ways they are maintained are outside anthropology, mainly in jurisprudence. The problem with this literature is that it avoids the problem of describing the stuff of organizations, their conceptual content. The most complete descriptions of the content, by contrast, are in anthropology, but because of the blinding effect of the theoretical dedication to determinism over most of the last century, these accounts have not been attached to a systematic analysis of how the content is used by the participants and how this use is sanctioned. A central empirical problem, then, is to draw these two bodies of analysis together, to see precisely what the conceptual building materials consist of and how they are imposed to form and maintain actual organizations.

Sanctions, generally, are what the jurisprudent Rudolph von Jhering (1913) describes as the coercive force that comes into play when one person fails to carry out their obligations to another (1913, 1915). Person A does not arbitrarily or whimsically make his or her behavior contingent on Person B doing something, and Person B does not arbitrarily make his behavior contingent on Person C, and so on. They do it, as Jhering stresses, in order to accomplish something. A depends on B, B on C, and so on in order to gain their common anticipated benefits. This dependency, however, necessarily means that members have the power to injure one another. This sets up the need for a mechanism to apply sanctions to prevent or redress such injury. In organized states, where the courts have a monopoly on the use of legitimate force, the task of the judge is to apply such force in a way that is orderly and predictable. What makes it orderly and predicable is that it is controlled by law. For Jhering, law was the "self-regulation of coercion" (1913, 262–65), the rules that the courts impose on their own use of coercive force when called upon to apply it.

Jhering's analysis provided the basis for the sociology of law of Eugen Ehrlich. Whereas Jhering focused mainly on the actions of courts, Ehrlich (1975) devoted most of his analysis to what he called the "living law of associations." What he meant by this was the vast bulk of the mutual agreements that we all make in our daily lives that are so important, so pervasive, and so strongly sanctioned by our mutual dependencies that we hardly ever seriously think of violating them.

By mutual cooperation, those who form an association can produce more of whatever it is they wish to produce together than they could separately. The difference between what they could produce individually and what they can produce if they work together provides the basis for exercising coercive sanctions on one another to assure each person's adherence to her or his commitments. But it also presents a problem of assuring allocative equity. If the benefits are not divided in such a way the members consider fair, those who are disadvantaged will see it as to their advantage, and even as necessary, to pull out. More broadly, the extent of the benefits and the ways they are divided provide incentives for making the organization more or less effective.

Notice that this analysis does not require that the benefits be denominated in money. Benefits are often so obvious that the question of denomination or relative shares is not important. Similarly, the logic is not restricted to productive activities in an economic sense. It applies equally well to people who join together to maintain any sort of public good and to organizations as ephemeral as a poker game or as enduring as a family.

Organizational purposes are the basis of community adaptation. If you make the pursuit of established purposes impossible by destroying a community's ecological base and forcing them to depend on handouts or employment in alien organizational settings, you have the decay of authority and interpersonal discipline often found on tribal reservations. If you provide no alternative at all, you have the dead-end despair that Colin Turnbull describes for the Ik of northern Kenya whose traditional hunting ground was made into a national park into which they were prohibited from following their game (Turnbull 1972, 21–33).

The questions that arise in this theoretical framework concern the way organizations are explicitly designated, the way the mutual adjustments of behavior are actually arranged, and the ways in which purposes are specified and pursued. What we will see is that the first two questions require us to understand a type of phenomenon that neither Jhering nor Ehrlich—or any other jurisprudent—had recognized. These are social information systems.

Social Information Systems: First Observations

Many ethnographers have noted that the ideas used to report social relations are not merely descriptive. They are, in Stanley Tambiah's (1973) useful term, performative. Ideas used this way must be shared, and to be shared they must have standardized definitions and associations. Such organized and shared ideas are what I call cultural information systems (Leaf 1972).

Cultural information systems, in turn, are of two main types: social and technical. Social information systems (or social idea systems) are cultural information systems that define social relations. These relational ideas are the conceptual building blocks of organizations. Technical and technological systems are cultural information systems that define sets of things and their interrelations.

Although there is no coherent literature reflecting the analysis of cultural information systems in the present sense at the present time, many of their important properties have been described in various disciplinary and subdisciplinary contexts. The analysis here mainly builds on information theory, the study of structural models and the like in social and cultural anthropology, the study of cultural models in cognitive anthropology, the study of indigenous knowledge systems and local knowledge in development studies, and cultural ecology.

In the last few years, the type of empirical formal analysis I will describe here has led to major advances in the analysis of social information systems. The most concrete and definite of these concern systems of kinship, and since kinship is the gateway to all other social relations, as will be shown, these gains have very broad implications. The essential point to start with is that all social idea systems involve ideas of reciprocity, and the way this reciprocity is defined imposes forceful formal constraints on such idea systems. But kinship is where this idea is learned first, and as such kinship must be structured so that it can be taught first. Other systems use other versions of the idea of reciprocity that impose different constraints. What these formal structures are and how they work to define the reciprocal relations that organizations depend on are described in chapter 4.

The main empirical questions concerning cultural information systems pertain to their precise character and limits. How do we locate them? How definite are they? What is their formal organization? How is their formal organization related to their content? What establishes their boundary conditions? How sharply are they distinguishable one from another? How are they established in consensus?

The quality and clarity of the answers we get to these questions is heavily dependent on the standards we hold ourselves to in seeking them. They are particularly influenced by the criteria for making two judgments. The first is the judgment that two ideas are connected. The second is the judgment that something is a matter of consensus. There seems to be a widespread fear that the more rigorous and clear the criteria are by which we indicate what we are talking about, the more difficult it will be to prove our claims. The argument here is exactly the opposite: if we do not employ the most rigorous possible criteria, we will not come up with any answers capable of holding up under critical examination.

To understand the ideas that provide the bases for organizations in human communities, we must be very careful to elicit and describe them precisely and cleanly from the point of view of those whose ideas they are. Strange nuances of usage that informants insist on to our annoyance have an odd way of turning out to be important. It is very important to curb our predilection to read past them and restate what we hear in terms that seem more objective, or familiar. In India, for example, people speak of themselves as being "in" households but do not speak of being "in" a faction. They speak of "supporting" a faction. Navajos do not speak of being "in" their father's clan but rather of being a "child of" their father's clan; they are "in" their mother's clan only. Americans "hold" or "occupy" offices, but they "are" kinsmen. (And, of course, the same concrete individuals who think and act as these Americans in one set of contexts may think and act as these Navajos in others.) Americans have rights as citizens, whereas Britons have rights as subjects. American officials are public servants.

Indian and Bangladeshi officials are government servants. The cultural definitions used to form mutual adjustments of behavior in named arrangements may be articulated in ways that do not resemble Western notions of a position or a group at all. Roy Wagner (1974) describes a social world in the New Guinea highlands in which relations are constructed in terms of a universal interchange of male and female sexuality. Such modes of expression have implications, and these implications need to be understood. To be understood they must first be taken seriously.

Technical information systems have quite different formal properties. They do not involve the idea of reciprocity. Instead of defining objects related reciprocally to the describer, they describe objects as though detached from the describer. Instead of systems of "I" and "thou," they describe "it" and "them." What these are and how they work are described in chapter 5.

Together, social and technological idea systems are used to create organizational charters (described in chapter 6), which in turn are important in creating actual organizations.

Situations

When social idea systems that define organizations are instantiated in behavior, they differentiate situations. Here, the relevant extant literature is mainly in sociology: W. I. Thomas's definition of the situation and its successors, Erving Goffman's presentation of self (1959), and especially Harold Garfinkel's ethnomethodology (1967, 2002). Ethnomethodology presents a far cleaner and more detailed account than Goffman's, although neither links the details of presentation back to the logical structure of the ideas being invoked. This is what will be supplied here beginning in chapter 6.

When situations instantiate organizations they automatically entail organizational purposes. Situations are formed by people trying to get something done, a fundamental point that pragmatists stress but that both Goffman and the ethnomethodologists ignore. The situation is not created by the ideas used to define it; it is created by the individuals using those ideas. In this context, the most immediate context of any given set of social relational ideas is the set of technological ideas that the organization in question associates them with. The practical contexts of the ideas that describe the roles and responsibilities of people in a legal trial are the ideas that define the accoutrements and apparatus of the courtroom. The practical contexts of the organizational ideas that define a military unit are the ideas that define its equipment and tactics. Accordingly, empirical questions about the uses of organizational ideas divide into two main groups: those concerned with their relational content and use and those concerned with what these relationships are intended to control or produce. Broadly speaking, in the last fifty years questions about content have usually been asked under the headings of studies of social organization, social structure, and culture. Questions about what they are used to control and produce have been asked under the heading of cultural ecology. The artificial separation of these two areas has been a major stumbling block in the way of formulating social theory that is genuinely comprehensive and penetrating.

Other Purposes: Subversive Agendas

It may be objected that in any given organization or situation there are often members who do not really share the organizational purpose or who pursue other goals or agendas on the side, secretly, or additionally. This is not inconsistent with my analysis. Since I recognize that individuals belong to multiple organizations, I expect them to pursue multiple goals. But they will recognize which goals belong to which organizations and act accordingly in minute communicative detail. It is consistent with my argument if people belong to a work organization and one or another kind of family organization so long as in the work situation it is the work goals that are the explicit framework of cooperation while the family goals are part of the hidden or personal concerns, and in the family situation it is the work goals that are hidden or personal. It would contradict my argument, however, if the family goals were the basis of cooperation in the work situation and the work goals were the explicit framework of cooperation in family situations. The way such goals are interrelated in personal strategies, how individuals move between them and balance them, and what this requires by way of rational action at the individual level are described in chapter 9.

Recognition of multiple organizational purposes is provided for by specific social mechanisms. To a very great extent, these are the same mechanisms that define membership in the individual organizations. That is, membership in multiple social organizations is a socially recognized and socially constructed fact presented by and for community participants.

Associations of Ideas versus Beliefs

Anthropologists are sometimes asked how they know their informants are telling them the truth. The answer is a counterquestion: truth about what? No one can speak without conveying some information. The problem is to know what that information is. Experimental design in ethnology is a dual process of fitting the situation of observation to the information sought and calibrating the conclusion drawn to the situation of observation.

Informants can easily lie or distort in response to questions about matters beyond the observable conversational here and now, but it is very difficult to lie about the accepted stereotypes and relations among ideas that even lies and distortions depend on. As an example, when I was just beginning fieldwork in

Sidhpur, the subject of cows came up in a conversation with a young man from a landholder family. Since it is often said that one of the reasons for Indian poverty is that they wastefully maintain huge numbers of surplus cows because they believe that cows are sacred, I asked how they were treated. He said, "We take very good care of cows. We never sell them; if we cannot keep them we wait until they are almost three years old, and then we either give them away or let them go free." I asked why. He said, "Because cows are like mother." This is certainly the kind of statement usually taken as an expression of the aforesaid belief, but in fact I had not observed either a belief or any actual treatment of cows. All I had observed was a set of conceptual associations: that a cow is like mother and that both should be taken care of unselfishly. In addition, since I knew that cows were not mature at three years old, I could infer that the reason that the cow was "like" mother was particularly associated with the further ideas of childbirth and lactation, as other observers had said. But this was all. I had observed a stereotyped response, nothing more. To find out how much of this response was actually "believed" in any strong sense would require another method—namely observing what people said and did when these kinds of topics came up more spontaneously among themselves on occasions when choices had to be made—and finding out if these ideas had anything to do with the way cows were actually treated required a village cattle census and the elicitation of the ideas that reflected cattle management in the context it provided (Leaf 1972, 42).

As it turned out, these ideas were not part of the idea system used for managing cattle. They belonged instead with the idea system of kinship. The statement was a kind of kinship parable whose implicit conclusion was "and if we treat cows this well because they are like mother, just imagine how well we treat our mother herself!"

Decision Models and Experimental Economics

Producing and dividing a benefit implies instrumental rationality. As with the idea of an organization, this cannot be fully described at this point. But I can indicate the direction we will be taking. First, the general conception of reason that I use is Kantian, as explained in chapter 2. Second, in contemporary terms, I am arguing that what Occhipinti and Siegal (1996) describe as a rationality of purpose is more basic than a rationality of process. A rationality of process is a view of rationality as simply following the rules of inference of a "formal, normative system." A rationality of purpose is reasoning "that is directed consistently toward achieving particular goals and may be constrained by bounds on information processing, such as the size of working memory" (Occhipinti and Siegal 1996, 510). Occhipinti and Siegal further argue that rationality "that leads to plausible and non-trivial conclusions must take into account the reasoner's construction of reality" (511). Their argument was focused only on the possibility of evolutionary selection of modes of reasoning useful in food procurement and was framed with an omnibus conception of culture unrelated to any specific sense of social organization. My argument here is much more comprehensive and the theory of social organization is specified. The main idea is that rational decisions utilize the same ideas that define the organizations that the decision makers are in. Rationality is therefore inherently relative and situational rather than universal and absolute. Formal rules of inference may indeed be used, but they are deployed in the context of socially defined purposes.

A great deal of excitement is presently being generated by studies of rational decision making in experimental economics and allied areas. These seem to their proponents to provide a way to expand Adam Smith's accomplishment by providing another, and possibly more inclusive, way to relate individual decisions based on self-interest to stable emergent patterns at the societal level. According to Avner Greif, the studies fall into two lines based on two different views of how these societal patterns emerge. The first line "considers the impact of the internalization of traits through evolutionary processes and learning on the set of relevant rules" and "utilizes evolutionary game theory and learning models to study the process through which decision makers with particular traits . . . emerge and the constraints on behavior that their interactions entail." The second, which includes his own work, "considers the impact of strategic interactions and exogenous and endogenous cultural features . . . on the set of relevant rules. It . . . concentrates on the origin and implications of (nontechnologically determined) 'organizations,' and the constraints implied by beliefs prominent in a society on and off the path of play" (1998, 81).

While most of these studies do not claim cross-cultural validity, there is an exception (Henrich, Boyd, Bowles, Camerer, Fehr, Gintis, and McElreath 2001, 73). This evidently grows out of the first of the two lines that Greif distinguished. According to their own account, the project design was built on a 1996 experiment by Joseph Henrich, who was actually a graduate student in anthropology at UCLA at the time, working among the Machiguengas. It is important for two reasons: its psychological evolutionism and its conception of experiment. The experimental method of these studies is radically different from what I am arguing for under the heading of participant observation. In participant observation, the phenomenon that the experiment is trying to capture is the situation as defined by those providing the information. In the economic experiments, the experimental situation is definitely not defined by the experimental subjects, and what it might correspond to in their world is usually not of interest to the analysts. The aim is to strip away cultural ideas in order to get at what the experimenters think of as universal psychological processes. Investigators set highly artificial problems, usually involving giving or promising money to the experimental subjects and requiring them to give or promise some of it to others in the group. The experimentalists identify the most stable solution—and the most rational one—as defined by the Nash equilibrium. A solution is at the Nash equilibrium when neither player would alter her or his decision given that individual's knowledge of the moves of the other players but provided that the players have no way to cooperate. Most designs of games of this sort are set up in such a way that if the players could cooperate, they would all do better. The researchers then measure the difference between this Nash optimal solution and the solutions actually chosen. The general result is that most experimental subjects do not behave as the models predict, and theoretical discussion focuses on how to account for the differences. The purpose of the Henrich et al. studies was to see if these disparities held up cross-culturally.

The group conducted three well-established types of experiments in fifteen societies and compared the responses. The experiments were the ultimatum game, the public good game, and the dictator game. The ultimatum game, for example, has one player get a sum of money (or something). He must then offer a portion of this to the other. The other can either take it or refuse it, but if he refuses neither player gets anything. The Nash equilibrium solution is that the giving player offers just one unit, and the receiver takes it. The public good game has each player give a sum of something like money and allows them to decide to keep it or put it into a common pool, which is added to by the investigator and divided among the contributors. The Nash equilibrium solution is for no one to contribute to the pool; the actually most beneficial solution would be for all to give everything.

They summarized the results as follows:

First, the canonical model is not supported in any society studied. Second, there is considerably more behavioral variability across groups than had been found in previous cross-cultural research, and the canonical model fails in a wider variety of ways than in previous experiments. Third, group level differences in economic organization and the degree of market integration explain a substantial portion of the behavioral variation across societies: the higher the degree of market integration and the higher the payoffs to cooperation, the greater the level of cooperation in the experimental games. Fourth, individual level economic and demographic variables do not explain behavior either within or across groups. Fifth, behavior in the experiments is generally consistent with economic patterns of everyday life in these societies. (Henrich et al. 2001, 73–74)

In short, none of the predictions were very good, but the more the experimental subjects had economic institutions that were similar to those of the investigators, the better the investigators' models predicted their behavior. Since the experiments were carefully done, the gap between what their models predict and what people actually do has just two possible interpretations. Either people who cooperate with one another are not rational, or the experimental models do not adequately represent what rationality is in the context of successful human adaptation. My argument is for the latter. The experiments carefully exclude organizations; I will show why they have to be included. The experiments generally seek to represent the reasoning processes they are concerned with as universal; my argument is that they are necessarily situational.

These experiments were subsequently described in still more detail as *Foundations of Human Sociality: Economic Experiments and Ethnographic Evidence from Fifteen Small-Scale Societies* (Henrich, Boyd, Bowles, Camerer, Fehr, and Gintis 2004), which was critically reviewed by Michael Chibnick (2005). Chibnick focused primarily on the authors' leap directly from the gap between actual choices and what the Nash equilibrium predicted to explanations in terms of evolutionary psychology. Although he notes exceptions and qualifications, his basic criticism is that this amounts to trying to explain a variable (the different reactions in different communities) with a constant (universal human genetics). I agree, although I think that Chibnick does not describe directly enough the recognized lack of a scientific basis for the idea of traits as genetically determined attitudes or conceptual predilections inherent in individuals that these studies are invoking. Beginning with Boas's demonstration of racial malleability in the 1880s, it is difficult to think of an idea that has been more thoroughly examined and more firmly rejected (Boas 1940; Montagu 1946). The old conclusions are only reinforced by newer understandings of what genes are and how different what they control is from the actual content of thought.

The second line of experimental economics described by Greif has the same focus on the gap between predicted and actual behavior but offers a different type of explanation. This focuses on the way decision rules come to be embedded in what they call institutions. I agree with their general drift, but looking for the ways game theoretic formalizations can represent the logic of actual situations is still not the same as finding the indigenous models that are actually constitutive of that logic, and a theory that merely recognizes organizations but does not clearly separate them from institutions or ask what they are and how they are built up is seriously incomplete.

The primary question regarding indigenous algorithms is simply whether they exist. If they do, then the experimenters are not investigating inherent psychological processes but rather what happens when they try to impose an alien decision algorithm over one or more indigenous algorithms that they are ignoring. In fact, such indigenous algorithms do exist and are of many different kinds, as described in chapters 6, 7, and 8.

Once we recognize indigenous decision algorithms, the next question concerns the ways they are used in individual strategies. If there is not one type of rational decision algorithm but many, we have to ask how individuals come to balance or arrange them. This is developed in chapter 9.

Culture and Structure

It is now generally accepted that culture can be regarded as the symbolic expression of structure. The confusing part is that cultural ideas used to form organizations may seem on their face to be either structural or cultural. When they directly describe specific positions, organizations, or sets of mutual relations, they seem to be structural. But when they take the form of myths, ceremonies, stories, canons of good and bad taste, or values, they seem to be cultural.

Sometimes the values that define an organization may be much clearer and more highly standardized than its specific roles and relations. A family, for example, is usually more clearly defined in terms of the quality of relationships they should exhibit than any specific number of social positions and relations. Generally, the members are supposed to have what David Schneider characterized as relations of "diffuse, enduring solidarity" (1968, 116). In any one community, we would expect all family members of a family group to be related to each other in these terms whatever their stated kin relations. We would expect them not to be related to members of other family groups in these terms. It may seem vague, but such a characterization would hardly apply to members of a military unit or participants in an economic transaction.

The values that define organizations of different kinds are always different and often in conflict. If they were not, the organizations could not be differentiated. Demanding immediate and full payment for a meal that one has served a customer in a restaurant is right and proper. Demanding such payment for a meal you have just served to your two-year-old daughter in your home would very likely be taken as an indication of lunacy. We do not notice that we hold such contradictory values because we are so habituated to moving from one type of organizational framework to another that we make the adjustments without conscious effort. But if we drag a principle from one organization into another where it does not fit, reactions are swift and forceful. We know this as cultural actors; the problem is to come to grips with it in social theory.

Institutions

Closely related to the problem of organizations in social theory is the problem of institutions. The way that writers have handled institutions is even murkier than the way they have handled organizations, and the relation between organizations and institutions has been murkier yet.

Broadly speaking, the idea of an institution has been taken in two major ways. Each reflects a different aspect of common usage. The first is as established process. One of the most important general points in Mead's *Mind, Self, and Society* is that we build up our sense of self by incorporating a sense of other through habits acquired in interaction. Self-definition comes about through self-discipline, seeing ourselves not only subjectively but also objectively. There are mutual adjustments of behavior at every stage and every level in this constructive process. The highest level is what Mead calls institutions, which he defines as socially established patterns of responses to situations that are built up through agreements among socially defined actors.

The problem with this is that Mead's phrasing conceptually compresses a complex chain of separate phenomena and processes. Society is not an undifferentiated mass that coughs up an appropriate response when presented with some kind of stimulus. Sometimes things are responded to, and sometimes not; sometimes responses are appropriate, and sometimes not. But most importantly, insofar as responses to anything are reliably established, they involve specific organizations. Society does not respond to a fire, but a fire department does along with those who call it in and who react to what it does. Society does not react to the need to eat, but farms and food production organizations do, and so on.

I am not saying that absolutely all patterned activities in societies are performed by people in organizational capacities. As noted, walking down the street without bumping into one another is not acting as members of an organization. It is, however, very probably the case that all of our important patterned activities involve or depend on organizations, such as the governmental departments that build the streets and those come that into play if someone knocks others down when using them.

The second sense of institution treats them as a specific kind of supraorganization, something that contains organizations but that is not quite an organization in its own right. We readily speak of the "institution of law" but the "organization of law offices" and the "organization of courts." We speak of the "institutional context" of economics or kinship as though it might include more than the organizations of economics and kinship. Although this sense of institutions seems more concrete than the notion of institution as process, the more its proponents have tried to specify what it applies to, the more apparent it has become that no actual referent can be established. Yet no writer reverses the relationship. Organizations are never spoken of as including or encompassing institutions.

Since positivistic theory has been especially committed to a unitary and hierarchical view of society, positivistic arguments have been especially forceful in insisting on the existence of institutions in the supraorganizational sense: organizations make up institutions, and institutions make up society. The idea of an institution thus becomes central to theory. It is the conceptual glue that holds the whole construction together. But since the idea of institutions cannot be given a consistent descriptive content, the dominant argument for it has been based on claims for theoretical necessity, which is usually some version of Durkheim's argument for what he called social facts.

A social fact is a fact that is known only from social theory as such. Every major writer in the positivistic tradition, in anthropology as well as sociology, has used a different version—and often several different versions—of this claim. Social facts (not ordinary facts) are what are supposed to confirm positivistic social theory, and positivistic theory is the basis for asserting the existence of social facts. As Garfinkel has said, "The objective reality of social facts is sociology's fundamental principle" (2002, 65). For Durkheim (1915), the existence of an idea of a totemic clan—an actual idea held by actual Australians—may be an ordinary fact, but the existence of *the* clan, as an all-encompassing unity expressed through ceremonies and manifested in behavior, was a social fact. The logic of Weber's ideal types is parallel, as is Tönnies's social will represented in *Gemeinschaft* and *Gesellschaft*. The same argument underlies Radcliffe-Brown's (1952) idea of relations of conjunction and disjunction as underlying joking relationships around the world, Evans-Pritchard's segmentary system (1967), Levi-Strauss's universal structural dichotomies (1949, 1955), Schneider's claim that "sexual intercourse" is the central "symbol" in terms of which kinship relations are "defined and differentiated" (1968, 33), and so on to and through Clifford Geertz's various ideas of culture as his own unitary interpretation (1960, 1964, 1966, 1973).

Dissatisfaction with the positivist conception of institutions as social facts played a central role in Schneider's turn to postmodernism in the mid-1990s. Partly for this reason and also because Schneider's argument provides such a striking example of how positivist assumptions have prevented their adherents from recognizing the significance of their own observations, the problem of institutions provides a particularly neat test case to demonstrate the difference in power and productivity between positivism and genuine empiricism.

By his own account, Schneider's early intellectual biography was woven mainly out of Marxism, positivism, and psychoanalysis. His parents were Marxists, and he was a graduate student in the Harvard Department of Social Relations. He recognized that these three schemes were mutually contradictory and that none could be proven empirically in any strict sense, but he never rejected them. They remained models for what social theory might be if a way could be found to prove it. When I was his student in the early 1960s, he seemed to think that the differences might be reconciled factually. Not long after, he evidently recognized that this was not possible. He did not recognize, however, that the cause of the impossibility lay in inherent problems with ideologies rather than in inherent problems with facts.

Schneider's rejection of empiricism crystallized in *A Critique of the Study of Kinship* (1987), which argued that a "quartet" of "rubrics," "domains," or "institutions"—kinship, economics, politics, and religion—were nothing more than "metacultural categories embedded in European culture which have been incorporated into the analytic schemes of European social scientists" (184). That is, they were European cultural ideas about culture with no real cross-cultural validity. And even for the West, Schneider rejected the idea that they could be regarded as the "building blocks of society" on the grounds that their "boundedness" was "dubious at best" (183).

This was elaborated in Schneider's autobiographical conversations with Harry Handler in 1995. Toward the end of the book, Handler says that "categories like kinship, politics, and religion have been 'deconstructed'" and asks where this would lead. Schneider accepts the implicit linkage between his position and the postmodernists. He then reaffirms the rejection of the quartet and holds that in their place we should simply use whatever native categories we find in the cultures in which we find them (without saying what these categories were categories of or why he would pick the particular Yap concepts he cited as examples). He then adds that "people don't believe the system that much" and that "the institutional notion has been going, too. So that 'topics' in anthropology now tend to be gender, political economy, race and class" (Schneider 1995, 194).

Schneider's arguments were especially liked by anthropologists committed to what George Marcus and Michael M. Fischer call anthropology as cultural critique. Marcus and Fischer characterize American kinship as "perhaps a model of repatriated anthropology, which offers an epistemological critique of our taken-for-granted social categories" (1999, 148). Exactly how far-fetched this is depends on which taken-for-granted categories they have in mind. Schneider certainly opposed ethnocentrism, but theoretically his argument was much more of a return to his intellectual beginnings than a new start. It was a return to Sigmund Freud in the importance that Schneider was willing to assign to incest as the central organizing principle of kinship—the central symbol—and to Talcott Parsons for his conception of theory itself.

Parsons, like Comte and Mill, saw science as imposing supposedly a priori theory on inherently unordered observations. Schneider recognized this and accepted it. He expressed it to a succession of his graduate students with the allegory of the baseball umpires.

The story, briefly, is this: There were three umpires, a young umpire just starting out, a middle-aged umpire, and an old veteran umpire. They were discussing how they called balls and strikes. The youngest said, "I calls them the way I sees them." After a pause, the middle-aged umpire said, "I calls them as they are." After a still longer pause, finally the old umpire says: "They ain't *nuthin* 'till I calls them" (Feinberg 2001, 10; Leaf 2001, 63). There was no doubt that Schneider thought the old umpire had it right and the greenhorn had it wrong. Facts are created by the imposition of theoretical categories and not otherwise.

For Parsons (1951; Parsons and Shils 1951), this justified what was irreverently referred to as the four-square gospel: a square diagram representing the societal whole divided into four functional subsystems by two supposedly universal, a priori, dichotomous pairs of functional orientations. The dichotomies were internal versus external and latent versus manifest. The four resulting quadrants were adaptation, goal attainment, integration, and latency. The meanings are still the object of unending explanation and counterexplanation. Each of these subsystems at the societal level was in turn supposedly analyzable into the same four functional subsystems at an indefinite number of subordinate levels. The smallest units were either individuals or action systems.

Parsons and his supporters commonly equated the four functional subsystems with institutions and identified them with the same four that Schneider designated as his quartet: the economy, government, family, and religion (among others). This is apparently what Schneider was alluding to in calling them building blocks. The correspondence was taken as showing that Parsons's postulational method was real science. Social reality did indeed follow a priori categories and not the other way around. Schneider's comments to Handler recognize a problem with this, although it is far from the most basic: if the four institutions correspond to the quadrants, they should fit together like quadrants, like four plots of land meeting at a corner. If they do not, there is no reason to take them as parts of a single whole. There should be some actions definitely within one and other actions definitely within others. They should also be objective and not situational, since after all they are being created by the imposition of Parsons's categories and not indigenous categories. And together they should be comprehensive, precluding more subsystems with still other characteristics. Schneider recognizes that we cannot observe this. Vague, circular, and hedged around with obscure qualifications as Parsons's argument always was, it was still contradicted by experience.

Arriving at this point, Schneider had a choice. On the one hand there were actually observable multiple organizations: your family and mine, the University of Chicago, and the Hi-Lo Grocery on 55th Street. There are also institutions in the sense of higher education, kinship, and the food industry, although they are hard to define and although we cannot relate the organizations neatly to them. On the other hand, there was Parsons's method of proceeding from metatheory to theory, starting with a postulated social whole and the postulation that it should be divisible into discrete parts. The observations and the postulational method did not fit together; one or the other had to go.

Schneider chose to reject observation. The choice is perfectly in keeping with the history of positivism, and he was therefore correct to call his position neopositivism. The results of field studies were not important because all fieldwork does is confirm the presumptions we bring to it. It has no crucial place in the development of theory (Schneider 1995, 215). This is straight positivist dogma, exactly what Schneider had encountered as a graduate student.

I take the choice that Schneider declined, observing the metacultural usage and confronting the althoughs. The metacultural idea of an institution as we actually experience it as cultural actors is as a feeling that there is something surrounding or encompassing organizations that is not an organization in itself and whose contents or composition we cannot describe in any consistent way. What we will see is that this idea has a perfectly good explanation, which in turn leads us on to other discoveries. It is a specific type of social projection, an idea that is unavoidably produced in certain specific organizational processes in all societies. The idea of society as a whole is the same sort of social projection. It is readily observable as a socially produced idea held in wide and firm consensus but not in any way observable as an object, organization, or social group. Such projections have an important social-psychological function. As will be described in detail in chapter 7, they provide a conceptual background against which individuals can speak as organizations take shape and interact, a conceptual horizon against which organizations become conceptually visible.

The definitive reply to Schneider in regard to the analysis of kinship is Feinberg and Ottenheimer's *The Cultural Analysis of Kinship: The Legacy of David M. Schneider* (2001). In addition to Feinberg and Ottenheimer themselves, contributors were Raymond Fogelson, Raymond DeMaille, Dwight Read, Robert McKinley, Susan Montague, Laura Zimmer-Tomakoshi, Ward Goodenough, and myself. Although the primary aim was to review Schneider's theoretical claims and contributions rather than argue for any one alternative, there is a very high level of theoretical consensus among the contributors pointing to what such an alternative would be. First, kinship certainly does exist as a distinctive type of cultural and organizational system. It is a definite cross-cultural reality. It can be and has been studied empirically, which is what most of the contributed essays actually do. Second, it is not one thing in the sense that many kinds of cultural ideas bear upon kinship relations, including but not limited to grammatical features of language, types of specific relations such as joking relations, systems of rules for marriage and the like, and terminologies. Third, such studies are not undermined by recognizing relativity of perspective and the social construction of kinship relations, as Schneider seems to have concluded, as long as the analyses recognize and describe this relativity and social construction as part of the phenomenon of kinship itself. Relativity and social construction are interrelated facts. Fourth, a key to understanding how this social construction is done is recognizing that kinship systems are not sets of names for certain kinds of relations, as though such relations might exist on their own in some way, but instead are elements in self-contained formal structures. They are not like a set of tags to be tied to objects one at time; they are like little systems of mathematics or logic whose constituent concepts depend on the logical structure of the whole. They do not define a set of objects in nature but a system of reciprocal relations with moral force. Actual kinship relations are constructed by applying these definitions in interaction.

The organizational perspective here is the same but is enlarged and more fully differentiated.

Cultural Ecology

Recent developments in cultural ecology generate still more empirical reference points to incorporate. From the 1940s through the late 1970s, studies of social organization and ecological studies in anthropology came to be sharply separated. Organizational studies came to be the main vehicle for arguments to support deterministic claims drawn from positivism, while ecological studies came to be the main vehicle for deterministic claims drawn from Marxism and Spencer's social Darwinism.

Since the 1970s, interest in cultural ecology has recrystallized in new ways and greatly expanded. Some of the lines of argument continue to be deterministic and grounded in positivist or Marxist ideology, but the most important are solidly empirical and pragmatic.

The main contemporary arguments for determinism seem to trace back to Roy Rappaport's *Pigs for the Ancestors* (1974), Marshall Sahlins's reply in *Culture and Practical Reason* (1976), and Rappaport's response to Sahlins and other critics in the extended appendices added when *Pigs for the Ancestors* was republished in 1984. Rappaport described a ceremonial cycle among the Tsembaga Marings in Papua, New Guinea. It begins with the planting of the *rumbin* tree as the initiation of a "truce of God" and ends some twelve to fifteen years later with a ceremony called the *kaiko* in which a large number of pigs are slaughtered and the tree is uprooted as a declaration that the truce is ended, after which war ensues. His argument was that this cycle and this ritual were in actuality the cause of warfare and were thereby both what responded to the balance between the pig population and the human population and what regulated them. The original conclusion summarized the argument this way:

> The Tsembaga ritual cycle has been regarded as a complex homeostatic mechanism, operating to maintain the values of a number of variables within "goal ranges" (ranges of values that permit the perpetuation of a system, as constituted, through indefinite periods of time). It has been argued that the regulatory function of ritual among the Tsembaga and other Maring helps to maintain an undegraded environment, limits fighting to frequencies that do not endanger the existence of the regional population, adjusts man-land ratios, facilitates trade, distributes local surpluses of pig in the form of pork throughout the regional population, and assures the people of high-quality protein when they most need it. (Rappaport 1974, 224)

The determinism was stated still more flatly in an article in the *American Anthropologist* published shortly before. The title was "Ritual, Sanctity, and Cybernetics." Cybernetics for Rappaport was about control mechanisms. The ritual acted like a thermostat, but "whereas the thermostat regulates only temperature, the Maring ritual cycle regulates directly the frequency of warfare, the size of pig populations and population density, and through these variations yet others, such as acreage in production, women's labor, and lengths of fallow" (Rappaport 1971, 66). Moreover, he argued, this regulatory function explains why rituals have the quality of sacredness or sanctity that had been so often recognized. It not only conveys the information but also makes it authoritative by sanctifying it (69).

Thus represented, individual choice and purpose as well as social relationships and social ideas were mere epiphenomena of material relationships. In Marxist terms, they were superstructure.

Although the argument was framed with the usual kinds of empirically ungrounded concepts of unitary culture, unitary ecology, arbitrary units of analysis, and determinism, a key set of variables was in principle observable: the human population and its demography over time, the pig population and its demography over time, and the occurrence of kaiko. We can see what the chain of evidence should be. But crucial links were missing. The argument did not, for example, have the actual incidences and rates of human death from different causes. Nor did it have full information on the pigs. Rappaport says that the pig population builds up naturally except that people kill pigs at times of individual or family stress, but he does not have data on how many pigs are eaten on these occasions during the period of buildup, only the number at the time of the feast at the end of the twelve- to fifteen-year cycle. The total pig population just before the kaiko was 170. He also says that in the two years of the study, he recorded a total of 32 shoats surviving in 14 litters. If these two numbers give the actual effective reproduction rate (16/170 per year), the total at the end of the fifteen years leading up to the kaiko would have been 150, which means that none would have been available to be eaten on other occasions. Nor did he collect information on the age and weight breakdown of the entire 170 pigs, only on the 13 pigs that belonged to the largest clan (Rappaport 1974, 61).

Rappaport's 1984 addendum was mainly devoted to defending his versions of the conventional unempirical assumptions, but he also included new information on pig demography. This is in his appendix 11, defending his claim that the ecology provided adequate protein when people most needed it, which was at times of stress. What he reported was that between November 1981 and July 1982, 37 pigs died of "natural causes," most of which were consumed. In addition, 41 were killed and consumed (Rappaport 1984, 476). This is a total of 78 pigs in nine months for a rate of 96 per year. For fifteen years, this adds up to at least 1,440 pigs as compared with 170 in the kaiko. With this ratio, to argue that the timing of kaiko is rigidly determined by ecological constraints on pig reproduction and survival would require that all of these other events for which pigs are consumed be no less rigidly determined, and this does not appear to be the case. He does not describe the natural causes, but he gives the reasons for the other 47. Only 11 were sacrificed in connection with illness and 3 with death, which might be construed as ecologically determined. The rest were associated with a variety of social events that clearly involve individual calculation and choice in creating or maintaining social relations, such as affinal payments, compensation for damage to gardens, legal penalties, and feasts for special events. One pig was killed by its owner because his wife had insulted him and she was "especially fond" of it (476).

Rappaport also argued that the pig population remained below the pig-carrying capacity even at peak times. The trigger for the ritual, he says, is not actually that the pig population reaches an ecological maximum but rather that the women, who grow the yams that the pigs eat, begin to complain about the work, and the men find the complaints unbearable. He does not explain how he knows this is the actual causal sequence rather than an indigenous just-so story told after the fact. A thermostat does not act as a thermostat if it is only used as a switch, turned on or off whenever someone wants to.

Rappaport increasingly qualified his substantive claims after his original publication. In the 1984 edition he finally wrote: "That *Pigs for the Ancestors* failed to meet the rigorous requirements of systemic analysis in all respects must be freely admitted" (1984, 364).

In the meantime, Sahlins had answered Rappaport's monolithic materialism with an equally monolithic idealism, asserting that cultures were self-determining and operated by rules of their own. Since then, the argument has been transformed from idealism versus materialism to an increasingly convoluted whirl about the relationship between nature and culture, drawing on Levi-Strauss's structuralism, and the question of which is dominant has been transformed into various competing views of a dialectic between them. Labels associated with this line of development include the new cultural ecology, new materialism, symbolic ecology, and symbolic cultural ecology. It continues to be only programmatic.

Aletta Biersack's (1999) review of ecological studies in the *American Anthropologist* clearly recognized the difference between this line of argument and the more pragmatic and empirical studies, which have been far more constructive both theoretically and practically. Good descriptive studies of indigenous technologies, particularly farming, have massively documented what deterministic theories persistently deny: individuals recognize problems and find solutions. These solutions involve forming organizations. People compare alternative forms of organization and opt for the more effective.

Analyses of how this happens have been developing in three main lines. The first has been a series of studies beginning with Sol Tax's *Penny Capitalism* (1953), treating economic conventions such as prices and the impact of market transactions ethnographically instead of purely as economists' definitions. These have consistently shown that they are ethnographically real and take different cultural forms in different places but that they nevertheless facilitate allocative efficiency. Tax's work has had important confirmations in economics, most notably in Theodore Schultz's *Transforming Traditional Agriculture* (1964).

Some would consider that the next major effort to make economic theory more ethnographically responsive was the substantivist-formalist controversy of the 1960s, but in the end the key issues were not so much empirical as a matter of differences in disciplinary perspectives. The main effect was that it led to some long-term working relationships between anthropologists and institutionalist economists in the Society for Economic Anthropology.

This was followed by *Agricultural Decision Making: Anthropological Contributions to Rural Development,* edited by Peggy Barlett (1980). Generally, the articles dealt with different types of decisions made by farmers or affecting farmers. There was no concluding chapter and no single substantive conclusion, but arriving at one had not been the purpose of the volume. It was, rather, to show that ethnographic methods could be applied to these problems and did yield improved descriptions. Despite the title, none of the contributions actually provided a description of how farmers planned their farming using their own cultural algorithms, as I will do here. The nearest was Christina Gladwin's "A Theory of Real-Life Choice," which described how one could model a decision to plant a crop as a binary decision tree incorporating choices that farmers actually would make (Barlett 1980, 45–85). Aspects of the formalist-substantivist arguments as well as the themes of this volume continue to be developed.

The second line is a wide range of studies of indigenous farming systems and other productive technologies in the context of studies of development projects. These have made three major points. First, they demonstrated the necessity of social analysis as a component of development planning and project design. Second, they have consistently demonstrated the efficacy and efficiency of indigenous technologies compared to modern technologies that are often not well adapted to local conditions. And third, they have shown that the effectiveness of projects introducing new technologies does not depend only on the technology. It also depends on the compatibility between the managerial design of the project and local organizations (Cernea 1991; Chambers 1983; Hopkins 1987; Lansing 1991; Leaf 1998; Kottak 1999a, 1999b). The result is an actor-centered instrumentally oriented outlook that its proponents characterize as putting people first. This is now the dominant approach in international development project planning.

The third line is the revolution that has sprung from the work of Ester Boserup (1965, 1981). Boserup's impact has been both substantive and methodological. Substantively, she reversed important ideas about the causes of technological development. Previously, the main cause was generally held to be invention, and analyses most often consisted in trying to infer and then test various scenarios that would make this or that specific invention, such as the plow, plausible or likely. It was assumed that once invented, the innovation spread, productivity increased, and population built up virtually automatically.

Boserup pointed out that what needs to be explained is not so much invention as adoption. There are usually many more technological ideas available in or around an area than are actually adopted, and we often find inventions that have no effect in one time and place but a great effect in another. Thus, the mere appearance of an invention is never sufficient to explain its spread, much less explain technological evolution in general. Boserup argued that population increase was the cause and the adoption of the invention was the consequence, under specified conditions. Under any given productive regime, population builds up to the limit that the technology can sustain. At that point there is a window in which very specific technical innovations are needed. If the conditions can be established for their widespread adoption, which usually takes some kind of public action or reorganization, they can lead to a new technological regime and support still higher population densities. Otherwise, the system is in crisis and can collapse.

Boserup's main methodological innovations were a measure of intensification and a measure of efficiency. Previous discussions of intensification had usually turned on some idea of input or output per unit area. We spoke of labor intensification, capital intensification, and so on. These are very difficult to specify in a way that can be applied cross-culturally or over long periods of time. Boserup's measure is the ratio of the area cultivated to the total area exploited. It is operationalized precisely for each field as the length of time that field is fallow compared to the time it is under crops and has provided a general comparative tool for farming systems past and present. For example, in a slash-and-burn system of shifting agriculture, if you return to a field every thirty years and farm it for one year, then the ratio is 1:30. In a system of settled agriculture in which each farm has three fields of the same size and one is left fallow each year, the ratio is 2:3. In a system with no annual fallow, the ratio is 1:1.

The measure of efficiency was equally incisive. Previous attempts had usually been stated in terms of economic cost and gain measured in money. This makes almost no sense across large cultural and temporal divides. In place of monetary budgets, Boserup used energy budgets: calories gained for calories expended, per unit of land area. Such ratios can be established quite precisely for crops that can be examined in the field and can be inferred with at least reasonable precision from historical and archaeological records. They allow comparisons across all different kinds of systems and often illuminate rules or practices that otherwise seem to make little sense (Bayless-Smith 1982; Turner and Brush 1987).

These conceptual changes have produced greatly increased precision in assessments and comparisons of different agricultural technologies and organizational arrangements. In anthropology it has yielded what Biersack, referring to the position of Daniel Bates and Susan Lees, describes as "a more assumption-free ecology, one that was less vulnerable to attack on empirical and theoretical grounds" (Biersack 1999, 7). The most comprehensive and accessible summary of this perspective is Bates's (2001) textbook.

These studies have provided three main findings. The first is that traditional systems are consistently efficient, and generally the more primitive the system (the lower the intensity) the higher the ratio of energy output to energy input. The second is that there are substantial bodies of instrumental ideas in non-Western societies that are quite comparable in their empirical precision and efficacy to bodies of Western scientific and technological knowledge. The third is that there is no deterministic connection between the technological ideas that an organization uses and its organizational ideas. Any given technology can be managed with a wide range of organizational ideas. We will see how in chapter 8. This had been recognized but not stressed by Malinowski and Firth in the 1920s. It was recognized again and given much more prominence by Scarlett Epstein in her *Economic Development and Social Change in South India* (1967), and I am sure I was clear about it in *Information and Behavior in a Sikh Village* (Leaf 1972) and elsewhere. But none of these seem to have had much general effect. Since Boserup, however, the recognition seems to have become something like common sense (Turner and Brush 1987; Schusky 1989).

Conclusion

A community is not a singularity. Communities always contain multiple and distinct types of organizations based on distinct organizational principles and values in such a way that they cannot add up or aggregate to a coherent societal whole. Individual organizations are ongoing consensual constructions of those who conceptually place their interactions within them. They exist in and through interacting human imaginations backed by sanctions rooted in interests. These constructions utilize ideas. Ideas define the relations, and their other ideas define the contexts of those relations.

Human beings think, interact symbolically and practically, and organize. No three points are more conspicuous. The question has been whether they are interconnected. The answer is that they are, and to fail to understand how is to fail to understand them individually.

CHAPTER 2

Skepticism, Pragmatism, and Kant

In recent years, skepticism has been enjoying renewed attention, emphasizing the issues of scientific method that concern us here (McGowan 1974; Burnyeat 1983; Fogelin 1985; Shapin and Schaffer 1985). There is a related but more broadly focused revival of interest in pragmatism (Meltzer, Petras, and Reynolds 1974; Goodman 1995; Hollinger and Depew 1995; Langsdorf and Smith 1995; Rosenthal, Hausman, and Anderson 1999).

Hollinger and Depew's *Pragmatism: From Progressivism to Postmodernism* (1995) retains a clear sense of what pragmatism was originally and how successive adherents to this original conception have distinguished themselves first from those who attempted to assimilate it to logical positivism and then from those who would assimilate it to postmodernism. The only problem is that contributions are confined to philosophy. There is no discussion of pragmatism in law and legal theory, for example, or in social theory.

Oddly, one of the most prolific modern writers in the pragmatic philosophy of science is Nicholas Rescher. Rescher was a student of Karl Hempel and originally identified himself with the Berlin school of logical empiricism. Now, however, he identifies his position as "pragmatic idealism" (Rescher 1991, 1993, 1994). Although, as Ernan McMullin says, the label "might seem close to an oxymoron" (1994, 219), Rescher accurately represents the pragmatic understanding of empirical knowledge, taken in the same broad sense that I do here. That is, he speaks for the fundamentally experimentalist outlook that the classical American pragmatists shared with their continental counterparts who described themselves as skeptics and Kantians, while he clearly distinguishes this position from crypto-positivists such as W. V. O. Quine (Rescher 1962), explicitly self-identified logical positivists such as Carnap, and neopositivists such as Reichenbach and Hempel, for reasons akin to my own.

With respect to social theory, Hans Joas's explicitly pragmatic (1993) critiques of positivist and postmodernist theorists from Durkheim to Habermas are consistent with this same classical pragmatic tradition. So are the contributions to

Alfonso Morales's *Renascent Pragmatism* (2003), representing issues and methods that interlink law, sociology, and anthropology. Ian Hacking's (1999) critique of postmodernist constructionism is pragmatic in fact although not in name. He does not discuss pragmatism as such or call himself a pragmatist, for reasons having to do with other contemporary claimants to the name that Hacking wants to separate himself from (Goodman 1995, 234–49). One of those contemporary claimants is Richard Rorty, whose sweeping rejection of all philosophy and all science in *Consequences of Pragmatism* (1982) has encouraged a great deal of contemporary confusion.

Unfortunately, the resurgence of interest in pragmatism has been accompanied by the idea that its origin was due especially to the impact of Darwin. Depew traces this to John Dewey (Hollinger and Depew 1995, 16n14). Whatever the source, it conveys far too narrow a sense of what pragmatism is. The first pragmatists were a diverse group of philosophers, lawyers, and experimental scientists who drew on four complementary bodies of scholarship: (1) the social, legal, and economic analyses of the Scottish moralists (Hume, Adam Ferguson, and Adam Smith) and their continuation in the evolution of American democratic theory; (2) the epistemological, legal, and social analyses of the particular kind of Romanticism associated with Emmanuel Kant, Gottfried Herder,[1] Johann Wolfgang von Goethe, and Wilhelm and Alexander von Humboldt; (3) the historical jurisprudence of Carl von Savigny and the subsequent sociological jurisprudence of Rudolph von Jhering; and (4) the psychophysics of Gustav Fechner and the subsequent ethnology of Adolph Bastian, the experimental psychology of Herman von Helmholtz and Wilhelm Wundt, and the *Volkerpsychologie* of Wundt and Wilhelm von Humboldt (Leaf 1979, 93–106).

Jurisprudence has always been especially important as a source of skeptical and pragmatic analysis because skepticism and pragmatism loom especially large in law, in contrast to the determinism that looms so large in Judeo-Christian religion. Lawyers and judges must recognize the reality of choice, chance, and purpose and the effort that must go into applying evidence to determine how and why choices were made. This legal theory has, in the past century, become the basis of the largest, most important, and most successful application of any social theory in history, namely the system of decentralized economic regulation of the American New Deal as an alternative to the authoritarianism of both the Right and the Left and its successor embodiment in the postwar Marshall Plan for European recovery and the parallel program for the recovery of Japan (Dulles 1993; Leaf 1998, 5–8).

Kant's Empiricism

It is difficult to see how anyone can understand the potential of modern social science without understanding Kant, yet he is rarely read. Kant demonstrated that all the enduring puzzles of philosophy concerning such seemingly inner or subjective matters as human thought, perception, and judgment could be resolved by empirical methods. They were questions of fact. When we read Kant as what he was—a constructive skeptic and not some strange and inconsistent sort of idealist—he is an astonishingly modern thinker.

Before Kant, skeptical analyses had long recognized many important properties of human perception and society that the drift into positivism has obscured for modern ethnologists. They had stressed that thinking was public as well as private, that perception was both culturally and individually relative, that communication depended on context, that societies were pluralistic, that moral thinking depended on recognition of reflexivity and reciprocity, and that effective law and government had to recognize this. The problem was that no one could say why. They could not find a coherent way in which all of these points were interconnected, a set of principles that brought them together. This is what Kant changed. Kant's analysis of objects was a description of the social creation of objectivity, of objectivization, in the various subject matters he dealt with. And in all cases, reflexivity and reciprocity were the cornerstones.

Reflexivity has been recognized in skeptical theory since Anaxagoras's "Man is the measure of all things." We see the world around us according to the criteria by which we see ourselves. Whatever we say about our context reflects our conceptions of ourselves, and what we say about ourselves has implications for our contexts.

The importance of reciprocity in the logic of social relations was powerfully developed by Montesquieu in *The Spirit of the Laws,* first published in 1748. Montesquieu's central claim was that law is nothing but human reason. This is not an original point in itself, but Montesquieu's use of it was. He made it very clear that reason in this sense was necessarily reciprocal. One could not simply deduce the nature of the laws appropriate to a monarchy from the nature of the monarch, for example. One had to see it as a set of reciprocal relations between and among the monarch and the subjects, and these all had to be reciprocally consistent with one another. Position A could not be superior to Position B in a certain way unless B was reciprocally inferior to A, and all such relations had to be consistent with the type of system they were part of. Seeking profit in office was essential for a monarchy but reprehensible in a republic. Hence the virtues of a subject in a monarchy were necessarily different from those of a citizen in a republic. It directly follows from this perspective that the degrees of freedom people have in asserting different types of social relations in any given society are far more restricted than what they could assert if there were no such constraint. Moreover, when we recognize that it is in general much more difficult for an individual or small group to invent new conceptions of reciprocal relations and get them accepted than it would be for them to work with relations that are already accepted, we can readily understand why people left on their own much more often preserve tradition than cast it aside. The importance that Montesquieu placed on historically established social pluralism as a basis of social stability followed directly.

Kant's analysis of moral judgment incorporated Montesquieu's recognition of the reciprocal logic of social relations, just as his political and jurisprudential views incorporated Montesquieu's recognition of pluralism and his focus on individual perception, needs, and interests. Montesquieu was explicitly opposed to centralizing authority; Kant was explicitly a republican. There is no doubt that Kant had read Montesquieu by 1770 (Zammito 2002, 260). Nevertheless, according to Kant's own statements, his starting point was Hume's skeptical critique of John Locke's materialistic theory of perception.

Locke's theory had two premises. One was the distinction between simple ideas and complex ideas. The other was the idea that the mind is a blank slate. Repeated sense impressions, acting on the mind, automatically and necessarily produce certain corresponding simple ideas. These simple ideas are combined in the mind by relations of cause and effect to produce complex ideas. Since the idea of cause and effect is the heart of this argument, this was Hume's focus.

To be consistent, Locke had to argue that cause and effect was itself a simple idea. Hume's counterargument was to propose an experiment. Hold up an object and release it many times. It falls every time. Hold it up once more and examine your thoughts. Is there really anything that *causes* you to believe that it must fall again? It is, as Hume said, "no contradiction" to imagine that it will stay or rise, and we can readily do so. That is all there is to it. It follows that the supposed cause and the supposed effect are not mentally conjoined. Repeated combinations of events in nature, no matter how regular, do not produce an invariable relation of cause and effect in our minds. They are inherently different, and whatever connections we make between them are, as Hume said, only the consequence of "custom or habit" (1748, 56–57).

Kant described himself as having been awakened from his "dogmatic slumbers"[2] by the recollection of this argument, whose significance he realized as he attempted to put it in general form (Kant 1783, 260).[3] But he criticized Hume for having run "his ship ashore, for safety's sake, landing on skepticism, there to let it lie and rot." His aim was to build on Hume's criticism and establish a "formal science" (262–63). Kant had previously written on Newton and the history of mathematics.[4] Evidently, what he meant by "formal science" here was something along the same lines.

Kant presented three different forms of argument, which he called critical or synthetic, analytic, and anthropological. The main critical writings were the *Critique of Pure Reason* (1781), the subsequent *Critique of Practical Reason* (1788), and the *Critique of Judgment* (1790). The critical writings took established philosophy as their starting point, set aside what could not be supported by experience, and related the rest to the experience it organized. The analytic writings gathered up these conclusions and presented them in what he called a less scholastic and more discursive manner, but he always cautioned the reader not to take the manner of exposition for the method of analysis. The *Prolegomena to Any Future Metaphysics* (1783) did this for the *Critique of Pure Reason*. The *Groundwork of the Metaphysics of Morals* (1785)[5] did it in a way for the *Critique of Practical Reason*, although in this case the *Groundwork* came first and served as an analytic preparation rather than a retrospective codification. It also served as the basis for *The Philosophy of Law* (1796),[6] Kant's most systematic analysis of the conceptual presuppositions of law. This was divided in two parts: *Metaphysics of Morals* (not to be confused with the earlier *Groundwork of the Metaphysics of Morals*), and the *Science of Right*. The translator W. B. Hastie describes the latter *Philosophy of Law* as the sequel to the *Groundwork*. Kant's anthropological work was *Anthropology from a Pragmatic Point of View* (1797).

Kant's social psychology and his analysis of the social construction of the self are mainly presented in the *Critique of Pure Reason*, the *Prolegomena*, and the *Anthropology*. The analyses of social relations, government, and law are the *Critique of Practical Reason*, the *Groundwork of the Metaphysics of Morals*, and *The Philosophy of Law*, while *The Critique of Judgment* focuses on aesthetics and emotions.

The *Critique of Pure Reason* began with the question that had been accepted as central in dualistic philosophy since Plato: "What can be known by the mind alone?" Kant narrowed this by focusing specifically on what we call observations of fact as opposed to observations of moral qualities. The question then becomes "What a priori assumptions are necessary to organize our experience of matters of fact?" This much could still be considered conventional, but not what followed. His next step was to question, on empirical grounds, the idea of a mind alone that the question assumed. Once questioned, there was no way the assumption could stand. This is what Hume's "custom and habit" opened up, and this is what led Kant to an entirely new view of the basic processes of perception.

W. T. Jones's *Kant and the Nineteenth Century* covers many of the issues that concern us here. He describes one main aspect of Kant's pivotal break with previous philosophy: "Abandoning the traditional view that minds are the essentially passive contemplators of independently existing objects, Kant held that objects are constructs in which the activity of minds plays an essential part" (1975, xx). In the traditional view, a mind does nothing but perceive or think. It does not work; it does not communicate. For Kant, minds (plural) are what direct action and interaction; they communicate and they work. Objects take on their identities in this process. On this basis, Kant's search for the a priori is not a search for ideas that are either built into isolated minds before experience or imposed on them by experience. It is a search for the ideas that the process of constructing and communicating common experience must presuppose.

Locke's theory had turned on the same supposed dichotomies that persist in contemporary positivism, Marxism, postmodernism, and interpretivism: between perceptions that are subjective and perceptions that are objective and between ideas in the mind as opposed to objects out there. Kant, however, recognized that the relationship was not dichotomous but instead was contingent. Objective judgments are not the opposite of subjective judgments but rather are built upon subjective judgments. All judgments are subjective, but some subjective judgments are also objective. The problem is to explain how they get that way.

The analysis began with the observation that the subject of a perception—the thing that has the perception—is not something internal to us. The world of our perceptions is not in our mind or head but in what Kant called sensibility, the world as presented by or in our senses. It is presented in what Kant calls our "sensory faculty of understanding." The out there between my eye and the farthest I can see or hear is not beyond my senses but how my senses operate. When we see a tree, we are not doing our seeing here while the tree is doing something else over there. We experience ourselves and the tree in a world as our ability to construct such a sensory display presents it. To fail to understand this is to fail to understand Kant.

Then, since this structure includes the sensory representation of time and space that mathematics represents, time and space must be principles that structure our experience. As Kant put it in the *Prolegomena:*

> Sensibility, the form of which is the basis of geometry, is that upon which the possibility of external appearance depends. . . .
>
> It would be quite otherwise if the senses were so constituted as to represent objects as they are in themselves. For then . . . the space of the geometer would be considered a mere fiction, and it would not be credited with objective validity because we cannot see how things must of necessity agree with an image of them which we make spontaneously and previous to our acquaintance with them. But if this image, or rather this formal intuition, is the essential property of our sensibility by means of which alone objects are given to us, and if this sensibility represents not things in themselves but their appearance, then we shall easily comprehend, and at the same time indisputably prove, that all external objects of our world of sense must necessarily coincide in the most rigorous way with the propositions of geometry; because sensibility, by means of its form of external intuition, namely by space, with which the geometer is occupied, makes those objects possible as mere appearances. (Kant 1783, 287, 288)

Richard Rorty insists that Kant holds a correspondence theory of truth: that like Plato, Locke, and Descartes (among many others), Kant is trying to "ground" observations in experience by showing that they "correspond to" a reality that is beyond experience (Rorty 1979, 4). Here is Kant's actual position. There is no problem of correspondence between the basic form of geometry and the basic form of the sensible world because they are the same thing. There is not one thing in the mind and another in nature, but just one set of structuring principles in our sensory faculty of understanding. Geometry "formalizes," or articulates it: "thought space renders possible the physical space, that is, the extension of matter itself; that this pure space is not at all a quality of things in themselves, but a form of our sensuous faculty of representation; and that all objects in space are mere appearances, that is, not things in themselves but representations of our sensuous intuition" (Kant 1783, 288). This is the alternative to the dualists' gap between appearance and reality or theory and fact and to the positivist claim that geometry is only a matter of definition. It is the basis of Kant's conception of knowledge that is a priori. It is also the basis of modern pragmatic theories of the social construction of reality in that such theories recognize that we develop and use the categories that constitute our perception in interaction with others.[7]

Kant is not suggesting that geometry represents a system of innate ideas that structures our perceptions. He recognized that geometry must be learned, but he also recognized that it *can* be learned. It comes naturally. The question is why. His answer is that we have a general sense of it, an intuition, and it is this intuition that specific geometries give expression to and formalize. We learn our formal mathematics, which then provides the structural categories of our world, but we *can* learn it because we have a human faculty to do so that is more basic and widespread than any formalization.[8] Together with the physical space it "renders possible," this faculty allows us to order our conscious perceptions, which Kant calls judgments. What we order them around is the relation we envision between subject and object, perceiver and perceived, and subjective and objective judgment.

Kant extends the analysis of the relationship between subjective and objective judgments to our sense of subjective and objective things:

> All of our judgments are at first merely judgments of perception; they hold good only for us (that is, for our subject), and we do not till afterward give them a new reference (to an object) and desire that they shall always hold good for us and in the same way for everybody else; for when a judgment agrees with an object, all judgments concerning the same object must likewise agree among themselves, and thus the objective validity of the judgment of the experience signifies nothing else than its necessary universal validity. And conversely when we have ground for considering a judgment as necessarily having universal validity (which never depends upon perception, but upon the pure concept of the understanding under which the perception is subsumed), we must consider that it is objective also—that is, that it expresses not merely a reference of our perception to a subject, but a characteristic of the object. For there would be no reason for the judgments of other men necessarily agreeing with mine if it were not the unity of the object to which they all refer and with which they accord; hence they must all agree with one another.
>
> Therefore objective validity and necessary universality (for everybody) are equivalent terms, and though we do not know the object in itself, yet when we

consider a judgment as universal, and hence necessary, we thereby understand it to have objective validity. (Kant 1783, 298–99)

That is, the judgment that our personal perception reflects an external object is the same as the judgment that all others, universally, will make the same attribution. This attribution, however, is not based on the perception as such but rather on the categories under which we make it. Notice that this agreement embodies the principle of reciprocity: I must know that my perception agrees with others, and they must know that theirs agree with each other and with me. We are all on the same footing. This is a fundamental point that separates Kant from idealists and links him back in time to skepticism and forward in time to pragmatism.

But how can we know when the categories under which we make a judgment will be shared? This is a crucial question. Kant knows that we cannot actually experience anyone else's perceptions, much less everyone else's. His answer is twofold. First and most explicitly, it is that the category says so on its face: to know it is to expect it to be shared. Space, as we all learn it, cannot by definition be just my space. It must be space for all. Time must be time for all. We learn that time and space encompass us and define our common externalities when we learn what they are. We learn that beauty is more personal and relative when we learn what it is.

The second aspect of the answer, developed most fully in the *Anthropology,* is that when we learn concepts from others, we do not just learn something like their literal content or referent. We learn the ways that others use them.

Kant thus recognized a social and consensual component in our most interior mental processes. What was his proof? Here again his experimental method comes into play. He does not offer to deduce it from undoubtable premises but (in the *Critiques*) takes us through a series of variations on situations of use that we can compare with our own experiences, looking at the judgments that we expect others to share and the ways we actually share them. He is talking about everyone's perceptions. Since you are one of everyone, what he is saying should be true for you. It is up to you to see if it is. Your next step should be to check it out with others. The analysis was social psychology in a strict and rich sense. Thought is human but not private. To perceive is to think, to think is to communicate, to communicate requires training in the means of communication, and to be trained requires life in a social group.

For Kant, mind was something we developed with others, in ways he described that we could clearly verify. But however powerful this discovery or realization may now seem, it was still only the beginning. This was only his analysis of what he called phenomena. The further analysis of noumena was built upon it.

Phenomena are objects as they are perceived. They are not sensations. They are the face of the mountain I see just now to the north, the tree I am leaning against, the you I see before me. Noumena are the next step. They are not just the mountain as I see it but the mountain that I feel I would also be able to see from a different position or at a different time. It is also the I whom I presume to be doing this seeing or leaning, the you whom I presume to be listening and understanding and to whom I might speak again in a few days. Noumena are the objects that we presume to lie beyond our perceptions of them. Kant describes noumena as transcendental objects of the understanding. Few concepts are more consistently and widely misunderstood and misrepresented.

Kant meant transcendental literally. To transcend something is to start within it and go beyond it; it is not to be entirely separate from it. The imagery is more dramatic in Kant's German. The term is *überschwänglich,*[9] and the sense from the etymology is of expansive fecundity, overexpansion, or exuberance. We experience such objects as manifested in perceptions but extending beyond them. In saying that they exist a priori, Kant is not making a dualistic claim about an ultimate reality beyond appearances. He is pointing out only that such a thing, by its very nature, cannot be encompassed *in* perception, and therefore such conceptions cannot be derived solely from perception. Since perception is relative and contextual, we cannot see *the* mountain; we only see what we take as part of it. The idea of the *whole* mountain is *überschwänglich*. It therefore *must* be, as Kant said, a pure creature of the intellect, but again in a very specific and empirical sense. It arises from the nature of the understanding, in the sense of a need of the understanding for organizing principles. It is in this sense only a pure idea. It is a projection, an imputation. As Kant said, noumena are hyperbolical. They are exaggerations, and in Kant's German just as in our English, an exaggeration is not a fiction.

For Kant, the most general examples of ideas of these types were soul (or mind), series, and universe. Perceptions of us as subject, for example, use the transcendental idea of a soul, a self, or a consciousness. Perceptions of things as distinct from other things are series. Perceptions or a sense of what all of these are in may be attributed to a universe. But "attributed to" is all that is being claimed for it. Apart from that attribution and the uses it serves in organizing our experience, there is nothing: "Hence, if even the pure concepts of the understanding are thought to go beyond objects of experience to things in themselves (noumena), they have no meaning whatever. They serve, as it were, only to decipher appearances, that we may be able to read them as experience. The principles which arise from their reference to the sensible world only serve our understanding for empirical use. Beyond this they are arbitrary combinations without objective reality, and we can neither know their possibility a priori nor verify . . . their reference to objects" (Kant 1783, 312–13).

That is, when we speak of things that are beyond experience, we cannot know what we are speaking about. How could he possibly be clearer? Since all of our knowledge is grounded in and derived from our experience, constituted by our sensory faculty of understanding, we have no way of knowing if we are making sense in speaking of what is beyond it. We have no way even to imagine things except on the model of experience. The only respect in which speaking of objects as being beyond experience makes sense is if we take them as props or counters to which to attribute experience in order to organize it. Kant could provide no philosophical guarantee of the existence of noumena, as many philosophers point out uneasily, but he obviously and rightly felt that there was no need to. We were justified in accepting them for the very basic reason that without accepting them we could not have orderly thought or communication. The passage is clear, but with respect to current failures to recognize the Kantian basis of modern pragmatism it is important to emphasize that this is exactly what Rorty refuses to recognize, in common with most idealists and all positivists.

Kant does not say that noumenal objects are in themselves synthetic a priori. Concepts that are synthetic a priori are prior with respect to judgments of phenomena, not noumena. But noumenal objects embody, or are based on, concepts that are synthetic a priori.

The rest of Kant's argument concerns the delineation of specific noumenal categories. The details reflect his understanding of the history of philosophy and logic leading up to his own time and need not delay us. But it is important to note that in the process he codifies the previous skeptical arguments to argue that they apply to all possible noumenal postulations without exception, so that "the transcendent cognitions of reason cannot either, as Ideas, appear in experience or, as propositions, ever be confirmed or refuted by it" (Kant 1783, 328–29).

That is, the transcendent cognitions of reason could not have the properties that dualistic philosophy had attributed to them. They could not be more substantial and less ambiguous than experience itself. This is a fundamental criticism of two thousand years of dualistic philosophy. The implication, in plain words, is that the reason you cannot start with an a priori scheme not based on experience and arrive at knowledge of experience is that the idea of such a scheme is nonsensical in itself. You cannot know what you are talking about. But revolutionary as this is, it is still not where Kant's analysis ends. He recognizes a further question. If such cognitions cannot be confirmed or refuted by experience, and if there is nothing beyond experience, then why do such cognitions exist? Why don't we get rid of them? The answer is a new form of the old skeptical emphasis on the importance of action. Kant argues that the major types of noumenal postulations are not merely descriptive and do not refer only to present and past experience. They are also normative and refer to all possible experience: "Judgments, when considered merely as the condition of the union of given representations in a consciousness, are rules" (Kant 1783, 305). They are not just attributed by their users; they are imposed in the process of use. They do not just arise from life; they order it. They are part of action.

The *Groundwork of the Metaphysics of Morals* and the *Critique of Pure Reason* make the same kind of analysis of moral judgments, but each does so in a different sense. The problem of the *Groundwork* is to determine whether there are in moral judgments any a priori postulations comparable to noumena in physical judgments. This is expressed in two ways. One is whether there is any judgment that is made on the basis of reason alone, or pure reason, rather than anything coming from experience or the desire to comply with a prior law or convention. The other is that it would be made by any rational being, meaning that it would be inherent in the nature of reason as such. The argument has three main stages: an analysis of our ordinary usages, or what we actually mean; an extrapolation from that to a philosophical theory; and an exposition of how that theory applies back to the circumstances of ordinary life.

The analysis of ordinary usage began with the observation that there is only one thing we recognize as good without qualification, which is good will. We deem this good even though the consequences of acting on it may not be. He is not saying that we should do this or must do this or that it is undoubtable that we do this. He is just saying that when we think about it seriously, this is how we think and speak. It is an observation to be explained. So his next problem was to say what a good will in this sense was, not normatively but analytically. What do *we* mean in this, and if that can be determined, what does this lead us to? The answer was that we consider a good will to be a will that acts according to duty. Duty in turn is determined by reason, and reason does this by comparing the "maxim" of the act with the "categorical imperative," which he says plainly is the *only* universal rule of morality. The categorical imperative is to "act only on that maxim through which you can at the same time will that it should become a universal law" (Kant 1785, 88).

This has often been misinterpreted by turning it into a kind of solipsistic idealism, that whatever I believe to be right is right for me, and right for me is the only right there is. As Christine Korsgaard recently restated it, "We should act only on a maxim which we could will to be a law," which as she interprets it might be any maxim at all. "Because the will is free, it must be its own law. And nothing determines what that law must be. *All that it has to be is a law*" (Korsgaard 1996, 98; emphasis in original).

In actuality, there is something that determines what that law must be, as already indicated. It is reason. Reason, not will, is the bedrock of Kant's analysis. The will is only the impetus to action and in a strict sense cannot be *any* law, its own or otherwise. What Kant meant by the categorical imperative was not just any principle that we might wish to be universalized but rather a maxim that reason tells us would have to be accepted universally.

Moreover, what Kant means by universal is not just everyone but everyone from all possible rational perspectives, reciprocally. It is not just a principle I would want everyone else to follow but a principle that reason says every rational being would want everyone to follow. The principle is *necessarily* reciprocal. This is precisely why it led Kant to the further principle that our sense of morality requires us to always treat others as ends in themselves and never just as means and thus to his final notion that acting morally in this sense embodies the idea of a society as a kingdom of ends. In such a kingdom, those maxims that are acted on will be the ones that most enhance everyone's freedom and capacity for self-fulfillment. Kant's categorical imperative was, in short, a precise version of "Do unto others as you would have others do unto you." An action that we judge to be moral in itself is one whose principle is consistent with it.

I trust that it is reasonably easy to see why this makes sense as a general statement of our fundamental notions of what makes an action seem right or wrong in a moral sense, obligatory in itself or not. The more difficult point to grasp is how Kant takes it to be a priori and, especially, why it must hold for all rational beings. This takes us to the nature of reason as such. The explanation is that you cannot *be* a rational being without adhering to it. To think rationally—really to think at all—requires contrast. But Kant does not construe contrast as requiring absolute dichotomies. He recognizes that consistent schemes of thought can involve contrasts of many kinds. What matters is that whatever they are must be mutually consistent and must be adhered to consistently. Moreover—and this is the particularly brilliant part—since thought is not private but something we communicate, this self-consistency must also hold up reciprocally. I must make sure that words and ideas apply the same way to me and to you, and you must do the same. So must all other rational beings; without this, coherent communication itself is not possible. The Kantian conception of the a priori is, therefore, an analysis of the preconditions for perceptions that can be shared and communicated,[10] and his idea of self-contradiction, as what is destructive of such communication, is far more complex and many-sided than anything in previous or subsequent dualistic philosophies.

Kant gives only a few examples of actions whose maxims are morally compelling, but they confirm this reading. The clearest are that one should not lie, should not make an agreement with the intent of not keeping it, and should not commit suicide to avoid difficulties. His explanation, in each case, involves demonstrating that if the maxim were to be adopted it would negate itself. When universalized, it is self-nullifying. In effect, Kant's supreme principle of morality is actually a fundamental formal requirement for rational interaction.

The *Critique of Practical Reason* applied the same type of analysis to judgments about relations of means to ends, and the idea of a self-contradiction took the form of a means that would undermine the end that it was intended to accomplish. You cannot rationally use a means to accomplish some end if that end will be destroyed in the process of using it. So in this case the categories that are synthetic a priori are most fundamentally the ideas of freedom and purpose in the context of the knowledge of human behavior and cause and effect obtained through experience.

The *Philosophy of Law* developed the implications of the *Critiques* and the *Groundwork* to establish the principles of "all laws, which is possible to establish by external legislation" (Kant 1796, 44). The argument is complex. In the main it seems to be a step-by-step refutation of Hobbes's argument that in order to have the security of law, reason requires individuals to give up their will to an absolute sovereign. Kant's alternative is based on the observation (not just a stipulation) that the will is inalienable and that reason is the means by which we can guide it.

A key point for Kant's conception of the difference between a state of nature and a civil society was that while reason can establish action that is obligatory in a personal way, for something to be obligatory as a right that can be asserted by another requires legislation to establish an external mine and thine. This requires a civil constitution. A civil constitution requires still further laws. Some of these would reflect principles that would be obvious without legislation, such as laws establishing the right not to be murdered or defrauded. Others would concern actions that would not seem right or wrong in themselves but only once we knew that they had been agreed to be such by the community. A simple modern example is rules of the road. There is nothing right or wrong about driving on either the right or left, but experience would readily show that it is in everyone's interest to do one or the other. Once either becomes accepted as the rule, it becomes morally obligatory to follow it just as surely as it is obligatory not to lie. It seems simple, but a huge proportion of the seemingly odd rules and practices we encounter cross-culturally are of this type and therefore require this type of explanation, as opposed to explanations based on differing mental capacities, what the X "believe," or simply "it's their culture."

Kant's *Anthropology from a Pragmatic Point of View* is an analysis of the development of the capacity for judgment described in the *Critiques* through the process that we now call acculturation. The *Critiques* say what the categories of judgment are; the *Anthropology* says why and how we learn them. This includes an analysis of the rewards for getting them right and the penalties for getting them wrong.

Anthropology from a Pragmatic Point of View is the notes Kant had used for a very popular course he had been giving for some thirty-seven years, beginning before the first of the *Critiques*. Saying they are notes does not mean that they are incomplete. They were kept unpublished only to compel people to attend the course, a common practice at the time to ensure some income. The topic is the development of effective thought and perception. The argument proceeds from simple to complex and individual to group. It is divided into four main sections: "the cognitive powers," "the feelings of pleasure and displeasure," "the appetitive power," and "anthropological characterization." The last includes sections on the character of the person, the senses, nations, races, and the human species. The opening section will give a sense of how modern the argument appears.

The first subsection is "On Self-Consciousness." It takes up the same theme of self-identification as the *Critiques* but in a simpler descriptive way that invites the reader to assess what Kant is saying in light of his own personal experience: "The fact that man can have the idea 'I' raises him infinitely above all other beings living on earth. By this he is a *person;* and by virtue of his unity of consciousness through all the changes he may undergo, he is one and the same person—that is, a being altogether different in rank and dignity from *things,* such as irrational animals, which we can dispose of as we please. This holds even if he cannot yet say 'I,' for he still has it in mind. So any language must *think* 'I' when it speaks in the first person, even if it has no special word to express it. For this power (the ability to think) is *understanding*" (Gregor 1974, 9).

That is, to be in possession of understanding is to be able, indeed to be required, and to think "I." Consciousness involves self-consciousness. Kant continues with an observation that was central for George Herbert Mead: "But it is noteworthy that a child who can already speak fairly fluently does not begin to talk in terms of 'I' until rather late (perhaps a year later); until then he speaks of himself in the third person (Charles wants to eat, to go for a walk, etc.). And when he starts to speak in terms of 'I' a light seems to dawn on him, as it were, and from this day on he never relapses into his former way of speaking. Before, he merely *felt* himself; now he *thinks* himself. The anthropologist may find it rather hard to explain this phenomenon" (Gregor 1974, 9).

The next step is the idea of egoism, that all thought is at first egoistic, with reference to this "I." The section begins thus:

> From the day a human being begins to speak in terms of "I," he brings forth his beloved self wherever he can, and egoism progresses incessantly. He may not show it (for the egoism of others checks him); but it progresses secretly, at least, so that his apparent self-abnegation and specious modesty will give him a better chance of being highly esteemed by others.
>
> Egoism can take three forms of presumption: Presumption of understanding, of taste, and of practical interest. That is, egoism can be logical, aesthetic, or practical. (Gregor 1974, 10)

Anyone familiar with Kant's other works would see instantly that these three forms of egoism correspond to the major types of judgments reviewed in the *Critiques:* judgments based on a claim of objectivity, judgments based on taste, and judgments based on practical morality (principles relating means to ends).

In each case, egoism means making judgments without recognizing a need to check such judgments with others. "The *logical egoist* considers it unnecessary to test his judgment by the understanding of others too" (Gregor 1974, 10). The *aesthetic egoist* does the same for judgments of taste, and the "*moral egoist* is a man who limits all ends to himself" (Gregor 1974, 11). Also in each case, such egoists are mistaken. Testing is necessary. Moreover, it is ultimately forced on the egoist by the need to live with others. The progression of topics follows that of the *Critiques*.

The problem that Kant is dealing with is hardly recognized by dualistic philosophers but looms large in all our lives. To some extent a capacity for perceptual judgment is inborn; our judgments are our own and subject to error that we may make or avoid. But in another sense our judgments also depend on agreement with others and on learning to impute concepts obtained from others. Judgment is relative and consensual but still can be either right or wrong. Kant's task is to show how these two aspects interrelate. It is also, as Gregor's introductory note stresses, to show people how to use this knowledge for their advantage. Kant explicitly promises that the *Anthropology* would help people obtain their ends in their dealings with others.

Kant's argument is that in order to make good factual, aesthetic, and moral judgments, one has to make one's judgments refer to others as well as oneself. Good judgment is a matter not only of perception but also of self-discipline. It is in large part a matter of finding the way to avoid excessive egoism in either of two ways: leaning too much on one's own predilections or submitting too much to others' predilections. For example:

> When we use "understanding" to mean the power of knowing rules (hence the power of conceptual knowledge), so that it covers the whole *higher* cognitive power, we should not include under it the rules by which nature guides man's conduct in the same way that it drives animals by natural instinct, but only the rules that man himself *makes*. When we learn something by mere rote we do it mechanically (by laws of reproductive imagination) and without understanding. A servant who merely has to pay a compliment according to a prescribed formula does not use his understanding. He does not have to think for himself. But when he has to look after the household affairs in his master's absence, and needs various rules of conduct that cannot be spelled out for him, then he does need to use understanding.
>
> *Right* understanding, *practiced* judgment and *profound* reason comprise the whole sphere of the intellectual cognitive power, especially if we include in it proficiency in promoting the practical that is proficiency for *ends*.
>
> Right understanding is healthy understanding, because its concepts are *adequate* to the end for which we use them. And since *sufficiency* ... and *exactness* ... combined constitute adequacy, so that the concept contains neither more nor less than the object requires ..., right understanding is the first and most eminent among the intellectual powers. For it answers its purpose with the fewest means. (Gregor 1974, 70)

Wherever you see a variant of "practical" in this, read a variant of "pragmatic." They are two lexemes for one idea. What Kant is saying is that the basis of all our mental powers and virtues is to be found in the practical relations of means and ends.

The discussion of normal and efficacious judgment leads to consideration of defects of judgment, which are of two kinds: mental illness and mental deficiency. Kant catalogs and analyzes them in the same manner as the cognitive powers. Madness is a general term for many extreme forms of mental illness, and in the concluding "random remarks" he turns to it directly.

> The one universal characteristic of madness is loss of *common sense* (*sensus communis*) and substitution of *logical private sense* (*sensus privatus*) for it; for example a man sees in broad daylight a lamp burning on his table that another man present does not see, or hears a voice that no one else hears. For we have to attach our own understanding to the understanding of other men, too, instead of *isolating* ourselves with our own understanding and still using our private ideas to judge *publicly,* so to speak. This is a subjectively necessary criterion of the correctness of our judgment generally, and so too of the health of our understanding. (Gregor 1974, 88)

Normalcy or sanity is maintained by holding one's perceptions up to the standard of common sense, meaning what one knows to be held in common. Sanity isn't something one has; it is something one does. One learns how to do it while learning to live in any community. It may become deeply habitual, but fundamentally it requires an act of choice or will. One can depart from it at any time and take the consequences. Mead would rephrase the analysis to describe the way we maintain self-consciousness: it is "an awakening in ourselves of the group of attitudes which we are arousing in others, especially when it is an important set of responses which go to make up the members of the community" (Mead 1934, 163).

In Kant's time, every educated person would have been familiar with arguments to the effect that civil society involved a contest of wills and that law was created out of such contests or in order to resolve them. It would have been immediately apparent that Kant's analysis was not only about individuals but also about law and organization. This would have raised the question of what kind of legal system Kant saw as most consistent with the development of healthy judgment in its citizens. Kant's answer was clear:

> *Freedom* and *law* (which limits freedom) are the two pivots around which civil legislation turns. But in order for law to be efficacious and not merely an empty recommendation, a middle term[11] must be added, namely power, which, when it is connected with the principles of freedom, provides the principles of law with effect.
> There are four conceivable combinations of power with freedom and law:
>
> A) Law and freedom without power (anarchy)
> B) Law and power without freedom (despotism)

C) Power without freedom and law (barbarism)

D) Power with freedom and law (republic).

We see that only the last combination deserves to be called a true civil constitution. (Gregor 1974, 190–91)

Kant rejected the idea of an inherent conflict between social development and individual development. Law was a part of common sense. By the same token, there was no conflict between the development of (good) law and individual freedom. As was spelled out more fully in his *Idea for a Universal History from a Cosmopolitan Point of View* (1784) and *Perpetual Peace* (1795), the corpus of laws that were morally obligatory in a community was the embodiment of choices freely made in that community's history, condensed and expressed where necessary or desirable by its agencies. The elaboration of law, in this sense, is the elaboration of freedom. Since Kant, and especially since World War II, we have increasingly realized the force of this. We cannot have true rule of law without simultaneously ensuring that a major function of the law is to protect individual liberty, particularly in the form of increasing recognition of what has come to be an almost universally recognized list of human and civil rights. Ronald Dworkin (1986) is an important contemporary representative of this analysis.

In the beginning of the nineteenth century Kant was widely read, and enormous excitement was generated by the burgeoning empirical science and spreading political liberalism that his analysis supported. Goethe and Beethoven are equally spokesmen for this vision. In Goethe's *Faust*, Faust bargains with Mephistopheles to gain power to attain his own interests and his own pleasures only. Faust then discovers that this yields nothing he values and demonstrates nothing but depravity, and he abandons it. In the end, to the bewilderment of Mephistopheles and despite Faust's original bargain, Faust's soul is saved by the heartfelt and spontaneous joy he takes in land reclamation:

> Below the hills in a marshy plain
> Infects what I so long have been retrieving;
> This stagnant pool likewise to drain
> Were now my latest and my best achieving.
> To many millions let me furnish toil;
> Green, fertile fields where men and herds go forth
> . . . .
> He only earns his freedom and existence,
> Who daily conquers them anew.
> . . . .
> Stand on free soil among a people free!
> Then dare I hail the Moment fleeing:
> *"Ah, still delay—thou are so fair!"*
> The traces cannot, of mine earthly being,

In eons perish, they are there!
In proud fore-feeling of such lofty bliss,
I now enjoy the highest Moment, this! (Goethe 1950, 241)

To relate Kant's analysis most directly to ethnology, the key question is whether the synthetic a priori categories and noumenal systems that Kant delineated are the only possible ones. Kant may have thought so; certainly he thought that he had accounted for all the major kinds that had been important in the history of Western thought. But in fact there are others. Kant's analyses included recognition of the ideas of the self, series, and other as culturally constituted social-psychological organizing principles in a generic sense, and he recognized the importance of the general idea of reciprocity in many ways beyond what I have described. But he did not recognize the nature and function of the social-organizational ideas that we use to define our different selves in relation to specific others in specific socially constructed contexts: self as father in family, self as professor in university, self as citizen in state, and so on. In general, he did not recognize the need to systematically delineate and analyze the systems of relational concepts that constitute kinship, government, religion, business, economics, or the professions. This is what I describe here.

Philosophical Misrepresentations

It was not hard to see that if Kant's arguments would prevail, dogmatic epistemology and social analysis would be out of work, and authoritarianism would have lost its best established defenses. On the other hand, if Kant were any kind of dualist, dualistic philosophy could go on as before.

Because of his focus on a priori knowledge, the most natural kind of dualist to make Kant into was an idealist, and idealists did so. They claimed, in the words of the influential idealist historian of philosophy Wilhelm Windelband, to develop "the principles won by Kant" into "the comprehensive systems of German philosophy" (Windelband 1901, 2:568) generally known as neo-Kantianism.

Fichte and Hegel

Misrepresentations began with Fichte, who styled himself as Kant's student and did indeed begin with an attachment to Kant and an endorsement by him. But as his writing developed, he sought to put Kantian philosophy on what he regarded as a firmer foundation. To do this, he inflated the individual ego to an absolute ego and that in turn into God. Kant never said anything of the kind; it turns Kant's idea of transcendence into just the kind of claim about realities beyond experience that he said made no sense.

Hegel followed close upon Fichte in time and approach but was far more aggressive. With a new form of philosophical writing that boils and surges with sweeping reifications, misplacing both concreteness and agency, he brought the self-contradictions of dualistic dogmatism audaciously to the front of his argument and treated them as proof that he was speaking for a higher than ordinary truth. Utterly rejecting Kant's concern with delineating what is observable, he twisted Kant's analysis of phenomena as actual perceptions into his own neo-Platonic "phenomenology of mind,"[12] a purely ratiocinative construction of a supposed mental force that is beyond our experience but directive of it, directive *because* it is beyond it. The force was Reason, or Spirit (*Geist*). (The German capitalization is often kept in English translations to convey Hegel's anthropomorphism.) Its qualities mirror those formerly assigned to God in Christian arguments for religious absolutism: it is the source of all general ideas, the single force controlling history, and subject to no law or morality but its own nature. Its own nature boils down to a continual dialectic of thesis and antithesis, affirmation and negation. Where Kant took the force of ideas as a fundamental problem, Hegel took it as the ultimate explanation. Hegel's conception in turn became Durkheim's idea of a collective consciousness and is now Jürgen Habermas's "metabiological" intersubjectivity (1996, 22).

Hegel's phenomenology was also his state philosophy, a theory of rule no less than a theory of knowledge. Historic religion was merely an early and crude recognition of the force of Reason, and state philosophy was its natural replacement, recognizing that Reason's real embodiment is not an otherworldly God but the this-worldly State. And since Reason was God and was purely general and all merely human perception and thought was the imposition of the general on particulars (by which they become known), it followed that the only criterion for truth was consistency according to the rules by which reason operates, which is to say conformance to the requirements of the state. For Kant, phenomena were what we would call social-psychological constructions, the appearances that things assume for us given our physical capacities and socialization. For Hegel, all general concepts were manifestations of unitary, generic, and absolute Reason in our individual consciousness, for its own purposes. We owe the state our minds, and any failure to see this is confusion.

Hegel was recognized as an extreme proponent of the subordination of the individual to the state and the state to a totalitarian ruler, but many less politically immoderate arguments—idealistic arguments—were similar in their sweep, pretension, and departure from Kantian concerns with what is actually observable. Jones (1975), again, provides the best survey.

More recent idealist and positivist misrepresentations of Kant's view of science through the 1960s need not detain us because they have been so well covered by Brittan (1978). But I should note a probably influential misstatement by Bertrand Russell regarding Kant's politics. Instead of acknowledging the clear contrast between Kant's republicanism and Hegel's absolute authoritarianism, Russell says only that Kant "is not himself politically important, though he wrote some interesting essays on political subjects" (Russell 1945, 703). The effect, for anyone who would believe this, can only be to divert attention from Kant's enormous impact on law and legal theory, which nineteenth-century anthropology grew out of and which nineteenth-century sociology was a calculated reaction against.

Richard Rorty

Since the time that Brittan wrote, Richard Rorty has provided yet another characterization of Kant as a dualist. This is especially important here because Rorty has been widely read outside of philosophy and describes himself as a pragmatist. For readers who are not familiar with pragmatism or Kant on their own, the inference has to be that pragmatism could not possibly be what I am describing. In fact, Rorty misrepresents all three: pragmatism, Kant, and the relation between them.

Rorty's explicit target is what he describes as the correspondence theory of Truth. What he means by this is not just the view that the truth of ideas or statements lies in whether they correspond to some set of experiences or conditions in experience but instead actually a view of philosophy itself. It is that the focus of philosophy is on the relation between what he calls Truth with a capital "T" and uncapitalized truth, which everything else deals with. Philosophy (with a capital "P") is the arbiter of Truth (with a capital "T"). It justifies, or "grounds," other types of truth by showing their correspondences to real Truth. This conception of Philosophy, he says, begins with Plato and Socrates, runs through Descartes and Locke, and includes Kant, the neo-Kantians, and everyone else before Dewey, Heidegger, and Wittgenstein, who were "in agreement that the notion of knowledge as accurate representation, made possible by special mental processes, and intelligible through a general theory of representation, needs to be abandoned" (Rorty 1979, 6).

Rorty's Philosophy (with a capital "P") is what I have previously described as dualism and am here describing under the heading of dogmatism. The term "dualism" calls attention especially to the postulated difference between the world of experience and the supposed world beyond it (Leaf 1979, 13–30). The term "dogmatism" calls attention to the basis for this postulation. Rorty recognizes the same features, but reflecting the modern linguistic turn in philosophy (Rorty 1992) from cosmological metaphors to linguistic metaphors, he usually describes the gap between the world of experience and the supposed reality behind it as being between different kinds of sentences, notions, claims, or truths. My objection is not with what Rorty finds unjustifiable about this; our criticisms agree. My objection is to the way he completely fails to recognize the skeptical tradition as the established alternative to it, puts Kant on the wrong side of the divide between them, and in consequence presents a truncated, confused, and shallow picture of pragmatism itself.

Philosophy and the Mirror of Nature (1979) begins by describing the view of philosophy that Rorty seeks to oppose:

Philosophy's central concern is to be a general theory of representation, a theory which will divide culture up into the areas which represent reality well, those which represent it less well, and those which do not represent it at all (despite their pretenses of doing so).

We owe the notion of a "theory of knowledge" based on an understanding of "mental processes" to the seventeenth century, and especially to Locke. We owe the notion of "the mind" as a separate entity in which "processes" occur to the same period, and especially to Descartes. We owe the notion of philosophy as a tribunal of pure reason, upholding or denying the claims of the rest of culture, to the eighteenth century and especially to Kant, but this Kantian notion presupposed general assent to Lockean notions of mental processes and Cartesian notions of mental substance. In the nineteenth century, the notion of philosophy as a foundational discipline which "grounds" knowledge-claims was consolidated in the writings of the neo-Kantians. Occasional protests against this conception of culture as in need of "grounding" and against the pretensions of a theory of knowledge to perform this task (in, for example, Nietzsche and William James) went largely unheard. "Philosophy" became, for the intellectuals, a substitute for religion. It was the area of culture where one touched bottom, where one found the vocabulary and the convictions which permitted one to explain and justify one's activity *as* an intellectual, and thus to discover the significance of one's life. (Rorty 1979, 3–4)

Rorty concludes the introduction with an explanation of his title: "The picture which holds traditional philosophy captive is that of the mind as a great mirror, containing various representations—some accurate, some not—and capable of being studied by pure, nonempirical methods. Without the notion of the mind as mirror, the notion of knowledge as accuracy of representation would not have suggested itself. Without this latter notion, the strategy common to Descartes and Kant—getting more accurate representations by inspecting, repairing, and polishing the mirror, so to speak—would not have made sense" (1979, 12).

I agree with his focus on images, but he does not have all the right ones. For the dualists, it is some version of the idea of two realities, as he recognizes, but it is also an image of the knower as an isolated individual. For Kant, by contrast, it is one world and people interacting within it, with knowledge as an aspect of that interaction. This is the dominant image of the skeptical tradition generally, including pragmatism.

Like the neo-Kantian idealists, Rorty assimilates Kant to the tradition he rejected. Throughout the work Rorty defines his target in phrases such as "the Cartesian-Kantian problematic" (1979, 8), the "traditional Cartesian-Kantian matrix" (11), and the "epistemological problematic" developed by "Locke and Kant" that "replaced the scholastic problematic" (262).

Pragmatism, by contrast, is described as abandoning this view of philosophy and the problem of grounding:

It is against this background that we should see the work of the three most important philosophers of our century—Wittgenstein, Heidegger, and Dewey. Each tried, in his early years, to find a new way of making philosophy "foundational"—a new way of formulating an ultimate context for thought. . . . Each of the three came to see his earlier effort as self-deceptive, as an attempt to retain a certain conception of philosophy after the notions needed to flesh out that conception (the seventeenth-century notions of knowledge and mind) had been discarded. Each of the three, in his later work, broke free of the Kantian conception of philosophy as foundational, and spent his time warning us against those very temptations to which he himself had once succumbed. Thus their later work is therapeutic rather than constructive, edifying rather than systematic, designed to make the reader question his own motives for philosophizing rather than to supply him with a new philosophical program. (Rorty 1979, 5–6)

The first problem with this, as I hope I have made clear, is that Kant's idea of grounding was not an effort to justify our fundamental physical and moral perceptions but rather to describe how we arrive at them in fact. The second problem is that it misrepresents the relation of Kant to the subsequent expansion of experimentalism and, in turn, to pragmatism as the philosophy that represented it. In consequence, it also greatly understates the scope and power of pragmatism. Rorty's alternative to the idea of knowledge as the mirror of nature is the idea that knowledge is "a matter of conversation and social practice," which he attributes to Quine and Wilfrid Sellars (Rorty 1979, 171).

These characterizations are even more strongly stated in Rorty's subsequent *Consequences of Pragmatism* (1982). Rorty begins by describing pragmatists in a way that contrasts the pragmatic tradition with the tradition beginning with Plato, again dualism but still without calling it that:

Pragmatists think that the history of attempts to isolate the True or the Good, or to define the word "true" or "good," supports their suspicion that there is no interesting work to be done in this area. It might, of course, have turned out otherwise. People have, oddly enough, found something interesting to say about the essence of Force and the definition of "number." They might have found something interesting to say about the essence of Truth. But in fact they haven't. The history of attempts to do so, and of criticisms of such attempts, is roughly coextensive with the history of that literary genre we call "philosophy"—a genre founded by Plato. So pragmatists see the Platonic tradition as having outlived its usefulness. (Rorty 1982, xiv)

This leads (again) to the argument that pragmatism and the Platonic tradition take the idea of philosophy in two different senses. In the pragmatic sense, which Rorty describes as "uncapitalized," philosophy is simply "an attempt to see how things, in the broadest possible sense of the term, hang together, in the broadest possible sense of the term" (1982, xiv, quoting Wilfrid Sellars). But,

In this second sense, it can mean following Plato's and Kant's lead, asking questions about the nature of certain normative notions (e.g., "truth," "rationality," "goodness") in the hope of better obeying such norms. The idea is to believe more truths or do more good or be more rational by knowing more about Truth or Goodness or Rationality. I shall capitalize the term "philosophy" when used in this second sense, in order to help make the point that Philosophy, Truth, Goodness, and Rationality are interlocked Platonic notions. Pragmatists are saying that the best hope for philosophy is not to practice Philosophy." (Rorty 1982, xv)

This leads to the argument that also lumps Kant with positivism and allied schools: "It is important to realize that the empirical philosophers—the positivists—were still doing Philosophy. The Platonic presupposition which unites the gods and the giants, Plato with Democritus, Kant with Mill, Husserl with Russell, is that what the vulgar call 'truth'—the assemblage of true statements—should be thought of as divided into a lower and an upper division, the division between (in Plato's terms) mere opinion and genuine knowledge" (Rorty 1982, xv–xvi). And from here on Rorty repeatedly refers to Plato, Kant, the neo-Kantians, Descartes, and positivists as if they were all aligned and occasionally combines them in phrases such as "post-Kantian metaphysical idealism" (143), "Platonist or Kantian philosophers' imaginary playmates" (167), and "the Platonic-Kantian notion of grounding" (168, 172).

What Rorty persistently misses in his representation of pragmatism is that it is empirical, and one of its most important observations is that what we say and how we understand it is embedded in and related to action, which is socially organized. Pragmatic philosophy is not just philosophical criticism of philosophical dualism or a therapeutic relief from it. It *is* constructive. It *is* systematic. And it also makes substantive claims about social, psychological, and physical reality. Pragmatism is empirical philosophy.

Rorty versus Dewey

Rorty does not support the associations between Kant and the dualists I have noted with textual analysis. He does, however, frequently suggest that his reading of Kant (and therefore also of pragmatism) is supported by Dewey.

Dewey's understanding of Kant, in relation to the kinds of issues Rorty focuses on, is clearly expressed in *The Quest for Certainty* (1929). This is mainly a response to those—dogmatists, of course—who attack empiricism on the ground that it is not certain and offer their own schemes as superior on that basis. Dewey's argument is that certainty is not a goal in science and does not need to be and that philosophical pretensions to it are unjustified. The argument is organized as a semihistorical review and comparison of evolving conceptions of knowledge in philosophy and science in which Kant is clearly a pivotal figure. Dewey explicitly takes science as I have; it is a body of experimental knowledge as opposed to a body of statements or the like.

In the introductory chapters, when Dewey first gets to Kant he describes his analysis in a way that Rorty might quote: "The Kantian method is of course but one of a number of the philosophic attempts at harmonization. There is one phase of it which may be said to continue the Cartesian attempt to find the locus of absolute certainty within the knowing mind itself, surrendering both the endeavor of the ancients to discover it in the world without, and of the medieval world to find it in an external revelation." But Dewey immediately continues: "In his search for forms and categories inherent in the very structure of knowing activity, Kant penetrated far below the superficial level of innate ideas in which his predecessors had tried to find the locus of certainty. Some of them were conditions of the possibility of there being such a thing as cognitive experience. Others were conditions of there being such a thing as moral experience" (Dewey 1929, 61). Dewey thus recognizes from the start that Kant was not seeking the basis of knowledge in an unjustifiable idea of the isolated individual mind but in the requirements of knowing activity as something social and interactive and also that knowing activity in regard to objects (cognitive experience) is different from knowing activity in regard to social relations (moral experience), as I have said.

Dewey next turns to Kant and idealism: "His idealistic successors pushed their way further on the road which Kant had broken:—even though he insisted that the doors were locked to traveling on it any further than he had gone" (Dewey 1929, 61). This is not the way I would put it because Kant did more than just insist, but it is certainly the sequence I have described. It is not what Rorty describes. In Dewey's view, Kant accepted his predecessors' problem of finding the basis of knowledge but resolved it in a different way, which his idealistic successors ignored.

More of what makes Kant pivotal in the developments leading to pragmatism is taken up in the chapter titled "The Copernican Revolution." The chapter begins:

> Kant claimed that he had effected a Copernican revolution in philosophy by treating the world and our knowledge of it from the standpoint of the knowing subject. To most critics, the endeavor to make the known world turn on the constitution of the knowing mind, seems like a return to an ultra-Ptolemaic system. But Copernicus, as Kant understood him, effected a straightening out of astronomical phenomena by interpreting their perceived movements from their relation to the perceiving subject, instead of treating them as inherent in the things perceived. The revolution of the sun about the earth as it offers itself to sense-perception was regarded as due to the conditions of human observation and not to the movements of the sun itself. Disregarding the consequences of the changed point of view, Kant settled upon this one feature as characteristic of the method of Copernicus. He thought he could generalize this feature of Copernican method, and thus clear up a multitude of philosophical difficulties

by attributing the facts in question to the constitution of the human subject in knowing. (Dewey 1929, 287)

Then, after a second paragraph elaborating the first:

> There is accordingly opposition rather than agreement between the Kantian determination of objects by thought and the determination by thought that takes place in experimentation. There is nothing hypothetical or conditional about Kant's forms of perception and conception. They work uniformly and triumphantly; they need no differential testing by consequences. The reason that Kant postulates them is to secure universality and necessity instead of the hypothetical and the probable. Nor is there anything overt, observable and temporal or historical in the Kantian machinery. The work is done behind the scenes. Only the result is observed, and only an elaborate process of dialectic inference enables Kant to assert the existence of his apparatus of forms and categories. (Dewey 1929, 289)

Note that in the first paragraph Dewey characterizes Kant's analysis in two ways. One is that he bases his explanation on "the constitution of the knowing mind," and the other is that he bases it on "the conditions of human observation." Unless we want to assume that Dewey is inconsistent, they have to be taken together. So we cannot take "the knowing mind" in a Platonic sense but as we find it in knowing experience, of Copernicus's sort. Dewey recognizes that Kant's focus is experimental knowledge. What he is saying is that Kant's own method was not of the same sort. This boils down to a question of whether Dewey or Kant had the better understanding of what the experimental method is. Notwithstanding my regard for Dewey in other respects, it seems to me that Kant did.

With respect to the first paragraph, the question is whether Kant misunderstands Copernicus's method by recognizing the way it included relativity of perspective and making such relativity a general feature of all perception. Dewey suggests that Kant goes too far in this, focusing only on the constitution of the knowing subject. But we have to ask what Kant is trying to explain. What is the perceived object in Kant's case? In fact, it is mental process; it is our own cognitions. So when Kant examines his own thinking, the thinking of others as it appears to them and to Kant, and the evident way that others see Kant's thinking, is he really looking at the perceiving subject alone as though in isolation, or is he looking at the perceived actions (mental and communicative actions) of that subject, which are objects? Obviously, it is both and the way they interact. Dewey did not recognize this, but Mead did. Kant's "subject" is Mead's "I" that observes the "me" (Mead 1913), and the "I" in this sense remains forever invisible. As Kant said, it is a *postulated* perceiver, a hyperbolical object.

With respect to the second paragraph, it sounds as if Dewey is deferring to the logical empiricists, who construed ideas such as Heisenberg's uncertainty

principle, first articulated in 1927, as supporting Mill's view that scientific statements could only be probabilistic. Dewey makes a similar criticism of Newton
for an absolutely fixed framework of time and space (Dewey 1929, 202–5).

Nevertheless, the inverse square law is not the probably inverse square law.
Priestley's conclusion was not that mercury, when heated, probably combined
with a gas in the atmosphere. The aim of experiment is to eliminate alternative
explanations. When this is done, introducing verbal fuzziness is pointless. The
finding should fit "uniformly and triumphantly" to the experimental event, in
context and until something else fits better.

Having said what he thinks is wrong with Kant, Dewey goes on with what is
right: "These remarks are not directed particularly against Kant. For, as has been
already said, he edited a new version of old conceptions about mind and its activities in knowing, rather than evolved a brand new theory . . . [that] forms a con-
venient point of departure for consideration of a genuine reversal of traditional
ideas about the mind, reason, conceptions, and mental processes" (1929, 290).
Dewey describes what this reversal is, which he takes pragmatism as embodying:

> The reversal has many phases, and these are interconnected. It cannot be said
> that one is more important than another. But one change stands out with an
> extraordinary distinctness. Mind is no longer a spectator beholding the world
> from without and finding its highest satisfaction in the joy of self-sufficing
> contemplation. The mind is within the world as a part of the latter's own on-
> going process. It is marked off as mind by the fact that wherever it is found,
> changes take place in a *directed* way, so that a movement in a definite one-way
> sense—from the doubtful and confused to the clear, resolved and settled—
> takes place. From knowing as an outside beholding to knowing as an active
> participant in the drama of an on-moving world is the historical transition
> whose record we have been following.
>
> As far as philosophy is concerned, the first direct and immediate effect of
> this shift from knowing which makes a difference to the knower but none
> in the world, to knowing which is a directed change within the world, is the
> complete abandonment of what we may term the intellectualist fallacy. By this
> is meant something which may also be termed the ubiquity of knowledge as
> a measure of reality. Of the older philosophies, framed before experimental
> knowing had made any significant progress, it may be said that they made a
> definite separation between the world in which man thinks and knows and the
> world in which he lives and acts. (Dewey 1929, 291–92)

This does not support the line that Rorty draws between Kant and pragmatism. Kant is concerned with the interrelationships between seemingly intui-
tive convictions, perceptions, rationality, and communicative habits, and his
method is radical empiricism. Rorty represents Kant as speaking ex cathedra
about realities beyond perception, Truth with a capital "T." This is just plain
wrong, and Dewey and the other pragmatists knew it.

Conclusion

In the introduction of *Reclaiming a Scientific Anthropology* (1997), Kuznar includes a section describing the basic assumptions of scientific anthropologists. He starts with quotations from Patty Jo Watson and colleagues and Russ Bernard to the effect that there is a "reality . . . out there." Kuznar then contrasts this with about the same list of contemporary philosophical views that I have described as misrepresenting Kant's difference between phenomena and noumena:

> For a philosopher, the realism expressed by scientific anthropologists may be somewhat uncomfortable. Immanuel Kant argued two hundred years ago that *noumena,* or reality that may underlie what we experience, is forever beyond empirical grasp; all we can observe is what we perceive—phenomena. Philosophers continue to debate ontology, or the nature of existence, generating various positions such as the phenomenology of Edmund Husserl and Martin Heidegger, positivism, and the realism of falsificationists. The realization that scientists deal only with phenomena led logical positivist philosophers of science to abandon the question of reality altogether, noting that the lack of empirical tests for reality renders the concept meaningless. Logical positivists assert that scientists need only accept phenomena as given. (Kuznar 1997, 27)

And then Kuznar notes, "Scientific anthropologists tend to be uncomfortable with abandoning the notion that the world exists, while at the same time being very critical of monolithic conceptions of reality. There is a mitigated realism that surfaces in their work. On the one hand, Bernard, Watson et al., O'Meara, and Roscoe simply state that anthropologists assume that the world is there, observable, and ordered. At the same time, these authors and other scientific anthropologists note that ideas about the world are indeed mental constructs and in need of constant reappraisal" (Kuznar 1997, 27).

Kuznar is right about the philosophers other than Kant. But Kant, again, did not say this. Transcendent objects are not unreal, they are just transcendent. Kant could not guarantee their existence beyond our perceptions of them, as noted, but he did explain why no such guarantee was needed. They exist as necessary hypothecations to order our thought in both a private and a public sense. I stress *necessary.* They are unavoidable; they are compelling.

Kant's position is what Kuznar says the anthropologists "simply state" but cannot explain. The explanation is what Kant provides. Noumena are not real in the way Locke or Popper say. Nor are they real simply as ideas in the mind of the isolated observer as represented by Husserl and Heidegger. They cannot be dispensed with as argued by Schlick or Carnap. They are real only and precisely in the way Kant and the pragmatists say, and as such ethnologists can readily elicit and examine them.

It is only by seeing organizational concepts as noumenal categories in a Kantian sense that we can recognize the ways in which they are at the same time psychological and socially constructed, mental and part of perceived nature, have a formal structure that depends on the properties of thought but are in no way simply arbitrary, and very importantly for social science why we find them in all communities among all people as the basis of culture as well as among ourselves as the basis of theory. Moreover, it also provides an empirically sound way to analyze them: searching first for the principles according to which such ideas are self-consistent (the a priori aspect) and then for the obligations, purposes, and activities that they allow people to articulate given this self-consistency (the synthetic aspect).

CHAPTER 3

New Tools

The problem of showing how large-scale social patterns emerge from individual decisions is central to social science. The first complete instance was Adam Smith's description of the way individual-level efficiency-seeking behavior leads to large-scale efficiency in the division of labor. But Smith's analysis was facilitated by the fact that economic outcomes are denominated with money. Money has been established and enforced to objectivize economic preferences, and this objectivization in turn permits this kind of emergence. The problem of building a comparable analysis in realms in which there is no such cultural device has been far more difficult to conceptualize. But now we can do it.

Strong growth in the general area known as human complex systems has produced several new families of computer models that can reproduce large-scale emergent phenomena. These are primarily agent-based models or multiagent models. The main units of such programs are agents, representing individuals or groups. What they do in computer simulations is make decisions and take action. They can be made to follow decision rules of almost any kind so long as they amount to something like "if x then do y, else do z" or "under condition x do y, else do z." The program then recalculates the position of the agent that made it and others affected before going on to the next agent and in this way can cycle through any number of agents any number of times, accumulating the interactive effects of all the decisions by whatever measures seem relevant.

With agent-based models providing a very general method for the computational side of the problem of getting from individual action to aggregate patterns, what remains is the conceptual side. Where do the parameters for the models come from? The parameters are of two main kinds: the constraints and resources that the agents are assigned and the rules for the decisions that the agents make with them. The constraints, in general, are assigned in one of three ways. They are purely hypothetical, invented by the analyst on the basis of generalized knowledge or a theory; they are estimates assigned to the problem on the basis of actual available data; or the agents can represent an actual population, and the constraints can be the actual constraints they face and the actual resources they have. Similarly, the decision rules may be hypothetical ("what if"). They may be derived from one or more theoretical models such as game theory, microeconomics, or a simple idea such as minimizing travel distance. Or they may be the decision rules that the people in a community actually report as what they follow.

Thus far, no social theory has explained such parameters systematically. This is what will be done here. Plainly put, I take resources and constraints as resources reported and confirmed ethnographically, and given this, I show that the decision parameters come from their cultural idea systems by way of the organizations formed on the basis of those idea systems. Ideas closely associated in cultural idea systems are closely associated as parameters in individual decision making. They are instantiated by being used to define the mutual adjustments of behavior in the context of the organizational purpose (or purposes).

Even without such theory, however, agent-based models have provided dramatic reaffirmation of the general point that we do not have to have conscious collective control to have coherent collective action, precisely as Smith showed for the division of labor.

A reliable feature of computers is that while they can "think" in the sense of follow rules, they have absolutely no imagination. They cannot make inferential leaps. The rules they follow must be mutually consistent and have no gaps. Otherwise, the computer either stops or produces garbage. This kind of consistency and coherence is one aspect of rationality. Another involves comparison. Rational people make comparisons between alternatives and choose the one that best meets some criterion. Finally, rationality also generally assumes some relation of means to ends. All of these are readily simulated, and it is usually easy enough to see if the program as written actually represents the action being modeled. There is no necessity for a black-box effect in which one is not sure that what the program is doing actually corresponds to what one is interested in. Properly designed computer simulations based on field observations allow absolutely clear and firm chains of evidence between those observations and analytic conclusions.

The types of programs needed to implement and test organizational theories work in three main ways: they represent associations between material objects and people, they replicate cultural idea systems, and they simulate decisions and their consequences. These involve, respectively, databases, generative system models, and simulations.

Databases

To computer scientists it seems odd to speak of a database as a model, but for ethnology there are solid reasons for doing so. Although ethnologists have sometimes spoken of objective information *about* a community as though it had no connection to the ideas *in* the community, in fact (as Kant implies) everything is objective only to the extent that it is made so in common experience, and there ought to be no confusion about whose experience we are trying to get at. It is theirs, not ours.

From an ethnological perspective, there are two main kinds of databases. The most common, represented by DBase and its offshoots including Microsoft Access and Filemaker, are primarily for handling numerical data. These are essentially large matrices of rows and columns that allow sorts and tabulations on different criteria, cross-tabulations, and statistical analysis.

A second type is represented by Ethnograph, NUD.IST, HyperRESEARCH, and Weft. These are designed for managing textual data and include algorithms for textual analysis. Some are especially designed for linguistic analysis. Quantitative and text-oriented databases have very different roles in the present scheme.

One of our central problems is to find systems of ideas and see how they are structured. For this, textual analysis can play a useful exploratory or confirmatory role, although not a primary one. Techniques such as frame analysis or simple measures of nonrandomness can show what terms go with what other terms in what patterns. This can suggest underlying idea systems, which we can inquire about with appropriately constructed elicitation methods, as will be described. After we have directly elicited such idea systems, textual analyses can also illustrate their uses and map the incidence of their use over a population. But textual analysis cannot be a substitute for direct elicitation. There would be no benefit in recording an interview in which one elicited a kinship nomenclature in diagrammatic form, for example, in order to analyze it as a text when one already had obtained the resultant kinship diagram and its explanations. This will become clearer when we describe cultural idea systems and how to observe them.

The more quantitative database lets us see how the use of ideas and objects is distributed in a population. To do this it is essential to categorize the data in indigenous terms. If the community places farming activities within households, the database should include farming under households. If men's associations or something else other than households do the farming, then the database should be set up that way. Moreover, items of information that would not be mixed together in the community should not become mixed together in the database. If fishing is part of farming, fishnets and hoes can be mixed together. If they are separate, fishnets and hoes should be separate in the database. If all property is divided between men's property and women's property in the community, it should be similarly divided in the database.

If the categories of the database do not accord with the indigenous ways that activities are classified, it becomes extremely difficult to enter data without double counting or leaving gaps. It is in this sense that a quantitative database has to stand as a model. It reflects analysis and should be testable as analysis.

Of course, one does not test a database in the way one tests a specific factual claim. Rather, one tests it in the way one tests a general understanding. Does it make sense? Is it clear rather than confused? Does it work? Ethnographic databases, like all other software, are subject to the iron law of programming: garbage in, garbage out. If we identify the indigenous ordering principles and make the database reflect them, we will be able to set up clear queries and get clear and powerful answers in indigenous terms. If we impose our own categories that confuse the indigenous categories, we will not be able to do this. We will get conceptual mush from the database and reactions from our informants that tell us, usually politely, that we are indeed alien. The ideal is to create a kind of community in a bottle, a snapshot of what the community was at a point in time that we can go back to—and they could go back to—just as if we could go back to the community itself.

In addition to ethnographic databases that the analyst may construct, there are often other databases such as censuses or land records, which can be used for supplementary information insofar as the categories are real in indigenous terms.

Generative System Models

While quantitative databases can represent the way information or things are distributed across categories, they cannot represent how the categories themselves are defined or structured. They can record who is in each house, what tools they have, what houses their relatives live in, what social class they belong to, or what is grown on each field they own. They can show material used in each ceremony or what ceremonies are performed in each house. But they cannot show what a household is. What is a father? What is a social class? What is a field? These questions take us to cultural idea systems, and representing cultural idea systems requires generative system models.

A generative model is any program that embodies a set of rules that act like premises and that can produce or check deductions from those premises. In this case, the premises are the central ideas of cultural idea systems, and the deductions are the rest of what they generate.

All idea systems have form in the sense of some fixed arrangement among their elements. This is illustrated concretely in chapters 4 and 5. This form may in principle be as spare and abstract as the theorems of modern set theory or symbolic logic, but so far in my experience they have always been imagistic, seemingly descriptive, and capable of being diagrammed or represented in plastic media.

In the last ten years there has been a substantial crystallization of interest in the formal patterns in cultural systems, mainly under the general headings of mathematical anthropology and formal modeling of cultural systems but also to some extent under the headings of cognitive anthropology and postmodernist constructivism. The theory here particularly reflects the discussions under the heading of mathematical anthropology. This group has converged from diverse starting points mainly around Dwight Read at UCLA and Michael Fischer of the University of Kent. Others working along the same lines include Richard Greechie, Gesele de Meur, Giovanni Bennardo, Robert McKinley, Stephen Lansing, Douglas White, Kris Lehman, David Kronenfeld, Richard Feinberg, Martin Oppenheimer, Paul Ballonoff, and Douglas White. Two online journals are associated with this work: *Mathematical Anthropology and Cultural Theory* at http://www.mathematicalanthropology.org/ and *Structure and Dynamics* at the University of California, Irvine, http://repositories.cdlib.org/imbs/socdyn/sdeas/.

In a series of panels that participants in the conversation have organized at the meetings of the American Anthropological Association over about the last ten years, we have tried to focus on what these interests and results seem to require for a general social theory. More recently, in 2002, 2004, and 2006, we also put on extended panels at the European Meetings on Cybernetics and Systems Research at the University of Vienna. The panels were organized by Read, Fischer, and Paul Ballonoff. The group has been much more in the nature of a loose collective search than an intellectual movement. They have produced no consensus statement but are recognizably working on the same sorts of cultural materials, share a common concern with making the closest and most exact possible analyses to find the generative patterns in these materials, recognize that computers are an important tool in this effort, and have made the problems of understanding such patterns much clearer.

The main work in this area has focused on kinship, for two reasons. The first is that kinship continues to stand out as one of the few clear cultural universals, something that occurs in all human communities and is clearly recognized as a distinct and important cultural system by their members; it is clearly not just an artifact of imposing our own conceptual categories. The second reason is that the arguments about kinship have always raised, and still raise, fundamental issues for understanding human nature and society.

In the 1960s, the main arguments over kinship were a three-way dispute between componential analysis/ethnoscience, alliance theory, and descent theory (reviewed in Schneider 1965). All three were based on positivist assumptions. Accordingly, all three viewed kinship terminologies through the lens of a referential theory of meaning in which the meaning of a word is seen as the thing it names. Given this, all three came to entirely different conclusions about the character and importance of such terminologies and the nature of kinship in general. From one author to another, it was often difficult to know if they were talking about the same thing, and indeed they often were not. The level of discord and obtuseness in these arguments severely depressed general interest in the topic and by the late 1970s nearly killed it off entirely.

In 1971 I published the diagrammatic analysis of Punjabi, an Indo-European language of north India, and argued that kinship terminologies were better conceived as kinship maps. They were coherent, formal, generative systems and could be elicited in the field as such. There was no need to treat them as only substitutes for constellations of supposedly universal kinship components in the way componential analysts had done or as a set of names for kinsmen as Schneider had argued (Leaf 1971). Their uses were a secondary issue that was easy to resolve once their basic character and structure were understood. The analysis did not seem to have much effect at the time, except that Sylvia Vatuk (1972) responded by affirming its wider applicability and added some elaborations and variations on the basis of her analysis of Hindustani.

In 1974 I presented to a seminar in the Department of Anthropology at UCLA a diagrammatic analysis of English constructed by the same methods. English is also an Indo-European language, but the shape and logic are very different, as will be shown. Dwight Read was in the audience. Read's graduate training was in mathematics rather than anthropology. He saw the importance of the point that it was a generative structure and developed the analysis from there. In 1974 he published "Kinship Algebra: A Mathematical Study of Kinship Structure" in *Genealogical Mathematics,* edited by Paul Ballonoff. The argument was that terminologies had their own logic, which was not dependent on reference to genealogy, and that this logic could be precisely specified in terms of set theory. In 1984 Read published "An Algebraic Account of the American Kinship Terminology" in *Current Anthropology.* This applied the set theory analysis to English, showing the parallels to the diagrammatic form I had produced (although at this point my analysis of English had been circulated informally but had still not been published). Then, working with Clifford Behrens, Read developed the first version of the Kinship Algebra Expert System (KAES), which generalized the analysis to identify the generative components of any kinship terminology and reproduce the component positions from the generative premises. The first description was published in Read and Behrens (1990), and development has continued.

The current version of KAES, written in Java by Read and Michael Fischer, is available at http://kaes.anthrosciences.net/. It can be downloaded with files for the kinship maps of American English, Punjabi, Shipibo, Omaha, and Trobriand (male terms only). The files are downloaded in zip folders. They should be downloaded to a single directory. When unzipped they will produce a folder headed "KAES" with the program KAES in it and another folder headed "kintermmaps" containing the map files with the file type xml. If KAES has no filetype label, it should be renamed kaes.jar. It will then run when clicked on in an Apple or other Linux system and on Microsoft operating systems if the Java Run Time Environment (JRE) has been installed. The latter is available for download at no charge from Sun Microsystems.

The KAES program allows the user to input a kinship map in graphic form. After the user begins with ego, the program asks for the generative terms and then uses them to ask for the names of new positions as in the field method I have described (Leaf 2006) and will sketch in chapter 4. It also, however, consolidates the results as it proceeds, building a graphic analysis on-screen. One important advantage of this method over the pencil-and-paper field procedure is that the computer version makes it easier to identify redundant generative positions and thereby arrive at the one set of generators that is most economical and in that sense logically most basic. Once the generative terms are identified and the full set of positions that they generate is obtained, the program can automatically reproduce various analyses, including both an algebraic form and a number of different reductions depending on the logical structure of the system itself. For example, if the system has sets of positions that are defined the same way but differ by some single feature, such as gender, it can identify that and replace the differentiated terms with a common cover term, such as "aunt-uncle" or aunt and uncle. If the system uses terms that mark gender but are not structurally similar, it can also recognize that and analyze out just a male or just a female terminology. The software can produce a matrix of kin-term glosses in which every position is defined in terms of relative products of the generative terms, such as "father's father" as the definition of grandfather. It can determine if the analysis is simple or complex (capable of being reduced) and if it is complex can reduce it. Once it is simple, the basic algebraic relationships can be displayed. Before KAES every one of these operations, if conceivable at all, was a matter of the deepest controversy packed solidly around with unresolvable methodological and philosophical argument.

Kinship is not the only such conceptual system that can be elicited and analyzed this way. It is only the most widespread, the entryway to the others from the point of view of individual developmental psychology, and in a strictly pictorial or graphic sense probably consistently the most complex of the systems that do not have to depend on writing to be remembered in wide consensus with accuracy and stability, as will be explained in chapter 4. In principle, the same basic type of analysis should be applicable wherever there are firm and clear interrelated definitions of social positions, particularly where these are regularly elicitable as diagrams in two, three, or more dimensions.[1] We will describe six major types of such systems in all that are in more or less worldwide distribution. There are many others less widely distributed. Each, as will be seen, has a quite distinctive logical and conceptual shape and, in consequence, different uses just in the way different ideologies or mathematical systems have different logics and uses.

Robert McKinley has characterized kinship as a philosophy for the same reasons that Read and I have been describing it as a generative system (McKinley 2001, 142). This may better convey the way such systems work subjectively. They do not generate what seem to their users to be views of just a part of their world; they generate what seem to be complete universes that blot out all other universes when they are invoked. From a kinship perspective, everything is kinship. From a religious perspective, everything is religion. From an economic perspective, everything is economics, and so on.

Technological information systems, described in chapter 5, have usually not been considered by social scientists to be as problematic or interesting as the social information systems, although their importance is increasingly recognized in development studies (Hopkins 1987; Chambers 1983; Cernea 1991; Ostrom, Shroeder, and Wynne 1993). Since it is easier for most people to say what they are about, there seems to be less curiosity about what they are. Our sciences are examples, and so are their folk counterparts: indigenous ideas of everything from systems of mathematics to house building, farming, hunting, and cooking. Some of these systems are very complex, while others are very simple.

Technological systems may include important computational algorithms, which sometimes require computer models to represent. Lansing has described one in the form of a kind of Balinese calendar called a *tika,* which, he says, "defines time as composed of interlocking cycles." It is a painted wooden device that "lays out a grid of thirty seven-day weeks" with each week having a distinct name. The thirty seven-day weeks occupy the horizontal axis, the seven days the vertical axis. In addition to these seven-day weeks, there are nine other weeks of different numbers of days, which are superimposed on the grid with specific symbolic notations. Farming agreements have to include the blocks of terraces that will be watered and the lengths of time in which the water will flow to them, which will vary by crop, and of course farmers will regularly grow more than one crop at a time. Therefore, for any given farmer, some of his land may be on one irrigation cycle and some on others, and within groups of farmers there must be agreement on grouping the crops and on cycling the water flows. To develop such a system ab initio for each farming year would require a level and complexity of negotiation that is almost unimaginable and certainly unmanageable. By having this reckoning system in common, as Lansing says, all of this can be "specified with ease and precision" (1991, 70).

In chapter 6 I describe an indigenous farm-planning algorithm used by farmers all over South Asia. Its formal structure is so like a computer spreadsheet that the spreadsheet is the natural medium in which to elicit and describe it.

Not all idea systems are equally important. American kinship is defined by a social idea system, but so is American baseball. Physical theory is a technological idea system (or perhaps two such systems), but so is macramé weaving.

Agent and System Models

The cultural idea systems are the bases upon which people form organizations and make agreements and decisions. The social relational ideas say who will be involved and define their relative rights and duties. The technological ideas define the practical activities. Representing the way these are brought together is where agent-based models and a few other types come into play.

The process of transforming a cultural idea system in the abstract to an organizational charter in use is instantiation, in a mathematical sense. I have mentioned baseball as involving a relatively trivial set of social and technological idea systems. By the same token, playing baseball is a relatively trivial example of the general process of instantiation. Another example is the game of chess and, in fact, all other games in which there are definitions of physical pieces as "men" and rules for moving them in relation to one another to accomplish some purpose, such as winning. A social idea system defines the pieces and their powers; a system of technological ideas describes the board and pieces as material objects. The rules of play bring them together to form two or more simulated organizations (or one game), and their action consists of carrying out their defined purpose. Such games are indigenous simulations of the process of instantiation that underlies all social groups. They embody the process of creating and deploying organizations in microcosm. They instantiate the idea of instantiation.

Instantiation produces knowledge that varies for different segments of the population (cf. Boster and D'Andrade 1989; Medin, Lynch, Coley, and Atran 1997; Nolan 2002). That is, ideas are not instantiated just once in one way by one set of individuals but instead are instantiated throughout a community in different ways by many sets. The result, therefore, is that each organization thus produced finds itself not as an isolate but rather as part of a universe of similar organizations. This sets up a distinctive dynamic that is extremely difficult to capture and describe in ordinary language but that computer models simulate very naturally. The models that can do this are of three main kinds: agent-based models, network models, and system models.

As noted in the beginning of this chapter, the purpose of these models is to connect individual behavior to aggregate or emergent patterns. Of course in a sense we can do this with statistics. This is the bread and butter of opinion polling, survey research, and the like. We can say who has what ideas or embodies what characteristics, and we can correlate such attributes with one another. But adding up and obtaining correlations in this way does not correspond to any actual individual or social process unless we want to return to the argument that it is somehow the community as a whole that forces this pattern on individuals rather than the other way around, or argue as Adolphe Quételet did that physical and social reality was shaped by statistical laws as such.

In the long run, aggregate patterns are the result of complex interactions among many decisions at the level of individuals acting for their various organizations. A family has so much land and knows what they need to eat for a year, so they plant the crops that will provide it. But the family also has an unmarried daughter, and they know their future depends on providing her with good marriage prospects. So they adjust the work so that she can go to school. Some of the farmland is irrigated, and their holding is downstream from an aggressive person who tries to take too long on his turn at the water flow, so the men of the family take part in factional alignments in order to have support in the event of a physical conflict, and this means time and effort. What actually happens at the community level is the outcome of a complex web of such local decisions, and until the advent of agent-based models and network models there has been no way to mirror them computationally. Now there is, and this makes it much easier to demonstrate the enormous superiority of the present type of theory.

With agent-based modeling we can construct an agent and assign him or her decision rules that correspond to the actual decision rules in each of these organizational contexts and can take the observed aggregate patterns as the target for this model to explain. Such models do not require all the decisions of any one agent to be mutually compatible with one another. An agent can be constructed to cycle through any number of logically separate decisions. So long as all the decisions for each agent in the model draw on common resource bases in the way that decisions do in reality, their effects will interact realistically in the simulation. The model will work out the way that this happens. If the aggregate patterns we arrive at from the model then match the aggregate patterns that we actually observe, then two conclusions follow. First, we have probably represented the actual decision mechanism. Second, we have certainly shown that it is not necessary to postulate a unitary social whole or some other high-level mechanism other than such individual decisions and their interactions.

Many examples of agent-based modeling in anthropology have drawn on modeling practices from biology, ecology, or to some extent economics. One of the first applications of models of this type was Stephen Lansing's *Priests and Programmers* (1991) and a follow-up article titled "Emergent Properties of Balinese Water Temple Networks: Coadaptation on a Rugged Fitness Landscape" (Lansing and Kremer 1993). Working with Kremer (a biologist), Lansing sought to explain the function and evolution of traditional water temples in regulating farming on the Balinese hillsides.

The agents in this case were *subaks*, groups of farmers who utilize contiguous fields and coordinate their cropping with one another. The crops have to be planted at the same time and harvested at the same time because of the requirements of the irrigation system. This effectively means that the farmers also have to plant the same crop varieties. So even though the *subak* has multiple individuals from multiple families, it farms as a cohesive unit. The simulation sought to find the optimal area over which *subaks* would aggregate into still larger cooperative units of the same sort. In Bali, the boundaries of these kinds of cooperating units are marked by water temples. The question was whether these temple units were optimal, which had implications for understanding both what they did and how they evolved.

In deciding how large an area to aggregate over, the *subaks'* problem was to balance the danger from water stress and the danger from plant pests, both of which reduced yields substantially. Pest control was achieved by leaving large enough areas fallow so that the pests could not live in them and could not readily move across them. Thus if the *subaks* coordinated their cropping over a large area, they achieved better pest control. But larger areas also aggregated water demands, which created demand peaks that were hard to meet in times of low water in the rivers. If they coordinated their crops over very small areas so that more of them planted and therefore irrigated at different times, water demand was spread out; however, pests could move from field to field, and total pest populations increased. It was an optimizing problem, but there was no available optimizing algorithm. In its place, Lansing and Kremer had their agents follow what is known as a hill-climbing strategy. The basic idea is that if you are on a curved surface and want to get to the top but do not know where the top is, you can still get there if you constantly look around for someone higher and move to where they are. When there is nobody left above you, you are on top.

Data on the crop varieties, water availability, effects of pests, and effects of water stress came from two actual water temple areas. The program predicted the crop yields for each *subak* from water and pest conditions and had the agents (*subaks*) compare these yields to those of adjoining *subaks*. If the adjoining *subak* had higher yields, the deciding *subak* would adopt those crops, which means that they would be joining with the other *subak*. With many runs under many different initial and environmental conditions, what Lansing and Kremer consistently found was that the optimal areas of cooperation were consistently arrived at in eight to thirty-five cycles (years) and closely matched the actual areas of existing water temples.

From the point of view of serving as a validation for the present theory, the weakness of Lansing and Kremer's analysis is that while it clearly argues for individually situated decision making, it does not show how the parameters of those decisions are derived from cultural idea systems. It only shows that whatever the parameters are, they recognize ecological efficiencies. A more recent agent-based simulation that focuses on more culturally specific decisions is Cathy Small's *TongaSim*. This is a multiagent model of Tongan society intended to simulate the relationship between warfare and traditional rules for marriage. It is described in "Finding an Invisible History: A Computer Simulation Experiment (in Virtual Polynesia)" in the *Journal of Artificial Societies and Social Simulation* (http://www.soc.surrey.ac.uk/JASSS/2/3/6.html). The article can be read on the Internet, and the program can be downloaded from an associated link. I will return to both of these models in the discussion of rationality and adaptation in chapter 8.

Still more recently, a particularly good example of a study based on careful efforts to estimate the actual constraints and resources of a situation and to derive the decision rules from observation of the community being modeled and others like it is Lawrence Kuznar and Robert Sedlmeyer's "Collective Violence in Darfur: An Agent-Based Model of Pastoral Nomad/Sedentary Farmer Interaction," published in 2005. By modeling one general environment for the low plains where the pastoralists usually live and another for the higher land occupied by the sedentary farmers and by postulating that conflict arises simply when pastoralists and peasants are in close proximity for extended periods, Kuznar and Sedlmeyer show that the present genocidal warfare in Darfur could have arisen simply as a consequence of household level responses to an extended and severe drought that began in 1982–84. While it has been exacerbated by the inflow of modern weapons and the involvement of the Sudanese government, it has not been caused by them (Kuznar and Sedlmeyer 2005, 22).

In archaeology, a striking application of multiagent models simulated foraging and farming strategies in order to postdict the observed cycle of prehistoric Anasazi settlement locations in Longhouse Valley, Arizona (Axtell, Epstein, Dean, Gumerman, Swedlund, Harburger, Chakravarty, Hammond, Parker, and Parker 1999). The question asked was "Given these subsistence activities, what settlement locations most economize the travel effort?" The program output was a map of where settlements ought to be at different times. A more recent study along the same lines used fuelwood consumption and regrowth as the basis for modeling settlement locations in the Mesa Verde area of prehistoric southwestern Colorado from AD 600 to 1300 (Johnson, Kohler, and Cowan 2005). The model estimated fuelwood production by a number of ecological parameters and fuelwood use by demographic and consumption parameters and then had the agents (households) minimize the distance to the fuelwood they would need. In all these cases, the models gave accurate predictions that could not be obtained by any other method.

While none of these studies based their decision models on the prior delineation of cultural idea systems as will be described here, such idea systems would clearly have included the parameters chosen. Small's decision rules were taken directly from the ethnography. For Bali, the values actually came from the farmers, and Lansing did in fact show his computer models to them afterward and filmed their reactions, so their agreement is on record (Singer and Lansing 1998). There was just no effort to see how the different ideas used in the model were conceptually interrelated. For the Anasazi and Mesa Verde people, who were of course not available to interview, the fact that they actually went to the resource areas that the models took into account was established by artifactual evidence, while the idea that they would have economized their efforts in doing so was consistent with virtually all ethnographic experience. Thus it is unlikely that systematically eliciting cultural idea systems would have led to rejecting any of the parameters. It only would have yielded more of them and more precision.

System models are more diverse. One package that some ethnographers have used is Stella, which was actually designed for engineering applications but can be used for representing organizational processes that depend on transforming flows of people or things. Small, Blankenship, and Whale (1997), for example, used a Stella simulation to test the coherence of Rappaport's model of the *kaiko* cycle. It worked, although they had to supply their own estimates of crucial information such as pig reproduction rates.

A different type of system simulation is a network model of the sort that has been pioneered in anthropology in the last fifteen years by Douglas White and several students and colleagues. This builds upon widespread contemporary developments in mathematics, computer science, business management, and a few other mainly applied areas. The result is some very powerful mathematical and computer realizations, although the social theory remains ad hoc. It is largely a matter of stressing the importance of mapping information and other flows and finding choke points and bottlenecks. The standard is now provided by a system called Pajek (Czech for "spider") that is available at http://vlado.fmf.uni-lj.si/pub/networks/pajek/ on a Web site maintained by Andrej Vlado. The site provides tutorials and an open-source network analysis program for downloads. Douglas White's site, maintained at the University of California at Irvine, has links to many other network sites, instructions, and papers by White and others.

The result is that network analysis as White does it is entirely different from the network analysis that enjoyed a vogue in the 1960s and 1970s. That analysis was mathematically empty, mainly a matter of offering the image or metaphor of an all-encompassing network as a way to sidestep the increasingly obvious difficulties in justifying the metaphor of an all-encompassing organic social structure. White, by contrast, describes his theory as strictly descriptive. Where networks are clear, his aim is to describe them precisely. It is not to pretend that they exist where they do not.

Network analysis in White's sense can be applied wherever social relations are established as relatively permanent bonds between specific individuals or groups, such as in marriage and kinship relations, long-term trade relations, or relations of mutual support or opposition. Essentially, using Pajek (or some similar system), the analyst enters information describing such relations as pairs of nodes, and the program, using graph theory, analyzes and presents its formal properties. Such analysis can cut through the particularities of specific forms of cultural expression to show how quite different rules or relational definitions can produce the same kinds of relational patterns, while conversely the same rule or idea, under different conditions such as differing distributions of persons who may be eligible in various capacities, can lead to quite different patterns. Equally important, it can also show with absolute clarity how different idea systems can produce entirely different patterns of relationships among the same physical people in the same community, overlapping but noninterfering and accomplishing quite different social and adaptive tasks.

Networks are not the same as organizations. The members of organizations can form networks, and groups of organizations can form networks; however, there are also networks that are not organizations.

The Evolving Computational Picture

To have a complete analysis of a human community, it is necessary to represent all of its cultural idea systems, material resources, organizational processes, and adaptive outcomes. The different parts all have to be modeled, and the relations among the models must reflect the relations among the phenomena that the models represent.

When I planned my first ethnographic fieldwork, in 1962, computers were just becoming available in universities. I had never personally used one, and no courses in their use were available in the Department of Anthropology. But I thought I understood the basics of programming from symbolic logic and the paper-tape Turing machine of Alan Turing and designed my fieldwork with this in mind. It took about seven years to implement the database component of my study on mainframes with boxes of punch cards and about another ten years to migrate to personal computers and much more readily programmable software. There continued to be problems with the amount of data that could be stored and the ease with which it could be extracted for statistical assessment, but this ended with relational databases such as Dbase IV and more closely associated statistical packages.

Modeling the cultural information systems has taken much longer, but thanks to Read and Fischer this too can now be regarded as established, not finished of course but firmly begun. We now have a full-scale working example with a topic of established importance that resisted other theoretical approaches by the leading minds in the field for more than 150 years, namely kinship. There should be no further doubt regarding the existence, integrity, and coherence of such systems or the general computational approach needed to represent them.

The analysis of instantiation has been the last piece to fall into place. This is only reasonable, since the scholars concerned with this problem are largely the same as those concerned with the formal properties of cultural systems, and the problem of cultural systems is intellectually prior. First, we have to see what the ideas are; then we can start trying to simulate their use. In 2001 Dwight Read and I organized a series of panels at the American Anthropological Association titled "Cultural Idea-Systems: Logical Structures and the Logic of Instantiation." With twenty-one panelists representing a wide range of ethnographic regions and substantive interests, the most striking feature of the papers was their degree of coherence and similarity. They were all focusing on the same kinds of formal analysis of cultural processes and finding the same kinds of relations to social organization even though there had been no previous panel of this sort and no specification of its content beyond the panel title and abstract.

At this point we know that such analysis is possible. There are enough solid examples to demonstrate the general feasibility of the approach. The problem is to do it. This can only be done on a case-by-case basis, but each case will show the way to others. The main barrier has been the lack of basic theory. The participants in the effort recognize that they have a common kind of focus, but they do not have a common way to describe it and hence also do not have a common way to discuss and share solutions. The reason is not hard to see. The studies are minutely detailed; they require researchers to develop genuine expertise in the cultural activities being studied, which are as diverse as Tongan politics, American bartending, Trobriand linguistics and poetry, images of Romantic love, Fanti kinship, and the aforementioned Balinese and Indian agriculture, among many others.

Conclusion

Human organization is wonderfully complex and variable. Organization accounts for our dominance as a species, and within our species organizational differences account for the relative success of one group compared to another. Our abilities to think and to imagine are part of this capacity to organize. Our thoughts are the inward display of our organizational associations, our communicative interface with one another. Each part of the puzzle of social organization must be seen in the context of the others.

Given the centrality of organizations in what human beings are and what they do, it would be logical to expect organizational theory to have a central position in the social and behavioral sciences. Yet the attention devoted to it has been declining. This is due only in part to the inherent difficulties of the topic. It is mainly due to the way these difficulties have been multiplied by the dominance of philosophical perspectives that would have made empiricism impossible in any subject matter. Having now said enough to set them aside and delineate the foundations on which a genuinely empirical science of social organization can be built, we will proceed to build it, piece by piece. This will necessarily involve us in a fresh understanding of the role of organizations in human thought, communication, adaptation, and evolution.

CHAPTER 4

Social Idea Systems

I have said that social idea systems are cultural idea systems established in wide and firm consensus. But what is consensus? How do members of the community establish it, and how do analysts observe it?

When we speak of consensus, we cannot actually mean agreement in what people privately think. We have no way of observing this. We mean, operationally, public expressions of agreement in or support for the ideas represented in public expressions or enactments. These enactments are of just three kinds. One is ceremonies or demonstrations, meaning stereotyped enactments in behavior. The second is folk models, meaning stereotyped descriptions of relations or organizations. The third is the actual relationships that the ceremonies and folk models are taken to represent or correspond to: marital relations that ceremonies represent, the rights and obligations of having an academic degree that graduation ceremonies represent, action on the basis of powers that oaths of office convey, the use of land secured by a ritual that recognizes possession (such as signing a title deed), and so on. Every idea system is represented in all three types of enactments. There is no community that has one set of ideas in its myths or laws and another quite different set in its ceremonies or behaviors.

Since all idea systems are expressed in all media, it follows that no one type of media can be associated with any one kind of idea system. Idea systems are identified only by their content and formal structure, independently of the type of media in which they are expressed. The only thing that holds idea systems together, and holds them in shape, is the conceptual relations among the ideas that make them up. This is a critical point to understand. It is why cultural information systems cannot be clearly delineated unless each one is elicited systematically, starting with its key elements (ideas), finding all the main ideas closely connected to them, and setting aside all of those ideas only connected fortuitously or occasionally in some contexts. You could no more elicit several cultural information systems simultaneously than you can take a course in several unrelated topics at once, which is precisely why we have to teach different topics at different times and places and in different ways.

General Considerations

Unfortunately, although cultural idea systems are not defined or shaped by their media, many anthropological studies have been. Lacking a theory focused on the ideas that underlie them, studies of ceremonies, folklore, and organizational processes have largely gone each their own way. Nevertheless, they largely followed a common pattern and converged toward a common recognition. The pattern was that each type of study suffered a loss of focus as positivist ideas became fashionable and led to dead ends. The convergence is that there has subsequently been a resurgence of interest along pragmatic lines, which in the nature of the case has allowed attention to shift from the medium per se to the relationship between the medium and the ideas it was used to convey.

Landmarks in the analysis of folk models go back to Laura Bohannan's "A Genealogical Charter" (1952), Paul Bohannan's *Justice and Judgment among the Tiv* (1957), and Holy and Stuchlik's *The Structure of Folk Models* (1981).

Folk models have also become a major focus in cognitive anthropology but with a different drift reflecting continuing adherence to positivist dogma. There have been several good reviews by leading participants (Rice 1980; Holland and ·Quinn 1987; D'Andrade and Strauss 1992; and D'Andrade 1995). These generally agree that such classification schemes or models are in some way objective, even though they are also ideas "in peoples' heads." The main concerns have been with how to pin such ideas down methodologically, how to measure the extent of consensus, the extent to which they can be considered to be general culture as opposed to simply personal views of it, and the ways they might influence behavior. There is also a substantial consensus on certain questions that are regularly not asked. There is, for example, little discussion of what forms of any given model are authoritative and why, how models may link up with one another as part of larger systems, or how to find the outer boundaries of such systems. Most importantly, none of the studies focuses on the conceptual basis of reciprocity. Even when topics are kinship, social organizations, ethnic groups, or schools, they are described only as systems of objective classification, parallel to color schemes or classes of plants and animals. Nevertheless, these debates have been an important component of the recent development of interest in the formal analysis of cultural systems and mathematical anthropology that we are concerned with.

Important ethnographic analyses of the way people in groups create their organization through instantiating organizational ideas in ongoing communicative behavior go back to Firth's "Authority and Public Opinion in Tikopia"

(1949); E. R. Leach's "The Structural Implications of Matrilateral Cross-Cousin Marriage" (1951), which in present terms is actually about the organizational implications of kinship ideas; and Barth's (1959) analysis of Swat Pathan factional balancing in terms of a zero-sum game in game theory. More recently, they include F. G. Bailey's later monographs beginning with *Stratagems and Spoils* (1969), through *Humbuggery and Manipulation* (1988), and up to *A Witch-Hunt in an Indian Village or, the Triumph of Morality* (1997). Garfinkel's documentary method (1967, 2002) and Goffman's dramaturgical method (1959) are describing the same process.

Comparable landmarks in the redevelopment of pragmatic analyses of ceremonies include Victor Turner's *The Ritual Process* (1969), Stanley Tambiah's "The Meaning and Form of Magical Acts" (1973), and Moore and Meyerhoff's *Secular Rituals* (1977). Moore and Meyerhoff's recognition that ceremonies have no distinctive association with religion, magic, or the supernatural was particularly clear. They described six attributes of all ceremonies: repetition, acting, "special" quality or stylization, order (the sense that the event is organized), evocative presentational style or staging, and an explicitly collective dimension (the idea that the event by its own definition has a social meaning) (Moore and Meyerhoff 1977, 8). As they say, such events include court trials, meetings, installations, graduations, and "other formal assemblies of many kinds" (4). I would add that ceremonies also have roles and scripts.

Many writers seeking to portray society as inherently monolithic, from Durkheim and Mauss to Gregory Bateson (1958), Levi-Strauss (1962), and Rappaport (1984), have claimed or suggested that a single ceremony represents the ethos or worldview of an entire people, which of course implies that one ethos or worldview is all they have. None has proved it, which would require showing that no other ceremonies portray a contradictory ethos or worldview. In fact, such contradictions abound. Ceremonies are of many kinds in every community and clearly fall into patterns and groups that are held together by ideas they share: there are life-cycle ceremonies, agricultural ceremonies, professional ceremonies, political ceremonies, military ceremonies, academic ceremonies, and so on, each representing a distinct ethos or worldview, a distinct system of values, and each based on a distinct idea system.

Each ceremony is linked to the others in its set by mutual references. One birthday refers to other birthdays, sowing rituals point to harvests, harvest to the next sowing. Weddings make implicit references to funerals, trials to pretrial hearings. Funerals do not refer to pretrial hearings.

Folk models make the same kinds of internal references to one another and are often closely tied to ceremonies. They are recited in ceremonies, they refer to ceremonies, and symbolic objects represent them in ceremonies. This pattern of redundancy aids memorization, strengthens consensus, and is recognized in consensus.

In doing ethnographic fieldwork, where we see patterns of mutual reference, we will be able to elicit an explanation in terms of the cultural idea system. Conversely, if we ask how the idea systems apply or what they mean in practice, we will be referred to the ceremonies, folk models, or actual instances of behavior. In other words, the apparent relation between ceremonies, folk models, behavior, and cultural idea systems is the actual relation. There is no third explanatory variable such as "social structure" or "social organization" apart from these. This is an important finding, all the more convincing by having been arrived at largely unwillingly.

Formal Properties of Cultural Information Systems

How do we find idea systems? It may seem like trapping smoke. But when ideas do indeed form a system in a strong sense, we can in principle start with any one and eventually go through all the others and come back to it. So the first problem is to find a starting point. There are several ways to do this. One is to use our own metacultural ideas as a frame and look for variations on them: different ideas of law, of kinship, of religion, and so on. This works reasonably well to the extent that the community we are trying to understand has ideas of the same general sort, but some important idea systems elsewhere are so different from our own that this method will not work. They will appear simply as noise or confusion.

Another good search principle is to look for recruitment criteria and the ways they are enacted. Since the criteria for fulfilling a position or role must be logically related to the definition of the position or role, if the requirements for membership in social roles or positions appear to be logically interrelated, the chances are good that the definitions of the positions will be interrelated. If the criteria are logically unrelated or contradictory, then probably the definitions of the positions are as well.

A third identifying feature of social idea systems lies in the way such idea systems are used. Although in fact highly formal and abstract, they seem to be highly normative or directive, as so much sociological theory claims that they actually are. Yet if their directive import really were clear, it would not be such a consistent focus of dispute. The basic ideas used to frame organizations are not normative but instead are pseudonormative. They do not provide formulas for actual behavior but rather provide an abstract framework within which such formulas can be invented and on which they can be hung.

The pseudonormativity of the ideas that are drawn from idea systems and used to define positions or roles is not a defect, and pointing it out is not debunking. It is a result of long evolution, and it is an essential part of human organizational technique. Cultural actors cannot act like positivist theoreticians and simply hypothecate that there are, somewhere, fixed and firm norms for behavior. They have to act here and now, and in order to do so they are forced to overcome the fact that they do not know what the norms for that here and now actually are in any detail. To know what a father is does not tell you what a father does. What should one do in title of being a professor? Profess, of course. But what is that? And what should one not do? Students may think that this is all neatly laid out somewhere, but professors know it is not. Such vacuity is evident to anyone in any position. The pragmatic consequence is that ambiguity that is not resolved by the idea systems must be resolved by the idea users. The content of the organizational ideas must be negotiated in the process of building organizational relationships. All such idea systems thus carry an implicit general instruction that amounts to this: "Since this is the rule you must follow, you must start by figuring out what it is." People are compelled to say what the rules are even though they know that what they are actually doing is saying what they think they ought to be and watching to see how others will respond.

Technical idea systems do not define social positions and therefore do not have recruitment rules and are not pseudonormative. The relation of the ideas to specific behaviors is generally much more definite than for social idea systems. It is much clearer what behavior goes with farming than with fathering, but if for example you saw wheat growing in a way that was not consistent with your definition of wheat, you would be very unlikely to think that having a conversation with the wheat about its deviant behavior was a reasonable way to act on this observation.

Implications of Multiplicity

As far as I am aware, the most complete single description of the indigenous social models and major technical idea systems current in any one community is still my *Information and Behavior in a Sikh Village: Social Organization Reconsidered* (Leaf 1972). At the time it was published, the dogma that societies were single monolithic structures was so firmly accepted that it was claimed as necessary theory even in studies that clearly showed the facts to be exactly the opposite. E. R. Leach's *Political Systems of Highland Burma* (1954) was a striking example. Leach had been a student of Malinowski and had done exceptionally thorough fieldwork, beginning as a civilian and continuing as a British officer organizing Kachin resistance to the Japanese during World War II. What he found were three distinct and contradictory indigenous models of society: Kachin Gumsa, Kachin Gumlao, and Shan. He clearly said that they were all in use simultaneously by the same people in the same communities. They thus could not possibly have been structures in the sense of quasi-physical wholes that people were in. They could only have been standardized cultural models that people used in interaction. Leach recognized this and described such interaction. He also recognized that this was the opposite of what current theory claimed. But his conclusion was only that the theoretical models that had up to that point portrayed societies as unitary wholes in a static equilibrium needed to be modified to recognize the reality of social change:

We can no longer be satisfied with attempting to set up a typology of fixed systems. We must recognize that few if any of the societies that a modern field-worker can study show any marked tendency towards stability. On the other hand I hold that it should be possible for anthropologists to develop methods for the analysis of changing social systems that avoid metaphysical generalizations of the type that Professor Popper has rightly condemned as "historicism."

Candid recognition that social systems are not necessarily naturally stable need not compel the structurally minded social anthropologist to abandon all his traditional techniques of analysis, for he will still be justified in continuing his use of scientific fictions. In practical fieldwork situations the anthropologist must always treat the material of observation *as if* it were part of an overall equilibrium, otherwise description becomes almost impossible. All I am asking is that the fictional nature of this equilibrium should be frankly recognized. (Leach 1954, 283–84)

Instead of taking the discrepancy between theory and fact as a reason to reject the theory, Leach uses it to justify the positivist claim that theory and fact are inherently different; that theory is, indeed, fictitious.

Of the few who recognized that such a disparity ought to have been grounds for rejecting this idea of theory, the most complete argument was in Bailey's *Tribe, Caste, and Nation* (1960). Bailey also found three structures, which are what the title refers to, and described them as "incompatible with one another, existing in the same field" (10). But instead of trying to fit the data to existing theory by holding that they represented change or that all theory was fictional, Bailey asked what kind of theory would be nonfictional. Flatly rejecting the idea of a monolithic whole and the determinism that went with it, he argued for recognizing their separateness and seeing it in the context of purposive, choice-making, rational actors. Frederick Barth (1959) in his game-theory analysis of Swat Pathan factionalism and T. S. Epstein (1967) in her analysis of the different strategies behind the reactions to irrigation in two Indian villages made similar cases for instrumental rationality and recognized multiple organizations implicitly but did not so clearly separate them out or call attention to their theoretical implications. However, no one was concerned with saying how many or how few such systems there might be in one community in total or with trying to specify what made them seem to be systems of ideas and not merely collections or sets of ideas in some less orderly sense.

Observation and Elicitation

The field methods used to elicit the cultural idea systems described in *Information and Behavior in a Sikh Village* were a combination of pattern seeking based on information theory, linguistic frame analysis, and the kind of open-ended questions that a clinical psychologist would ask in a therapeutic interview. I did not have a predetermined order in which to take up topics but instead sought to take whatever was pointed out or seemed to be identified as an event or behavior by those around me. Understandably, I was told about the more recognizably public topics first and was content to reserve the more sensitive or private sets of ideas for later when I had established my legitimacy. In Sidhpur Kalan, the first events I was invited to were mainly religious. Kinship came next, then farming, and then household economics. Politics, in the sense of factional politics, came last. The order of what is more or less sensitive would be different in different cultures.

I would attend events or be present during activities and would also ask about them. I would ask about them before, during, and after they took place. Sometimes those I asked were the main participants, sometimes witnesses, and sometimes they had not been there at all but had come to know by hearsay. What I was trying to get at was the stereotypes on the one hand and the ways they were used on the other. As I engaged in these conversations, I would encounter ideas as little packages of interrelated definitions that the event or behavior evoked. As the records accumulated, I found that I could arrange them by mutual internal reference, as one would assemble a text that one found in scattered pieces. Finally, when I had accumulated enough to make what seemed to be a closed or nearly closed system, I would verify its shape with direct extended interviews with appropriate groups: families for kinship, recognized religious practitioners in a religious context for religion, and so on.

As already suggested, the basic method for eliciting any system of ideas as a system is to start with any one clearly established idea and trace out everything firmly and closely linked to it. Take any idea that seems well established in a firm and uniform consensus and ask for an explanation. What is kinship? What is Sikhism? This will yield other ideas that you can ask about in turn. What is a father? What is a Granthi? Look for the kind of definition that is absolutely firm in each case. Then inquire into all the ideas equally firmly linked to it, and so on. Also, discard all links that are recognizably nonstandard, such as the view that some American informants might offer to the effect that while Americans believe that religion and politics are separate, really there is a gigantic religious conspiracy behind everything.

If the ideas truly form a system, the method will lead to boundary conditions. An example of a boundary condition is when you are consistently told something such as "That is another matter" or "Beyond that a person is not a relative." When all such boundaries are delineated, you can write up the results cleanly, check the description with the informants to be sure you have not inadvertently introduced any alien ideas, and consider this finished. Then ask what other ideas you had encountered that this particular system did not contain or entail, and repeat the process to find the idea system it is part of, and so on. If there are a limited number of idea systems (again, an empirical claim that the method will confirm or confute), there will be a limited number of times you can do this before you sweep up all the ideas that are well established in general consensus.

In Sidhpur Kalan there were six systems of ideas that were held by substantially everyone. Of these six, five were social idea systems that defined reciprocal roles of different kinds, and one was the technical idea system that defined the ecological basis of the local system of agriculture. The social idea systems defined kinship, the Sikh religion, political parties or factions, economic transactions and calculations, and management. Other social idea systems were used to define organizations that only a few took part in, such as the village postman, teachers, doctors, members of the cooperative, and those employed in nearby towns, the government, or the military. Other technical systems served as specialist knowledge for various craftsmen: weavers, potters, the doctor, the masons, and so on.

Since 1972 my argument and the related arguments of Bailey, Barth, and Epstein have been repeatedly confirmed or reinvented. Instrumental rationality is now the operating assumption in ecological and developmental studies. Indigenous idea systems have come back into focus, albeit without the present strict sense of system or a theoretical concern with delineating their formal properties. As just one illustration, Peter Blunt, Michael Warren, David Brokensha, and others have recently edited a series of volumes in which organizational ideas are the focus of one volume (Warren and Blunt 1996) and technical ideas, described as indigenous knowledge systems, the focus of another (Warren, Slikkerveer, and Brokensha 1995), although they do not use this terminology. Nevertheless, up to now no one else has attempted to delineate systematically all such models established in general consensus in any one small community. The dominant practice continues to be to focus on just one system at a time: the religion of X or farming in Y, with no clear field method by which unrelated ideas can be excluded. The consequence usually is to exaggerate the importance of the system chosen while obscuring its logical structure and blurring its boundaries. Most idea systems can be made to seem to include everything. Economists have no trouble making everything seem economic, kinship analysis makes everything look like an aspect of kinship, religious perspectives make everything seem religious, and so on. Since situation switching is easy to ignore if one's theory provides no way to recognize it, it has not been widely documented. I will adhere mainly to what I am sure of from my own observation and those relatively few accounts by others that are clear about which situations the organizational ideas they describe are not salient in. The systems I will describe are mainly those I have encountered in my own experience in India and the West.

Types of Social Idea Systems

Formally, social idea systems appear to fall into two main groups: kinship and all others. This is an important finding with many implications for our understanding of human social learning as well as long-term cultural and social evolution. Systems of kinship ideas are ego-centered; the others are not. We will begin with kinship.

Kinship

The best way to think of the overall organization of systems of kinship ideas is in terms of a core and added layers. The core is the set of ideas that has in recent years been most often described under the heading of kinship terminology but, as noted in chapter 3, is better thought of as a kinship map. What is of primary importance is not what the terms are in a phonemic sense or what they name or refer to but rather the ways they allow us to reason from one position to another. The basic definitions say what kinds of relatives there are and how they are interrelated. The additional layers define various kinship classes and groups and specify behaviors, legal obligations, and the like.

Kinship Maps

Systems of kinship definitions are usually considerably more complex than other idea systems that define local-level organizations in traditional communities. This complexity is directly related to the formal property that they are ego-centered.

Ego-centered means two things. First and most simply, the positions are generally defined only with reference to a specific user. There is not a definition for father or mother in general, in the sense of a father as a father against all comers in the way the president of the United States or the queen of England is defined against all comers. The primary definition is only for an individual's father, a father in relation to a specific person who is a son or daughter. Moreover, such definitions occur in fixed reciprocal pairs in the sense that if you are my father then I must be your son, and vice versa. By contrast, if you are my president I might be your supporter, opponent, vice president, speech writer, or any number of other things.

Second, since the main body of the positions in any kinship system is defined in this way, the most economical and natural way to represent them is usually, perhaps always, as though the positions are arrayed around a central user, the self or ego. There are, however, subtle differences in different systems in the way this ego is conceptualized. In some, for example, the definitional systems are different for a male ego and for a female ego, so self is gendered. Some systems are easier to elicit if the elicitation includes a specific named position such as "my," and some are not. All such subtleties have implications for the overall logic of the system.

The recruitment rules in kinship systems incorporate an idea that it is based on birth (in some locally defined sense) and holds relatively constant through life. In part because of this, the reciprocal pairs of relations that the ideas define are strictly reflexive and cannot be transposed. By strictly reflexive I mean that if you have a defined relationship to someone, that person has an equally clearly defined reciprocal relation to you. It is not escapable or negotiable. If you are a father to

X, X cannot decide to be a mother or cousin to you. Nontransposable means that if I am the son of X, I will always be the son of X and will never be the father of X. There are variations, of course, but they only qualify or adjust the basic idea of nontransposability to specific challenges that arise from the general logic of the system in relation to the constraints of birth, life, affiliation, and death. An example is the Navajo practice of adjusting positions when people die so that the position of senior woman of one's clan is always filled by a living person.

Kinship maps seem always to utilize a spatial imagery. People commonly speak of "sides," "lines," "distant," or "close" relatives and reckoning "upward" or "downward." Because of this, the best way to capture the conceptual structure of systems of kinship definitions without using one's own cultural conceptions as an obscuring screen is to ask for diagrams, not lists. My own experience includes elicitations in most North Indian languages, many European languages, and Hausa. I have also constructed diagrammatic analyses of definitions collected by others for several more South Asian language groups (Tamil, Malayalam, Kannada, and Purum) as well as Hopi and Navajo. My conclusion is that it can always be done by starting from ego and working outward, provided that all the indigenous concepts are represented by a unique graphic form that is appropriate in the view of those from whom the information is being sought and that no nonindigenous concepts are introduced. If ego is specified as male or female, that must be represented. If other positions are male, female, or neutral, that must be represented. If a system uses an idea such as marriage, you need a symbol for marriage. If it has no such idea, you do not include such a symbol. If it uses an idea of rank, you need a way to represent that. It is up to those whose system it is to say what the underlying ideas are. The ethnographer's problem is to find if, and how, they make up a system. Other questions will follow from the answer to that one.

Elicitation shows that there is always a very restricted set of direct relations arrayed immediately around ego and that all other relations are connected through these direct relations. More formally, all positions in the kinship map are defined either as direct relations of ego or as relative products of such direct relations.

The direct relations are not identical from culture to culture, but by and large they are similar. For present purposes, I will deal only with American English and Punjabi. The configuration of core positions is given in figure 1 with their standard English and Punjabi names. Nonstandard names are recognized as having the same definitions in terms of the other relations as the standard names, such as "Pop is another word for father," although in fact such seemingly casual or informal forms often appear to be survivals of earlier formal terms. In the end, however, it is not the terms that matter but the ideas that they evoke.

The English and Punjabi definitions seem the same in terms of the other positions within the core, but as we will see, they are not the same in terms of their implications for the positions beyond it. The differences accumulate to important overall differences in the logics of the systems as wholes. In both of these

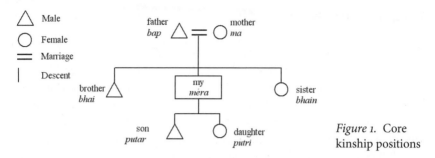

Figure 1. Core kinship positions

systems, ego may be male or female, here symbolized by a square. The definitions of relatives do not change with gender of ego.

Reciprocal relationships are those whose representations are symmetrical across ego in the diagram. That is, the positions one link up from ego are the reciprocals of the positions one link down. The positions one link to either side are reciprocals of each other, allowing for gender and other represented attributes. If you are my brother and I am male, I am your brother. If I am female, I am your sister. If you are my father (one link up, male) then I am your son or daughter (one link down, differentiated by gender). Reversing the path from ego to any position yields the path to the reciprocal of that position.

The rest of the system is obtained by using this core as an eliciting frame and applying it outward: father of father, mother of father, brother of father, and so on. Then we group the results so that we can say something like "one's grandfather is the father of one's father *or* the father of mother" and "one's uncle is any brother of one's father or mother or the husband of a sister of one's father or mother." As elicitations proceed outward, we usually find that multiple paths of links lead to each named position. In English, father's father is the same relation as mother's father: grandfather. If we ask whether these relations that all have the same name actually are the same, it is logically possible that we could be told either that they are or that they are not. In my experience, however, the actual answer has consistently been that they are. The general rule is one term, one position. When it is, we need to draw the graph to show it by making all the different links converge on that graphic element. The one symbol then corresponds to the one relational concept (such as grandfather), and the various paths to it correspond to different parts of its final, complete definition. For a more complete description of the procedure, see Leaf (2006).

When all the end points are reached and all the graphic symbols used in the elicitation are gathered so that there is just one graphic representation of each recognized position, the result is an experimental trace of the system of kinship concepts that exactly parallels a photographic exposure or an instrument reading in a physical experiment. It is a trace that will let us see how each positional idea is related to all the others and thereby let us predict its use. Figure 2 is the

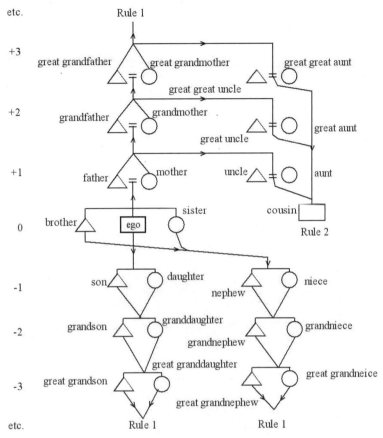

Figure 2. American kinship positions

main portion of the diagram that this produces for American usage, and figure 3 is the diagram that the same procedure produces for Punjabi (Leaf 1971, 1972). The diagrams are slightly simplified in that they do not include additional positions for relations acquired by marriage relatively late in life, terms for relatives of spouses of relatives. In both of these systems, however, the basic rule is that you treat them like actual relatives and take the connection from the relative they are connected through, allowing for the difference in gender.

In the American English case, because of the ways collaterals are distinguished from lineal relatives, it is particularly important to remember to read the definitions as developing in the direction of the arrows, from ego out but not the reverse. A great-uncle is anyone who is the brother of a grandfather, but a grandfather is not anyone who is the brother of a great-uncle. The configuration including uncle and aunt relations on the superior generations, which connects them by both a line indicating common blood and an equals mark indicating

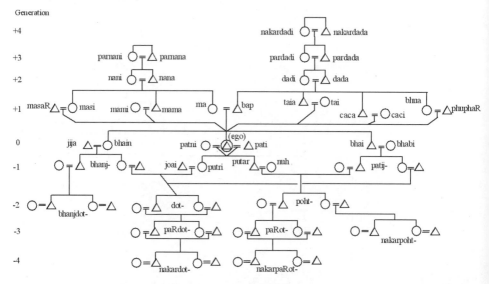

Figure 3. Punjabi kinship positions

marriage, is to be read that an uncle is either the brother of an aunt or the hus-band of an aunt and an aunt is either a sister of an uncle or a wife of an uncle but not both because there is a rule that one does not marry a sibling. For the same reason, father is understood as not being brother to mother, and a grandfather must be either the father of mother or the father of father but not both, and so on. There is no reason to draw the two sets of uncles and aunts or grandparents as separate any more than there is a reason to draw each brother as separate. The drawing represents the relationships, not the people who take them.

The conceptual outer boundaries of the system are indicated in the horizontal dimension by the cousin line and in the vertical dimension by Rules 1, 2, and 3. Cousin is a boundary because it is a conceptual limit beyond which a person is defined as not a relative. Rules 1, 2, and 3 are limits because they are rules for indefinite extension. Ascendant and descendant relations go on forever according to the rule, but there is nothing beyond the rule. Rule 1 is that for each succeeding ancestor beyond great-grandfather one simply adds a "great." The same is true for the reciprocal—each successively more remote descendant beyond great-grand-son or great-granddaughter. Rule 2 is the comparable rule for collaterals, the uncle and aunt positions and their nephew and niece reciprocals. And Rule 3 is that any descendant of a cousin is a cousin. With these rules, the system is complete and logically closed, with every term defined in relation to every other term. For any person, it will be possible to know if they are a relative or are not, and if they are, their relation to oneself and all other relatives will be specified consistently.

I leave out qualifiers for the cousin relation such as "first," "second," and "removed" for three reasons. First, I have never conducted an elicitation with a group that has agreed on a consistent set of definitions. Second, the terms are not usually part of the system of address. And third, they do not alter the basic point that cousin is the outer boundary. I leave out terms for in-laws because they are not part of the reciprocal address system, do not change the basic structure, and would make the graph much more difficult to read.

Since readers are probably familiar with this system in practice, even though they would normally have no reason to elicit it in the manner described here, there is no need to review the details. The most important points are the ones we can see best from the contrast with Punjabi. The most evident point is also the most important. The shapes are not the same. This immediately tells us that the ways the definitions are interconnected differ in the two systems.

First, the main structural feature of the American system, in contrast to Punjabi, is that all ancestors and descendants are grouped together as one single line down through the generations, while all collaterals are separated and branch away. In Punjabi, as in all other major South Asian terminologies regardless of language family, it is the contrast between mother's and father's sides.

Second, note that in the Punjabi case the positions below ego's generation fall into groups of four, each marked by a unique stem and a common set of four endings. The endings indicate gender and marital status. The ending for a consanguine male is *a*, the usual masculine noun ending, except in a few cases where this would be ambiguous and the more definite *aR* is used instead. For a consanguine female the ending is *i*. For an affinal male it is *joai* (the term for husband of daughter), and for affinal female it is *nuh* (the term for wife of son). The stem indicates the descent-relation to ego in which relational distance is suggested by similarity of sound. It is actually a kind of kinship poetry that can be readily heard reading down the groups, the phonetic combinations mirroring the graphic pattern. Thus, in Punjabi all relatives in generations below ego are distinguished according to their generation, gender, whether they are connected by descent or by marriage, and whether they are connected to ego through only males or by one of several possible linking females. Relatives above ego are distinguished by generation, gender, and whether they are connected on the mother's or father's side but not by whether the link is by marriage or descent. American positions, by contrast, are grouped by gender, generation, and whether they are direct ancestors and descendants or collaterals.

Finally, a third contrast is that in the American system there are distinct limits beyond which one is not kin in the horizontal direction but is kin in the vertical direction, while in the Punjabi system there are distinct limits in the vertical direction but not the horizontal. In the American system, a descendant or ancestor is always a relative, but no one beyond a cousin is a relative. In Punjabi, if we ask what is the *bap* of *nakardada* the answer is "nothing" (no relation), and the question strikes people as outlandish. By contrast, however, everyone in one's parental generation is some sort of uncle or aunt, and everyone of one's own generation is literally (not fictively or by extension) one's brothers and sisters.

The final shapes of the English and Punjabi definitional systems can be so different even though the cores seem so similar because the way the core ideas are concatenated embodies very different basic notions of what a kin relationship is. In the American system, the idea of a brother and a sister is restricted only to children of one's own parents. In Punjabi, they are all the children of one's own parents or their siblings, and those parents' siblings in turn are all children of their parents' siblings, a class that is ultimately infinitely large. The American idea is thus very strongly an idea of common descent, common blood. The Punjabi idea is more social-interactional. The American ideas define those who can be recruited as relatives as a very small set out of a much larger world of strangers and define kinship relations substantially as something that comes down from ancestors. The Punjabi ideas allow recruitment of an indefinitely large set with the only ultimate distinctions being between different types of relatives rather than between relatives and nonrelatives and define kin relations as something that one builds outward from oneself.

If we continue the elicitation of the Punjabi ideas to ask what distinguishes, for example, one's closest brothers from more distant brothers, we find that the crucial idea is not anything to do with descent but rather is the idea of shared rights in a unit of ancestral property. The American definitions make kinship a very clearly ascribed category based on descent, while the Indian concepts make it more an achieved category based on degree of mutual involvement and cooperation.

As indicated in chapter 3, the conceptual consistency of both of these systems has been confirmed mathematically by Read and by the Kinship Algebra Expert System (KAES) computer program of Read and Fischer. The program allows the user to input a kinship map in the same general way that the above graphic representations were elicited in the field, starting with self, then entering all the direct relations, and then extending the input outward to all positions defined as relative products of those direct kin. The resulting representation is not visually identical to the graphic forms I have given, but it is logically equivalent in the sense that every position in the graphic form is isomorphic to one in the KAES form, and all the definitions of those positions are the same.

The program then allows the user to test whether the diagram is simple or complex, which means whether it can be reduced algebraically or not. If it is complex, it allows the user to ask the program to simplify it on up to nine bases, such as by reducing all terms differentiated only by gender to a common cover term or replacing all reciprocal pairs with one member of the pair. Each simplification process is defined by an algebraic equation. The program works by looking for pairs or sets that the equation applies to and replaces them with the cover term or term that is more basic plus the equation. The equations are recorded in a list that builds up as the map itself is simplified. The program then can regenerate the map from the algebra.

For the American system, there are six such structural equations plus a rule for gender marking and a rule for cousin terminology. The first three of the six are, for example, parent of child = self, spouse of spouse = self, and spouse of parent = parent. When the graphic form is fully simplified, the list of structural equations is therefore fully specified. The user can then have the program regenerate the graphic representation from the structural equations. If the graphic structure were not algebraic in a very strict sense, this would not be possible. So in the nature of the case, the program proves that the map is a single, coherent, logical/mathematical structure.

Figure 4 is a completely simplified version of English, arrived at by reducing all terms that were structurally similar, then all that were differentiated only by gender so as to leave only the male counterpart, and then all descendants.

Figure 5 is the KAES regeneration of the American kinship map from this simplification based on the algebra. The isomorphism with the directly elicited graphic version should be obvious. The "etc." positions have the same meaning in the two charts. "Self" replaces "ego" in the hand-drawn version for logical reasons. In Read's view, it better represents the way in which that central position is defined mathematically as an identity relation in English as contrasted with a "my" in Punjabi.

On-screen, the individual positions can be moved by clicking and dragging to bring out one or another relational aspect more clearly. When a position is dragged in this way the lines indicating definitional relations remain attached and move elastically with the positions. In this case, I have arranged the positions to straighten the central line whose names involve the terms "father," "mother," "son," and "daughter" in order to make the parallelism with my hand-drawn version easier to recognize. Even without this, however, there can be no doubt that the two are equivalent.

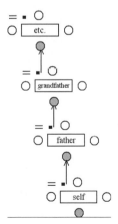

Figure 4. Fully simplified American kinship

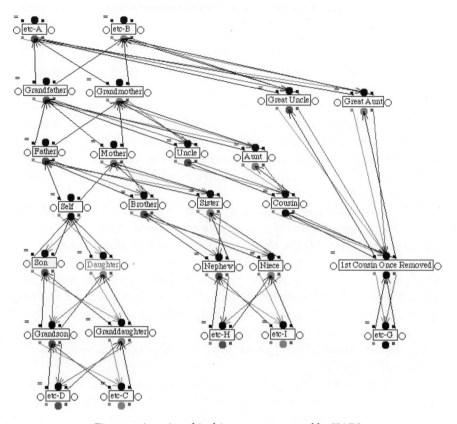

Figure 5. American kinship map regenerated by KAES

In KAES, the arrows mean "defined in terms of." Their color, starting, and ending points indicate what those terms are. Color is lost in the grayscale reproduction here, but on-screen the red means female, blue is male, and gray is either/both. The little dots on top of each position indicate the origins of a relation; the big dot indicates the destination. The little blue dot is on the left, and the little red dot is on the right. The generative positions are indicated by darker shading, which is not visible here. In this case, they are father, mother, son, daughter, and spouse. Every other position is defined as a relative product of these, plus a marker for gender and generation except in the case of cousin. Ego is "self." Thus, for example, the red arrow from the little red dot under father to the big red dot above sister indicates that a sister is the daughter of father. The blue arrow from the little blue dot under father to the big blue dot above brother indicates that brother is the son of father. The fact that another arrow goes to brother from mother means that brother is also defined through mother. So, strictly speaking, a brother is not defined as a male child of father but as a son of father other than self.

The simplifications are not only important as steps toward proving the general coherence of the terminologies; they are also analytically useful in themselves. Figure 6 shows what American kinship looks like when all pairs of terms distinguished only by gender are reduced to single positions. This makes even clearer the main structural distinction between the line of ancestors and descendants, ancestors and descendants of siblings, and collaterals who branch off and whose descendants appear in the undistinguished mass of cousins who make up the boundary between kin and strangers.

Figure 7 shows the results of the same simplification for Punjabi. In this case, the Punjabi term *mera,* meaning "my," replaces the term "ego" or "self" as the name of the central position.

Note that in this case all the positions did not collapse into positions that include both genders. This is because in Punjabi, gender of linking relatives separates different structural segments. In English, it does not. In English, therefore, gender can be considered to be added on to the basic structure; in Punjabi it is integral to it.

The KAES analytic process is experimental and predictive. The original graphic version of the map is stored in an xml file, as is the simplified version. The file is a list of definitions of positions, one position at a time, in a fixed

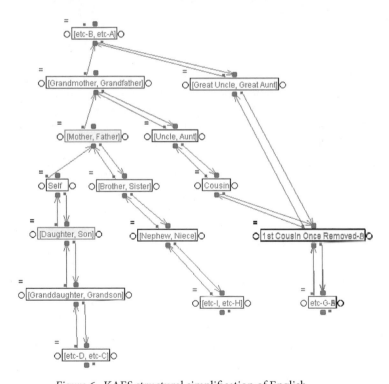

Figure 6. KAES structural simplification of English

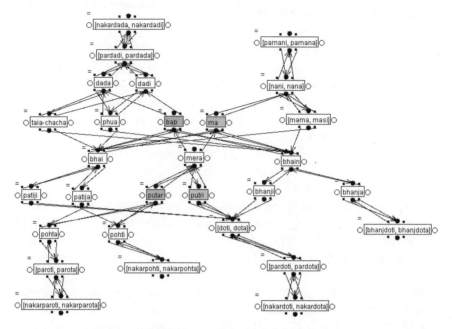

Figure 7. KAES structural simplification of Punjabi

format. Each position is defined in terms of the attributes that the graphic form represents. These include gender (if it is an attribute), whether it is or has a cover term, whether it is a generator, generational orientation, the generators that define it, and the other kin positions that are defined as kin-term products with it (that is, for example, *ma* is part of the kin-term product of *bap,* who is spouse of *ma,* and of *nana,* who is *bap* of *ma*).

Each step in the process of regenerating the map involves going to each position in the simplified graph and applying a general algebraic definition of the type of relation being considered. If, for example, the term in the simplification is only the male line, as in the present example, the algorithm asks what the definition of a female counterpart would be. What would the generators be that define it? What would be the products it would help to define? It then goes to the original xml file and looks for a definition with matching characteristics, and if such a term is found its definition is added and tested for consistency. Each step thus provides more conceptual handles for further steps. The generative process does not, therefore, precisely replicate that of the field elicitation but rather complements it. In the field elicitation, we build out the terminology in all directions and then check for consistency. The algebraic method checks for consistency as the way to build out the terminology. That the two methods converge, therefore, is a powerful mutual validation.

Table 1. Cayley table for simplified Punjabi base algebra

o	P
I	P
P	PP
PP	PPP
PPP	PPPP

The regeneration first creates a base algebra. The generators of the base algebra in the Punjabi case are I and P, meaning roughly male self and father (actually parent, but at this point no gender contrast has been introduced). I say roughly because their meaning in a more precise sense lies in the way they are constrained as the logic develops. The equations are two that define recursion and one that defines the end of the chain. The equations that define recursion are $I\_ = \_$ and $\_I = \_$, which mean "my X equals X" and "X's me equals X." The equation that defines the end of the chain is PPPPP $=$ o, which means that the P of PPPP (in this case the father of *nakardada*) is not a relation. The terms within the chain are defined by basic operations of algebra. IP is *bap*, IPP is *dada*, and so on. These equations can be printed out in a matrix, called a Cayley table. At each stage in the reconstruction as the algebra operations are built up, the Cayley table becomes increasingly more complex. The Cayley table for simplified Punjabi base algebra is presented in table 1. To read the table, take the term in the right column as the algebraic product of the term in the left column and the term at the top of the right column so that, for example, IP $=$ P, PP $=$ PP, and so on.

After constructing the base algebra, the next step is the sibling structure. This adds another generator, C, defined as C-brother and two more equations. One is CC $=$ C (C-brother of C-brother is C-brother). The other is PC $=$ P (C-brother of male parent is male parent). The latter equation would not apply in English and does not apply in all of the Punjabi positions, but it does apply in this line of positions. The next step is to construct the reciprocals. This adds two more algebra generators, A and B (son and younger brother), and a large number of additional equations. These are all the equations that can be applied that satisfy the general algebraic form of a relation that is symmetric in both directions; that is, for every link in one direction (sibling or descent) there is a link in the opposite direction. The Cayley table at this stage is table 2.

The next step is to regenerate the female counterparts of the male terms according to the general algorithm that says algebraically what a contrasting gender term for each existing term would be and then looks for actual terms that match that definition. This step also adds the resulting female generative term *ma* and its algebraic definition to the list of generators. After an intervening step involving

Table 2. Cayley table with siblings and reciprocals

The Algebra Cayley Table				
O	**C**	**P**	**A**	**B**
B	I	P	A	B
A	A	I	AA	A
I	C	P	A	B
P	P	PP	I	P
C	C	P	A	I
AA	AA	A	AAA	AA
PP	PP	PPP	P	PP
AAA	AAA	AA	AAAA	AAA
PPP	PPP	PPPP	PP	PPP
AAAA	AAAA	AAA		AAAA
PPPP	PPPP		PPP	PPPP

testing for consistency with definitions of descendants of siblings, the next major expansion comes from adding reciprocals. This is based on yet another general algebraic pattern. Two examples that should suggest the general logic are SP = I (son of father equals me) and PS = I (father of son equals me, with the further definition that sibling is not equal to me). The positions whose definitions satisfy pairs of equations of this form are reciprocals of one another. Adding the reciprocity relation restores a descendant counterpart to every ascendant position and thus reproduces the simplification in figure 5. At this point, the Cayley table becomes too large to be reproduced here, because as the map expands the number of pathways to each position increases disproportionally.

Another step adds tests for a further set of equivalences between various sons and daughters of the positions already present. The final step is to add positions that meet the requirements of a general definition of affines. For Punjabi, this reproduces the entire original terminology. At this point, the number of algebra generators has increased to ten, and the number of kin-term generators is the original core set of five: *mera, bap, ma, putar, putri.* (In the algebraic analysis there is no need to use the core sibling terms *bhai* and *bhain* as generators.)

Because the reconstruction involves a large number of comparisons, position by position, it is important to be patient. Each of the last two steps can take twenty minutes or more to run on a fast computer.

Ultimately, every different kinship system is generated by a different set of algebraic equations applied to a usually somewhat distinctive simplest version in a different sequence.

The ability of full terminologies to be regenerated from small portions of themselves is a feature of enormous importance. This is how such complex and sophisticated systems, so powerful in their ability to generate a wide range of relationships while keeping them all in single coherent framework, can exist in communities where many of their users do not actually know the whole system and its implications and yet can re-create the system precisely whenever they come together. The same generative power is what explains how such systems can persist with little or no change over wide regions and for very long periods of time. With one of the minimal descent lines, the fundamental ideas of reciprocity and relative products and a few of the basic rules peculiar to the systems, any group of users can reconstruct the whole using the same kind of naturalistic queries as the KAES model.

Since the graphic analyses and algebras are generated automatically and always by the same algorithms, the structures can be compared cross-culturally in a way that we have every reason to expect is culturally neutral and logically universal. We can therefore now ask and answer a number of questions that previously could not even be formulated. For example, do all kinship terminologies have the same generative positions? The answer is that they do not. In some, a term such as "brother" is generative; in others it is not. Do they all have an "ego"? The answer is not exactly; they all (so far) have a focal term, but this is not always defined as an "I." It is possible that these deep structures have historical or evolutionary significance in the way language families do, although at this point we have not analyzed enough systems to know.

The relations among the definitions have the distinctive mathematical properties of algebraic structures known as semigroups. The structure is in the definitions, and it is real. It is not external and imposed.

Before Read's analysis, the phrase "kinship algebra" was sometimes connected to componential analysis. There is an important similarity in that the componential analysts did indeed recognize that patterns in kinship terminologies were formal in a logical and even quasi-mathematical sense. It was an important insight, but the understanding of what a formal pattern was and the method of exposing it were entirely different and the difference turned out to be crippling. That was algebra as a metaphor. This is actual algebra, fundamental concepts of mathematics.

The componential analysts thought of their problem in positivistic terms: words were tags, and their meanings were what they denoted (referred to objectively) in contrast to what they connoted (suggested subjectively). The purpose of the method was to describe the meanings of the terms in this sense in such a way that for each term in the indigenous vocabulary "no term overlaps or includes another; every component is discriminated by at least one term; and all terms can be displayed on the same paradigm" (Wallace and Atkins 1960, 62). The order in the words, then, was taken as coming from what they objectively referred to. They assumed among other things that each term could have only one referent in this sense, an assumption that is not in fact true, as Punjabi illustrates. The discovery procedure, which was also the formalization, was as a priorist as the concept of meaning. In Roy D'Andrade's terms, it was an "*emic* analysis*,*" and "to carry out an *emic* analysis one began with a set of categories brought in by the scientific observer and then tried to find out which of those categories really made a difference with respect to the way the natives understood and responded to things" (D'Andrade 1995, 18–19).

In the specific case of kinship, the categories brought in were kintypes, which were also the components. These were a priori in the sense of prior to any particular analysis. They were, rather, thought to reflect certain universal features of biology and reproduction that all kinship systems had to recognize. For any particular system, the analyst's problem was to see which of these features were actually distinctive and how they fit together. Wallace and Atkins (1960) and D'Andrade (1995, 17–28) give substantially the same account of the general method. The kintypes were symbolized by one or two letters so as to seem abstract and schematic, but in the end the ideas they represented were only those of the American kinship system: M or Ma for mother, F or Fa for father, S or So for son, D or Da for daughter, B for brother, Si or Z for sister, and H or W for husband or wife, sometimes with added qualifiers for age and the like. A concept that was un-American, such as the Purum concept of a brother that includes all brothers older than ego but not those younger or the Navajo "grandmother" that means the eldest living woman of the clan, could not be represented.

Formal analysis in the present sense does not depend on finding what the terms refer to but only on how their definitions are mutually interrelated, and for this purpose the very simple but rigorously defined concepts from abstract algebras are both appropriate and adequate. Although the KAES diagrams do not have exactly the same visual look as my type of elicited graphs, they are clearly isomorphic and confirm that the elicited graphs are what they seem to be: coherent and complete systems of definitions of positions. In sum, the way to think about kinship concepts is not as applying a set of terms to divide up a set of material objects but rather as the Kantian idea of formalizing an intuition. We recognize that there is a something there but also recognize that there are many different ways to articulate it.

Other Kinship Ideas

The kinship map is the conceptual skeleton onto which the rest of the kinship idea system is attached. Common additions include rules of incest, rules of marriage, rules of inheritance, and conceptions of kinship groups apart from ego-centered sets of kinsmen, such as families, extended families, hearths (relations who store and prepare food together), households, wards, sides, lineages, clans, generations, and elders.

Such attached concepts and rules may be relatively superficial and imposed from without, or they may be tightly integrated. They may be purely traditional, enforced locally by mutual interaction, or they may be supported by law. Traditional ideas and legal ideas may exist side by side, and they may agree or disagree. All such differences have organizational consequences.

Although in the West as a matter of kinship folklore the explanation of incest rules is commonly sought in biology, the more salient reason lies in their logic. As formal systems, kinship maps must be logically consistent. Incest rules, at minimum, are rules that are logically needed to maintain that consistency. The most clearly forbidden relations are always among the core positions: parent-child and siblings. The reason is obvious if you ask what would happen (logically) to the terminology if the offspring of such unions were to be recognized as kin. What would happen in English, for example, if brother and sister could have offspring who would be sons or daughters? The first thing that would happen is that there would be no basis for the distinction between sons and daughters as against nephews and nieces. For the same reason, there would also be no distinction between grandchildren and great-nephews and great-nieces, and so on. The map would therefore collapse in its horizontal dimension. In the same way, if a position in the kinship map were to be accorded to the offspring of mother and son or father and daughter, the map would collapse in the vertical dimension. The entire conceptual system would vanish in two puffs of self-negation. In short, prohibitions on incest may or may not be necessary from the point of view of biology, but they are immediately and obviously essential for maintaining kinship as a formal structure.

In addition to the basic incest rules that arise from the particular generative structure of each system, there may be additional rules imposed for other reasons such as rules in some American states specifying which types of cousins are or are not marriageable, rules of caste, or religious preferences.

Inheritance rules vary greatly in the extent to which they are integral to the map's logical structure. In English-speaking countries, the same terminology has been associated with many different rules of inheritance. Inheritance seems to be much more a matter of governmental policy expressed through law than of kinship as such. In Punjabi, on the other hand, the idea of property being passed on through male descendants in a village seems to be absolutely integral to the terminology, and in these communities the courts do not impose law on kinship but instead have consistently imposed kinship on law under the heading of customary law.

It is probable that the contrast between Punjabi and English kinship systems in regard to the relative firmness of attachment of different inheritance rules bespeaks the adaptation of the two systems to different social circumstances. It may very well be that the English system is as devoid of implications for inheritance as it is because in England and its cultural descendants an effective system of laws and courts has been available for many centuries to handle these matters, while the Indian systems carry this burden because there has been no such court system to hand it off to. At this point we do not have the answer, but up to now we have not even had the question.

Kinship and Socialization

Ethnologists study kinship in part because it is one of the very few apparent sociocultural universals. But why is it? As long as kinship was viewed through the clouded lens of epistemologies that required us to impose ideas on it that were actually alien to it, this question could not be answered. Now that we have it out in the open, the answers begin to emerge. Part of it has to be the way its massive logical redundancy supports its logical stability, and another part must be the way this logical structure supports its cultural transmission. But there is more. I have noted that kinship is the gateway to all other systems of social relations. It is the first set of social relations we learn, and through it we learn what we need to know to move on to others. The logical structure is also what gives it the ability to do this.

Piaget's developmental psychology (1953, 1962, 1970) provides the connection. Because of the particular way the details of the system are generated from the core terms, systems of kinship ideas are uniquely appropriate to the problem of introducing infants to the idea of social relations in a form that can be learned in the sequence of developmental stages that he has documented. Kinship maps are designed (by cultural-evolutionary variation and selection) for teaching what it is to have a social self, that is, to occupy I-thou-it relations.

Piaget and his colleagues have shown that cognitive complexity develops in three major stages, generally marked by the ages up to five, from about five to about nine, and from nine to about twelve. In Stage I, logic is strongly tied to sensorimotor activity and is limited to one-to-one relations: some one definite thing, sound, or action goes with some other definite thing, sound, or action. If a task cannot be broken down to this kind of relationship, it cannot be learned. Children at this point may play in each other's proximity, but they cannot play together in the sense of playing according to a common set of rules.

Stage II, from five to eight or nine, involves the beginning and development of the concept of a class and the differentiation of an individual/element from it: if this is an X, it must have property Y. This includes the beginning of the formation of the concept of "I," the ego, as Kant described it, although Piaget takes it through several very specific logical substages. It also includes the beginning of hindsight and anticipation and of what Piaget calls the differentiation of prelogical operations from sublogical operations. The former involves discrete objects in the realm of abstract representation, while the latter "relates to elements in the spatial continuum" (Piaget and Inhelder 1964, 282). That is, this is the beginning of the differentiation, in thought, of thought from its objects.

After about age nine the complexity moves to classes but in a way that is limited to simple operations such as juxtaposition or equation but not class inclusion. Finally, beginning at about age twelve, conceptualization moves to classes of classes or sets of sets in such a way as to form hierarchical arrangements and the fully formed type of hindsight and anticipation that Piaget and Inhelder call "equilibrium" (1964, 285). This means that the child can recognize that certain basic class operations involving negation and complementarity are the reverse of each other and can "shuttle" back and forth between them (288). In social terms, it is only at this point that one can formulate fully reciprocal thinking, a thought such as "If I were in your place that is what I would do," and also recognize its negation.

The design of kinship maps both reflects and exploits this logical progression. Because of the way they are structured around a focal term or an ego and because one becomes such an ego at birth, a person can start learning the core concepts at the earliest stages of cognitive development, and this foundation will not be abandoned or rejected in later stages but instead will only be expanded, refined, and qualified.

To learn one's most immediate relatives, it is not necessary to learn any concept of classification. A baby has one mother, one father, and perhaps a few siblings. In this context, one face goes with one or very few vocalizations, one to one. The vocalization eventually turns into the idea of a position or relation: mother, son, brother, etc. But by about age five children learning English have begun to be exposed to relatives who are more distant and have, for example, come to recognize that while they have one father, they may have many uncles. This requires a different kind of cognition. The first step uses the idea of a class: an uncle is someone like Uncle Bob. This is what we see up to perhaps ages seven to nine.

Eventually, however, a child will meet more and more relatives who have the same objective attributes as Uncle Bob but who are, for example, cousins. To make the distinction that this requires, it is not possible just to change the visible characteristic of the class. One must move to a definition in terms of classes of classes: relations of relations. An uncle is the brother of a parent or the husband of an aunt. And this is evidently why it is only between about ages eight and twelve that children start to learn that an uncle is any brother of one's mother or father or any spouse of an aunt, finally arriving at a position defined wholly by its relation to other positions, which also involves a full-blown and reversible concept of reciprocity (Piaget's equilibrium) and a clear sense that one is dealing with a definition as such (Piaget's abstract class) and not just a specific set of physical objects. At this point, finally, one has learned all one needs to know to think in terms of kinship with complete mastery. It is also, however, all one needs to know to think in terms of any other kind of social relation.

While there have been many studies showing that Piaget's stages of conceptual development hold up cross-culturally (Saxe 1983, 139), only a few have focused on the acquisition of kinship terms, and none have utilized the present analysis of kinship terminology or any other system that would allow them to extend their queries to relations very far beyond the basic core. Nevertheless, what has been documented is consistent with my argument here.

Hy Van Luong (1986) described four studies—his own and three others—focused on the conceptual process of de-centering. De-centering is the ability to take the perspective of another rather than acquisition of kinship terms as such, but there is enough overlap to address the present question. Luong's aim was to identify the specific mechanism by which de-centering is acquired. He considered three alternatives: the empirical theory of Piaget, a Chomskyian theory of inherited and universal capacities,[1] and a position based on information theory that related what is learned to difficulty of learning.

Luong's subjects were fifty-six immigrant Vietnamese children in a bilingual program in an elementary school in the Boston area. The age groups were four to six years old, seven to eight years old, nine years old, ten to eleven years old, and twelve to sixteen years old. The other studies in the series involved children in Geneva (Piaget 1976 [1928]), American Jewish children (Elkind 1961), and rural Hawaiian children (Price-Williams, Hammond, Edgerton, and Walker 1977). Additional data and interpretations were drawn from about a half dozen other studies that were not full replications.

In the four main studies each child in each group was asked to do the same three tasks that involved de-centered reasoning. Two of the tasks involved knowledge of kinship terminology. One kinship task was to correctly take the point of view of a sibling; the second was to provide general definitions of sibling relations and a few others. The third task was to recognize that when you are facing someone, his or her left is your right and vice versa.

Vietnamese kinship ideas are unlike the others in the group because they require siblings to be distinguished by relative age as well as gender. Elder brother and sister are distinguished from younger brother and sister in both reference and address so that in any given group of siblings each individual would apply the terms to a different constellation of the others, reflecting and expressing their unique position in the birth order. The children were asked to identify themselves and their siblings (perspective comprehension) and to define the relations in the sense of saying why they called that person by that term (category definition). The answers were scored as right or wrong according to whether they did or did not accurately replicate the underlying logic of four levels of conceptualization of reciprocity in Piaget's terms, as restated in a study of English kin-term acquisition by Susan Haviland and Eve Clark (1974). The responses were tabulated showing the number of children in each age group that got the answers right at each conceptual level.

Luong's main question was whether the groups of children would learn the different tasks in a different order and if so whether the pattern supported one or another hypothesized mechanism. A subordinate question was whether the Vietnamese children would learn how to de-center earlier, since they had what amounted to more cultural pressure and prompting to do so. The answer was that the groups did learn them in a different order, but the order was not easy to explain. For acquiring perspective comprehension, sibling category definition, and left-right transposition, the Vietnamese children's ages were seven to eight, ten to eleven, and ten, respectively. For Piaget's Geneva group the ages were ten, nine, and eight. For the Jewish American children the ages were seven, nine, and seven, and for the Hawaiian children the ages were nine, eight, and ten.

Luong considered that the results generally supported Piaget's empirical theory, and this was what Luong's discussion mainly focused on. Although he attempted to account for the variations between the groups, there was no conclusive result because relevant contextual parameters were not consistently recognized across the other studies. For example, while Vietnamese embodies exceptionally intensive relativity of perspective in the sibling terms, it also, like Punjabi, defines a kin universe that is essentially open-ended. So while the instruction for de-centering is clearer, the problem that it applies to is more difficult. Comparable information on the extent of use of terms from the other studies had not been collected and could not be since Luong and the other investigators lacked an appropriate analysis of kinship itself.

With respect to my own theoretical concern, the important results lie more in the constancies than the variations. First, although the children began learning whom to apply the terms to by age four, none of them could explain why or provide definitions before age seven. Thus, the more abstract concepts came after learning the generative core and after Piaget's first major level of conceptual maturation. Second, the fact of the variation as such means that cultural learning is involved, and different concepts are taught by different mechanisms (pluralism).

Moreover, for the more detailed information that was presented on the Vietnamese children, it seems highly likely that the order of learning reflects the logical structure of the terminology as it would be revealed by the methods used here for English and Punjabi. Luong's results for Vietnamese were that the sibling terms were more difficult to learn than the terms for mother and grandmother. "Sibling perspective comprehension" was exhibited correctly by 36 percent of the four- to six-year-olds and by age nine by 100 percent. Knowing siblings' relations to ego was similarly mastered by age nine. But only 27 percent of the children in the four- to six-year-old group could define "elder brother" with the most complete logic; for ages ten to eleven and twelve to sixteen correctly defining "elder brother" still only reached 75 percent. "Elder sister" was still more difficult, and there was no age cohort with 100 percent getting it right. The ability to define the relation correctly began at 7 percent for ages four to six, was 82 percent for ages ten to eleven, and (perhaps surprisingly) only 75 percent for ages twelve to sixteen (7 percent is one person). By contrast, the most complete concept of "mother" was provided by 28 percent of those ages four to six, 82 percent of those ages ten to eleven, and 100 percent of those ages twelve to sixteen. Definition of "grandmother" was 8 percent for those ages four to six, 67 percent for those ages ten to eleven, and 100 percent for those ages twelve to sixteen (Luong 1986, 29).

In terms of the analyses here, there would be two obvious reasons for this pattern. First, Luong's description implies that "mother" is a core term and generator, while the elder and younger sibling terms are core terms but not generators. The elder-younger distinction makes no difference in reckoning through the sibling terms to more distant positions. That is, the father or mother of an elder brother is not different from the father or mother of a younger brother. The generators would be more memorable because to function as generators they need meanings that are simple and stable rather than complicated and contingent, and as generators there would be more sustained exposure to their deeper implications. Second, while "grandmother" is a generated term just as the elder and younger sibling concepts are, it is conceptually simpler. It is mother of mother, a simple relative product. Elder brother is son of mother (relative product) plus an attribute derived from comparing that person with ego.

In light of the present theoretical framework, these studies appear to have implications well beyond what their own authors described. They suggest that over the long haul of human evolution our capacity to learn while maturing has coevolved with our cultural devices for teaching. Moreover, there are many such devices, which give shape to our capacities in different ways. With respect to Luong's effort to compare Piaget's perspective with Chomsky's, I should add that if Chomsky's claim is that the entire evolutionary development is genetically driven and universal it is surely wrong, not only because of the differential patterns of learning that Luong describes but more basically because of the differential patterns of logic in the kinship terminologies themselves and between kinship and other idea systems.

In most systems of social relations apart from kinship, the definitions of the positions begin at the third level of logical complexity, definitions in terms of classes of classes: the idea of a set of positions defined with full reflexivity and reciprocity and the complementary idea of a set of people who can occupy them. All the positions in a system, uniformly, are conceptualized as completely detached from actual individuals and are defined only in relation to each other and to the set of individuals who can occupy them. On Piaget's analysis and in accordance with ordinary observation, this is not the sort of thing a young child can learn.

In short, kinship is the primary course in which we learn the linguistic, conceptual, and organizational fundamentals of self-construction, role taking, and reciprocity. It has widely been recognized that the family is an essential instrument of socialization. What has not been widely understood is why. The reason is not just that it is the organization that supports us when we are most helpless, for that is true of the young of many species, who do not thereby acquire the organizational abilities of human beings. The reason is that in addition to getting us through our early physical dependency, the human family also organizes itself with the logical structures of systems of kinship definitions and therefore cannot avoid teaching them.

Kinship Ideas and Kinship Organizations

A kinship map is not an organization. We have noted that ideas of kinship organizations are generated from the basic idea systems by selecting subsets of the ideas, emphasizing one or another set of aspects or implications, and combining them with additional ideas. In this, the definitions of the basic social idea systems cannot be violated, but beyond that they cannot be thought of as controlling or determining the organizations created with them.

In communities using English terminologies, variations in inheritance rules associated with the terminologies can lead to important corresponding differences in the way kinship ideas can be used for defining household organization. The sibling relation in a system of primogeniture does not have the same significance as in a system of birthrights for all. An idea of a lineage can be combined with the ideas of vertical links in the core relations to generate genealogies, which are important for some users of the English system but not others.

In Punjab, most families have recognized family genealogists who reside at two major sites on the Ganges River where families customarily take the ashes of their dead relatives to scatter onto the water. These genealogists keep genealogies that go back for centuries, even though the kinship maps end at the +4 generation. In English, by contrast, where the terminological "etcetera" allows people to identify relations back in time indefinitely, people rarely know who their great-grandparents were.

Ideas of generations can be used to define age grades such as we find in Africa, generations within families, or seniority within clans. Among aboriginal Australians, blocks of positions are associated with totems to define sections and section systems, as we find in the Arunta and Kariera. The range of permutations is well known (Fox 1967; Parkin 1997). What is new is that we can now see what they are permutations of.

In Punjab, important ideas drawn from the basic kinship definitions and extended to define general classes are male versus female, father's side as against mother's, and ideas that define the household, lineage, and the life cycle. A household, as noted, is defined as a group of kin cooperating in some common property. Property in this sense always implies both a means of earning a livelihood and a residential unit: a house or perhaps only a hearth (*chula*) in part of a house, stores of food, utensils, and the like along with the capital and tools of a common occupation. Distant relatives who cooperate in using and maintaining the property are part of the *parivar* (household) no matter how great that relational distance may be. Brothers are not in the same household if they do not cooperate. Actual households are groups that take the conceptual model of a household as their main description. Most households in villages are linked to at least some other houses by common clanship.

In most of India the property rights are transmitted by patrilineal descent, although for a few groups they are matrilineal. The most common marriage rule among communities in the Indo-European language area in the north is clan and village exogamy. That is, a man marries a woman from outside his own village and from an unrelated clan. A person cannot marry anyone of the clans of one's mother's mother, mother's father, father's mother, or father's father. A clan (gōt, gōtra) is a group of people descended from a common ancestor, usually eponymous but unknown. The marriage rule in Punjab is that you do not marry anyone in your pura char (complete four), meaning the clans of your mother's mother, mother's father, father's mother, and father's father. Kinship positions as a rule do not group into clans except that in Punjabi the line putar-pohta-paRota will be in one's own clan. Rajasthani and Hindustani, among others, have exact equivalents. Otherwise, it follows from the marriage rule that the nana-nani relational group and the dada-dadi side both include people from an indefinite number of clans.

Caste is another idea added to the basic kinship positions but not implicit in them. A caste (jati) is defined as an endogamous group sharing a common occupation based on common inherited property. The definition follows logically from the notion that marriage is a social and managerial partnership and should therefore be between households with the same occupation. The units within the caste are, again by definition, clans (gōt, gōtra), and the units within clans are local lineages (pattī, literally leaves or divisions) and families. Caste is thus the outer limit of marriage eligibility as clan is the inner limit. These stereotypes are the basis of what often appears in scholarly descriptions of the caste system or jajmani system as a unitary social system in which caste ideas control all social relations. In fact, this is another instance of taking ideas that seem to define an organization as evidence that such organizations actually exist without checking whether the criteria for recruitment make practical sense or are actually used.

Censusing actual occupations in any South Asian community always shows that families have many occupations and that most of these are not predictable from their caste identifications. Claims about the caste system are therefore consistently qualified by the claim that while it existed in the past it has broken down in the present, yet another version of the dualist's gap between theory and reality (Hutton 1946; Wiser and Wiser 1960; Dumont 1970; Srinivas 1976). In fact, however, there is no evidence from the past that matters were ever any different. The Laws of Manu, often cited to indicate the antiquity of the caste system, is a two-thousand-year-old version of exactly the same just-so story we find in the present. Manu's caste system is not claimed as a description of what he actually experienced. It is what he said existed in the past and wanted to restore. So what he really documents is what we still see: the marriage rules and the logical possibility of inferring such a system from them by taking them out of their practical context and exaggerating their importance. Nothing more.

The varieties of group definitions that can be created in this way are limitless. Only a small part can be captured in any given analysis, but whatever this may be it is usually readily apparent that what holds all such systems together as kinship systems and not systems of some other kind is their common use of the vocabulary of relational concepts whose most fundamental definitions are the positional cores.

Managerial Control

We cannot assume that because management of resources is everywhere important every society will have a system of ideas explicitly focused on it. Nevertheless, every community I know of personally does have such a system, meaning an idea system that includes ways to say what the managerial units are, who their members are, who is in charge, what rights the members of the groups have in their output, and how this is enforced. "In charge" in this context usually means two things: who has the decisive say in assigning people to tasks internally and who represents the group in transactions externally. Such ideas may be defined as being formal and public. In the West, this is the idea of workplace and its variants: the shop, the studio, the farm, the boat, the company, the office, and the job. Or they may be considered in various degrees covert, informal, or hidden, such as the Navajo idea of the outfit. For the Trobriand Islanders (Malinowski 1922), the *kula* trade in prestigious but useless ceremonial goods is conducted according to an overt idea of management in the sense that the trade is conducted in a highly formalized and ceremonialized way, with no bargaining, and spoken of as though it were of great social importance, closely tied to the social rank of those who take part in it. The *gimwali* trade that accompanies the *kula*, by contrast, is defined as hidden, secret, and informal, something that the Trobrianders do not talk about (or rather something that they say they don't talk about when they talk about it), but it is here that important practical goods are obtained by trade that could not be obtained otherwise, and in Malinowski's account the haggling is commonly intense.

The distinctness of management ideas is made evident in many ways. In Western urban areas, a workplace is physically and legally distinguished from a residence. A workplace is for management organizations. A residence is for kinship organizations. A person goes to work and comes home. To say that a person appears to sleep in his shop or office is to suggest that an expectation is being violated, and so is saying that a person's residence looks like a shop. In America, city and town zoning laws usually expressly forbid people from using their residences for business purposes, where the phrase "business purpose" actually means management purpose. It does not mean that you cannot engage in economic transactions or even make a profit while in your residence. It means that you cannot use or store material for productive activities and have the kind of traffic that production involves. Legally, workplaces are subject to inspection to protect the public, while residences are private and are protected from such intrusions.

By contrast, in India and most of the less-developed world workplaces are not expected to be separate from residences physically, but households as management units are still distinguished from households as kinship units organizationally. The two need not have the same membership and will certainly not have the same defined relations. A son is one thing; the family tractor driver is another. Permanent hired workers may be in the household in a managerial sense but are not kin. Some members of the family organization in a kinship sense (such as girls who have married out) are not part of the household as a managerial organization.

In northern Indian languages, the general term for management is *parbaNDhi*,[2] literally "bound together."[3] A manager is a *parbaNDhak*. The term *parbaNDhak* would not normally be used as a term of address, just as one would not use the term "manager" in North America. It would not be offensive; it just seems overdescriptive. It is normal as a term of reference. As in the West, the convention in India is that the *parbaNDhak* coordinates the activities of the household internally and stands as its representative to other managerial organizations externally. What the *parbaNDhak* promises to others outside the management organization can commit everyone in the organization to some activity or priority. What someone else in the organization promises would normally not have this force. If the management organization is a household, the senior male in kinship terms will not be recognized as the *parbaNDhak* if he is not actively engaged in organizing the actual production.

While the *parbaNDhak* is generally understood to be male, this is not a logical necessity. Furthermore, there is a sharp sense of difference between men's and women's spheres, and in the latter, such as dealing with those who provide household services in contrast to those who work in the fields, the senior capable woman of the house—usually but not necessarily the wife of the *parbaNDhak*— is considered to act for him. There are also female-headed households, and in such cases there is no question that the woman is a *parbaNDhak*. Internally, the men and women work out their responsibilities in their separate spheres. There is no general complement to the term for manager, as there is not in English, but there are many that have somewhat different implications depending on the types of tasks involved: a person might be described as a worker (*mazduri*) in general terms but also as a rights holder if the aim was to distinguish someone working as member of the household rather than as hired help. The term *parbaNDhak* is equally applicable for managers outside of the household and kinship context, which is another strong indicator of the formal separateness and autonomy of this idea system.

The ideas of the management system can be elicited in the same way as the ideas of kinship. First, collect fortuitous observations that appear to be relevant until such observations become repetitive and you can form a rough notion of how they fit together. For India, such observations include the terminology just noted, what tasks are done by men and what by women, and how the decisions are made and enforced regarding who does what in any actual context. With these points as guideposts, undertake systematic elicitation with a relevant group, beginning with whatever is the best candidate for a managerial concept. In this case, the obvious starting points were the ideas of the *parbaNDhak* and *parbaNDhi* themselves. I simply asked what they meant. What is a *parbaNDhak* expected to do, not this or that *parbaNDhak* but a *parbaNDhak* in general? This produced additional concepts including the ideas of the division by gender, as noted; ideas of cooperation and duty; ideas of acceptable and proper goals; ideas of respect and deference such that elders are generally relieved when younger people are available to replace them; and ideas of motivation. For example, while there is a general sense that some tasks are women's work and some are men's work, in agricultural households this is more a matter of convenience than an absolute rule. The more basic principle is that people rotate through different tasks according to who is available and what they can do. When sugarcane needs to be cut, which requires a lot of people at once, everyone joins in. When sugarcane needs to be pressed, which only requires two people, the youngest who are able might do it, while old people do lighter tasks or rest.

Management ideas for assigning people to resources also involve ideas for securing resources. In Punjab, these include the character and uses of a large number of specialized storage drums and other devices for securing the family's property. In America, such an elicitation should lead to the idea that possession requires meeting certain legal requirements, such as having receipts as proof of purchase.

As the description emerges, it can be checked by asking about the specific instances that have been observed. In each such instance the prediction being tested is that if the observed behavior were indeed organized with these ideas, they would be used to describe it. If it were not organized with the managerial ideas, some other idea would be used to describe it. If such other ideas were used and you specifically prompted your respondent with ideas from the management system, you should get a response such as "that is another matter." And finally, you should be able to return to opportunistic observations and find that the ideas used to describe such activities are also used to create them.

Outside the village system, managerial ideas in South Asia are largely the same as in the West. They define the powers of heads of departments in government units, the owners and managers of business firms, the distinctions between owners of various types and managers of various types, categories of employees, arrangements of specializations within them, and the relations among employees, agents, other representatives, and those they deal with. Nothing is mysterious. Managerial ideas exist and can be elicited, and when elicited they can be seen to form coherent systems. Then when we look at the kinds of behaviors these descriptions pertain to, we see that they are not just accounts as though from afar but that the same ideas are used by those within those relations to make them accessible for discussion and agreement.

In the West, in addition to the recognizably similar folk notions, we have a great deal of written law in which such ideas are increasingly elaborated and specified. The powers and duties of managers and those they manage is the main topic of the vast body of corporate and labor law and a large part of tort and contract law. But while the law itself is largely new, the basic ideas that underlie it appear to be ancient.

Computer simulations of management decision making are widely available in many different forms. This is what system analysis software such as Stella does in a very general way or programs for work or project scheduling in more work-specific ways. In communities that do not rely so extensively on written information storage and do not have access to this type of technology, there are similar algorithms in other forms, such as the Balinese calendar model and the South Asian physical farm budget model noted in chapter 3, that can be readily computerized. But since these have more to do with how specific managerial organizations are formed than managerial ideas in general, they are described in chapter 6.

Economics

Economic ideas are different from management ideas, and economic organizations are different from management organizations although contemporary economic theory thoroughly mixes them up. Where a managerial organization is defined around a type of production, an economic organization is defined by the idea of profit and loss. In the West, the term for an economic organization as distinct from a managerial organization is "firm" or perhaps "business," both of which carry more of an association with the idea of making profit than making things (as opposed, for example, to terms such as "shop," "studio," or "factory").

As the idea of a manager is the logical starting point from which to trace the ideas of management, the logical starting point for the economy is the idea of money.

All money is culturally defined, and all of these definitions are bound up in cultural idea systems. There may even be more than one such idea system per community. Walter Neale, in *Monies in Societies* (1976), describes the several moneys available in the colonies around the time of the American Revolution and the process that led to the silver Austrian taler, or thaler (named after Jáchymov, or Sankt Joachimsthal, the famous sixteenth-century silver-mining center), becoming the prototype of the American dollar. A more recent instance is the joint use of American dollars and Israeli shekels in Israel described by Virginia Dominguez (1990). The shekel is maintained by the Israeli monetary authorities and the dollar by American monetary authorities. Even though the latter had no jurisdiction in Israel and the American dollar had no legal status, it was in practice the main standard of value and store of wealth, as it also is across the border in Palestine (Dominguez 1990, 16). Dominguez's interest was in money as socially constructed yet real. The article explains how the two moneys were maintained side by side in terms of their relative stability and rates of inflation, and the explanation is applicable far beyond this one case. It makes perfect sense in terms of instrumental rationality in a world of multiple cultural systems, as do the processes described by Neale.

Systems of economic conceptions attached to the idea of money are just as definite in their formal structure and normative in their semantics as ideas of kinship and managerial control. Part of the formal logic of money is of course the logic of common arithmetic, but there is more; to establish money requires cultural conventions to apply the logic of mathematics to the money stuff, and these conventions must be enforced. These conventions concern the definitions of economic organizations, commoditization, and transactions.

Economic organizations are represented conceptually by their books. Bookkeeping models represent the formal structure of economic organizations just as scheduling and division-of-labor models represent the formal structure of managerial organizations. It is unlikely to be an accident that money, receipts, shipping records, and bookkeeping appear in history together at substantially the same time and place, in the ancient Near East.

The conventions concerned with maintaining the money stuff involve its design and production, the arrangements for preserving its value, ideas of what this value represents, ideas of who can handle it, ideas of who can or must accept it (the idea of legal tender, the idea of a negotiable instrument, and so on), and in modern communities all the laws and practices concerning counterfeiting and the use of money substitutes such as checks, bank transfers, and the like. So long as this all works, however, most of it generally remains specialist knowledge out of sight of most people who use money in daily life and need not concern us here.

The conventions for calculation are the cultural forms of monetary mathematics. The basic rules of arithmetic are probably formally unavoidable with any notion of the sequence of cardinal numbers, but the way they are embedded in monetary calculations is not. A simple example is that in Indian villages interest is usually stated on the basis of "twelve rupees in the hundred" or "eighteen rupees in the hundred." Although this may sound like a rate of simple interest in the Western sense, it is actually an algorithm for calculating interest that compounds monthly. The full meaning of twelve in the hundred is that for each hundred rupees borrowed, the borrower pays the lender one rupee each individual month that the loan is held. Thus at the end of the year the lender would have been paid twelve rupees, but the rupees paid earlier would have been in his hands longer. However, if the borrower does not pay the charge monthly in this way, he adds the additional one rupee to the debt in each subsequent month and calculates what he owes for the rest of the year with that amount included, which would be one pice (one-one hundredth of a rupee) per rupee. The result is a very neat way of calculating compound interest over any period with no mathematics other than addition. To compute the rate of eighteen rupees in the hundred everything is the same, but the monthly payment is a rupee and a half.

Economic transactions are mutual adjustments of behavior, but in comparison to the adjustments organized by means of other idea systems most of these are of very short-term duration. It is their effects that are intended to last. The conventions for making transactions include such matters as what the different transactions are called, what the parties are called, what symbolic actions indicate agreement or disagreement, and what kinds of records must be made. There must be rules to distinguish legitimate transactions from fraudulent transactions and fair from unfair. There must be definitions of different kinds of transactions that entail different kinds of expectations. In America we rent goods but hire people, and the legal and customary rules regarding rental are very different from those regarding hiring. A lease is different from a rental, and a mortgage is different from a lease. They entail different modes of payment and the payments have different social and legal implications. All of this is part of the system of ideas governing the use of money and is therefore tied into a single system by the use of money.

The conventions for commoditization are much more than just a set of assignments of numerical values to things on the positivistic model of terms and their objects. They are standardized procedures. As an example, the way Indian farmers conceptualize their labor rates is directly related to the way farm households calculate their income and plan their cropping activity. They calculate their income as a surplus or loss against a fixed set of maintenance requirements for the year. They plan their cropping activity and hire their labor by operation, not as so many hours, so much tool use, and so on. They do this because this is what the crops require. At one point in time the crop must be sown; a few weeks later it will need to be weeded, then perhaps irrigated, then weeded again; and it will then be harvested and then perhaps threshed or otherwise processed. In between, it must be tended and watched. This is what has to be arranged for. Sometimes intermediate operations yield usable by-products, and sometimes they do not. The work that can be done on a daily basis is usually done by the farm family. But the main operations usually are best done in short periods of time that require organized teams, hired from without.

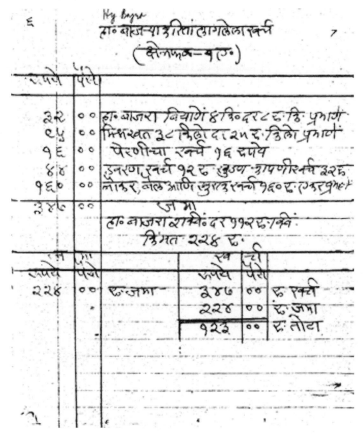

Figure 8. Farmer's cost record, India

Figure 8 illustrates this. It is a page out of an Indian farmer's personal farm record from a village in the Pus irrigation project in Maharashtra state. It was provided in the course of my activity on the Irrigation and Water Management Training Project, sponsored by USAID and the government of India from July 1987 through August 1989. One part of my project responsibilities was action research. The idea, which originated with Sol Tax, is now a common feature of development projects worldwide. Pus command was the state action research site, and four of the villages within the command area had been selected as representative action research villages. The plan was that innovations would be introduced there under controlled conditions, properly documented, and if successful they would then be spread more widely. The action research staff from the state irrigation department had been working for about a year before my arrival under the supervision of a very capable chief engineer with long experience in the field and a genuine interest in helping farmers.

On this occasion, I was interviewing a group of farmers in the presence of several irrigation engineers in order to try to show the engineers what the farmers' concerns were and why they often declined to take the irrigation water (and pay the seemingly very nominal fee). The reasons turned on cost, and when the farmers present realized what I was asking about they immediately sent for this particular farmer, who was known for especially careful record keeping. He very graciously let me borrow and photocopy his entire record book. This page records the costs and gains from one crop, high-yield *bajra* (pearl millet), on one field in one season.

The leftmost two columns are rupees and pice. The right column is the description of the operation, including the material and labor costs. The second section down the page is the sum of all costs and the record of the gain from sale of the grain, and the bottom section is a comparison of costs and gains giving total profit. The record is built up on a running basis through the season as the operations are performed. The totals are calculated after the harvest. The record book was arranged season by season.

Government economic departments in India have been doing farm budget analyses since the beginning of the twentieth century using what they consider to be the theory of the firm and Ricardian notions of returns to factors of production. None of their records look like this. They do not price things as farmers do but instead assign their own economic values for what they consider to be all the economic costs, including the farmer's own labor, maintenance of tools, depreciation on equipment and the like, over all the farming activities. For example, they typically assign one rate for family labor and another rate for hired labor. The rates are assigned by hours or days, not by operation and not by gender. In fact, however, family labor is not regarded by farmers as a running expense but rather as a sunk cost, so an important strategy is to minimize expenditure for hired labor. Also, farmers and hired laborers have different relative bargaining powers for the different operations. Weeding is less crucial than harvesting and does not have to be done in such a short time span. So the daily rate for weeding is usually substantially less than the daily rate for harvest. Some work is also more difficult. Men commonly do the heavier work; women do the work that is lighter but more repetitive. Men usually get a higher daily rate but also work longer days. To reduce all this to flat rates for nonfarm labor and for farm family labor cannot in any way capture farmers' or laborers' decisions or let us predict what happens when the total amount of funds for work increases or decreases.

If pressed by lack of money, the farmer will cut out the operations with the lower payoff. He might cut some weedings, or he might keep the weeding and cut down on fertilizer. The indigenous system of pricing conventions facilitates such a comparison because it makes fertilizing one operation with one price and weeding another operation with another price. The economists' measures, conceptually abstracting labor as an input out of all transactions that use it and doing such things as assigning costs for the active components of fertilizer separately (one charge for nitrogen, one for phosphorous, and so on), make such comparison literally inconceivable. The result is that if I know the indigenous pricing conventions and I know that a farmer is short of cash, I can predict with very near certainty what operation he will leave out and what the effect will be. The economist could not, assuming he could trust his data at all. If prediction is a measure of the power of science, there should be no doubt that close and careful ethnography is far more scientific than standardized and decontextualized economic quantification.

In the 1950s, Neale traced the information in the Indian farm budget studies and related crop economics studies back from the final reports to the field survey forms on which they were supposed to be based. What he found was that at the field level the forms were unintelligible. Most of the crucial information was apparently inserted subsequently (Neale 1958, 1959). Nevertheless, the field survey questions and methods remain the same to this day.

The practice of pricing by operations has a direct connection to the way the economy as an indigenous knowledge system acts as an information source in the fullest possible sense, not only as a system of cultural definitions but as a store of transactional experience. Since different operations have the same costs for different crops, farmers can hardly avoid thinking of their cropping choices in terms of an organized matrix of pricing information that consists of an expanded version of figure 8 with columns representing each crop and with rows representing each operation from sowing to harvest (as in Leaf 1998, 66–67). With this, they can readily compare each crop against all others for the return to its inputs and also each input against all others for their return to the crops. An example of an indigenous price matrix of this kind from the same area as the previous farmer's record is provided in table 3, also from Pus. The variables and the values were elicited from several groups of farmers and officials before eliciting individual farm budget models because this information is one of the inputs that the budget model requires. I repeated the elicitation several more times over about the next year and a half, and of course some of the prices changed.

The first two rows give the yield of main product and by-product. The latter is usually fodder but may also be fiber or fuel. The rest are all items of cost. There are three columns for each crop. The first column records the quantities of material divided by items of gain and items of cost. The second column is the unit prices for each item. The third is total gain or cost. The net gain is the total value produced less the total cost of inputs. In addition, it is important for farmers to know how long the crop occupies the field and what times it does so, because their economic goal is not to produce the maximum return per crop but rather the maximum for all their land for the year. Of course, I cannot know how farmers picture this information for themselves subjectively, but nobody had difficulty understanding this representation when I showed it to them.

Table 3. Market prices, Eastern Maharashtra, 1987–88

Kharif (Summer) 1987

Crop	Peanut			High Yield Variety Jowar			Cotton			Tur with Cotton		
	Peanut	Prices	Values	Jowar	Prices	Values	Cotton	Prices	Values	Cotton	Prices	Values
Yield, quintals/hectare	11.34	700	7938	25	125	3125	7.5	700	5250	1.75	750	1312.5
Fodder, bundle/hectare	800	0	0	2000	0.75	1500	0	0	0	0	5.5	0
Seed, kilogram/hectare	100	13	1300	6	26.34	158.04	4.62	17	78.54	1.6	0	8.8
Canal irrigated	1	360	360	0	0	0	0	0	0	0	0	0
Fertilizer, 50-kilogram bag			0			0			0			0
Urea	0	167	0	4	105	420	0.98	105	102.9	0	115	0
10-26-26	0	140	0	4.33	127	549.91	0	140	0	0	140	0
18-18-10	3	135	405	0	138	0	0	138	0	0	138	0
19-19-19	0	153.35	0	0	153.35	0	0	153.35	0	0	0	0
Mixed	0	135	0	0	140	0	0	140	0	0	0	0
Plowing	1	100	100	0	0	0	0	0	0	0	0	0
Sowing	1	68	68	1	61	61	1	55.38	55.38	0	0	0
Harrowing	1	80	80	1	24	24	1	12.21	12.21	0	0	0
Weeding	1	100	100	1	58	58	1	86.15	86.15	0	0	0
Plant protection	0	0	0	0	0	0	1	326.15	326.15	0	0	0
Harvest rupees	27	7	189	0	0	0	0	169.23	0	1	40	40
Other costs	0	0	0	6.75	106.67	720.0225	1.5	246.15	369.225	0.38	160	60.8
Market costs	0	0	0	0	0	0	1	115.38	115.38	0	0	0
Net return			5336			2634.028			4104.065			1202.9
Days to harvest	112	January/February to May		120–35	June to November		123–270	June to March		195	June to January	
Waterings	9											

Rabi (Winter) 1987–88

	Canal or Well						Perennial		
Crop	Wheat	Prices	Values	Sunflower	Prices	Values	Cane	Prices	Values
Yield, quintals/hectare	15	225	3375	7	500	3500	725	23	16675
Fodder, bundle/hectare	700	0	0	0	0	0	0	0	0
Seed, kilogram/hectare	142.86	3.5	500.01	7.5	15	112.5	30782	0.04	1231.28
Canal irrigated	1	75	75	1	175	175	1	811.75	811.75
Fertilizer, 50-kilogram bag			0			0			0
Urea	2.86	167	477.62	0	167	0	5	167	835
10-26-26	0	140	0	0	140	0	0	140	0
18-18-10	5.71	135	770.85	0	135	0	0	135	0
19-19-19	0	153.35	0	0	153.35	0	4	153.35	613.4
Mixed	0	140	0	5	135	675	0	135	0
Plowing	1.43	100	143	0.83	25	20.75	1	30	30
Sowing	1	105.71	105.71	1	53.33	53.33	1	280	280
Harrowing	1	85.71	85.71	1	16.67	16.67	0	0	0
Weeding	0	0	0	1	120	120	1	520	520
Plant protection	0	785.71	0	0	458.33	0	0	0	0
Harvest rupees	1	200	200	1	188.33	188.33	0	0	0
Other costs	1	135.71	135.71	1	83.33	83.33	2.2	160	352
Market costs	1	128.57	128.57	0	75	0	0	0	0
Net return			752.82			2055.09			12001.57
Days to harvest	105	November/December to February/March		105:120	November to March		ca. 360	January to December/February	
Waterings	8			5			20		

This was made from the table based on interviews in October 1987 and updated from interviews of March 8 and 23–24, 1988.

The matrix shows that sorghum is more profitable than rice on one dimension but also that a second weeding is less profitable on some crops than a dose of fertilizer. The effect is an indigenous equivalent to a production possibility frontier. It relates inputs to production outputs and is continually updated by farmers' choices as they observe their results and watch the shifting prices. The way that farmers use this information is appropriately modeled by ordinary microeconomics as long as we remember that economics is only one system of conceptualization among several. It is perfectly possible for someone to see X as the best option economically, in terms of monetary return, but to select Y because a return of some other sort is more important.

As a cultural device for enabling individual farmers to coordinate their actions with others to make optimal use of scarce resources over a wide region, a price mechanism working through this kind of indigenous information system is brilliant, and the spreadsheet can perfectly replicate its operation. Other such matrices exist for other types of activities: masonry, well drilling, and cattle raising and of course in nonrural contexts as well. Such different price arrays interact in the sense that some goods appear in several of them, and the price changes driven by the relative values in one will necessarily affect others. But it is unwarranted to leap from this fact to the conclusion that one can make up one general price matrix that is equally meaningful as a representation of a supposed national economy. In general, real (ethnographic) cultural price information systems of this sort emerge in consensus wherever people interact through market conventions and a market mechanism but not beyond such interactions.

Economists assume that indigenous economic models, if they exist at all, could only be limited versions of what is presented in economic theory. In fact, all the indigenous models I have found have been considerably more powerful than their academic counterparts, and the few studies by economists who have tried to test indigenous economic pricing systems in a similar manner have come to the same conclusion (Hopper 1965; Schultz 1964).

Factions

In every community there must be a way to enforce what is recognized as right. Rights and obligations may be clear, but there is always a temptation not to recognize them if you might be the loser for doing so. In large-scale societies such lapses, if serious enough, can be met by calling on some sort of police agency. In small communities, what we usually find is an enforcement organization that can be mobilized as and when needed.

In South Asia, activities of this kind are organized through what are usually called factions in English and parties in the northern Indian vernaculars. In my first fieldwork, I knew from the literature that factional activity was considered secretive, disruptive, and not the sort of thing one talks about to outsiders. In fact, factions were more often described in terms of breakdown or cleavages in village organizations than as an organization in their own right. I therefore initially refrained from showing interest in them, although I noted privately whatever mentions occurred spontaneously. Finally, after about four months, I had occasion one morning to spend several hours in a room with the men of one of the village factional groups while they discussed an upcoming election. I practiced inconspicuousness, saying nothing. Afterward, one of those present, Naranjan Singh, invited me to lunch. In American terms, Naranjan was a friend who had always been interested, helpful, and supportive. I accepted, and we went up to the guest room on the top of his house.

For most topics, I tried to conduct systematic elicitations in appropriately constituted groups, not with single individuals. This generally had the logical effect of defining the situation as public so that what I got was public information, which was what I wanted. In this case, however, such a procedure would have defined the situation as an outsider asking villagers about secret matters, and the answer would have been "We do not have them here." The interview situation had to be constructed as private. Naranjan asked his sister to prepare the food, and I knew this would take about an hour. She left, and we were alone. I then explained that I wanted to know about factions and asked if he could draw me a diagram of their organization. (He had previously taken part in one of my kinship elicitations, so the procedure would have been familiar.) He immediately said he "did not know about" them. I reminded him where we had both just been and explained that I did not want to know who was in them (which I guessed was the most delicate part of the secret) but only what they were. I also described what I had already gathered and explained why it was confusing in American terms. He then agreed to draw the diagram.

My practice for taking notes was to use large pieces of newsprint that I could fold to whatever size or shape might suit the topic. I handed him such a sheet and a pencil. He spread it across his knees, paused, and carefully drew a single vertical line down the middle. He then handed it back with a perfect air of completion. That was factions. One line. I could make nothing of it. I asked a series of questions to be sure he understood what I had meant by a diagram. He said he had. I did not want to suggest an American-style diagram of party hierarchies for fear that he would accept it out of politeness or frustration and that I would thereby corrupt the experiment. So I tried an alternative diagram, a set of about six horizontal lines, to see if he would reject it. He did. That, he said, was caste; that was different. Assured that he would reject a wrong suggestion, I then offered the downward-branching diagram usually used for representing an American or European type of political party down through its national, state, and local divisions. He rejected that equally firmly. I was both relieved and perplexed. I explained my drawing. He then offered to expand on his. I handed back the paper. He added what is shown in figure 9 and again handed

Figure 9. The faction idea system

it back with an air of completion. That was it; there was no more to add. But by this point I could query specific possible elaborations or adjustments and the explanation that proceeded from doing so brought in everything else that I had encountered up to that point.

This is the simplest social idea system I know of. The core idea, which the vertical line represents, is opposition: flat, absolute and unqualified. The space on each side of the line is a group. Since the group is secret, it is logical that we do not see it. It only becomes visible in conflicts. The basis of the conflict is that one says "yes" on some principle or issue, and the other says "no." The issue, it turns out, is which of a pair of opposed figures or positions in some contest will dominate: political figures in an election, sides in a court case, or groups of men in a physical confrontation. People in one's own faction are friends; those in the other are enemies. More elaborately, factions are alliances of men who see themselves as defending themselves against the efforts of the others to gain control of their property (according to an often-quoted saying, specifically land, water, and women). All understand the relation as an all-out struggle for dominance, a covert war (Barth 1959; Bailey 1960, 51ff.; Izmerlian 1979, 37ff.; Srinivas 1976, chaps. 7–9). Each also sees its own group as acting from principle, while the others are simply "opportunists" (Leaf 1984, 205–22).

The most obvious reason that factions are defined as secret is that according to the other systems of ideas that define relations in the village, there should not be any need for them. If people carried out their kinship obligations, honored their managerial commitments, or were constrained by religious ideals, there would be no conflict. So the fact that there is conflict implies by definition that something is wrong. Exactly like a fight in a family in the West, it is therefore something not to talk about to strangers. The factional model is thus a model for covert alliances to deal with covert problems.

Since factional power is defined as hidden, factions have no names. They cannot, logically, openly recruit. Nor can they take public positions on issues. Outsiders are invariably told that they do not exist, and anyone who asks if they exist must be an outsider. Also because they are covert they have in a strict sense no local leaders. A leader would have to be acknowledged. There are no public faction meetings or faction ceremonies, since what is not openly admitted cannot be openly signified. Nevertheless, they are not nonexistent or merely mythical. There are covert meetings and in a way also covert ceremonies.

The main function of a factional group is to support its members, but in orderly villages where people behave rationally and the balance of power is clear, such confrontations are rare. Most often, what one has is covert symbolic displays of factional affiliation, a kind of symbolically hidden muscle flexing that also continually revises the available evidence on who is allied with whom. If a person prominent in one faction sponsors a public gathering for some purpose, such as an annual village harvest celebration, it is certain to be boycotted by members of the other faction. If he has a wedding for a son or daughter, people of the opposed faction will not attend unless they are such close relatives that the pull of kinship obligations overrides the push of factional hostility. If there is a dispute that goes to a formal court, the witnesses will be the factional associates of the litigants, not people who by chance happened to see or hear things favorable to one side or the other.

Village factional groups reach out to regional, state, and national political figures to gain advantage over one another, and it is by these links outside the village that they are most likely to be spoken of openly within the village. One group may be described as supporting one regional or national political party or person. If so, the opposed group will almost certainly support an opposed party or person, although exactly what group is supported will not be fixed. There may be one pairing for one event, such as a local election, but another for a different event, such as a national election. The idea is simple, complete, and widely used. In fact, as the original drawing of a single line implied, it organizes all inter-community public conflict in South Asian society. Newspapers report political gatherings in factional terms. They state the purpose of the gathering but barely bother to indicate what was said, focusing instead on who attended, who did not, and sometimes what reasons were given for attending or not attending. The underlying, unstated understanding is that those who attended support the principal person, and those who did not oppose him or her.

But while the basic imagery of factions is obviously far simpler than the Punjabi system of kinship ideas that it complements, the logic of instantiating it is consistently more complex, and one must learn this complexity all at once. There is no way to ease into it. To begin to think of factional relationships, you have to be able think in terms of classes and reciprocity from the outset, and you have to be able to think simultaneously of the way such relations are seen from the point of view of each individual subjectively and from the point of view of generalized others objectively. By definition, what faction you are in does not depend only on your actions but also on the actions of others, not only toward you but toward yet others in turn, and it also depends on the issues that are current at any give time.

There is a formal algebra to factions just as there is to kinship and all other such systems of positions. In terms of Read's notation, there are two positions: friend (F) and enemy (E), and both are generators. The structural equations are $FF = F$, $EF = E$, $FE = E$, and $EE = F$, which can be arranged in a Cayley table.

Further inferences follow as permutations of these. For example, FFF, . . . , Fn = F (All friends of friends are friends). But all enemies of enemies are not enemies. Rather, EEEE, EEEEEE, etc. (all sets of E of E) are F, while EEE, EEEEE, etc. (all sets of E of E of E) are E. Furthermore, strings of EF are the equivalent of strings of E, and so are strings of FE. There is no self or ego position as in kinship terminologies; the logic is objectifying, not ego-centric.

The logic by which factional ideas are instantiated, as opposed to the logic of the definitions as such, is that of a zero-sum game, as Fredrick Barth (1959) recognized for the factional groups in Swat, Afghanistan. Barth's key question was: Given that the powerful side completely dominates, why does anyone join the weaker side? The answer has two aspects. First, the benefits of being in a faction are not distributed evenly to all members. Not everybody is equally under threat at any time. Thus, the advantages of being on the winning side are not distributed evenly among the members of that side. Second, the weaker side has an incentive to bid more for recruits. The result is that there is almost always someone on the winning side whose share in the benefits of being on that side is less than their benefits would be for joining the weaker side. This keeps the two groups in very close equilibrium.

Prominent people of each group, on occasions understood as reflecting factional conflict, act very much as an attorney does arguing for the rightness of the positions of its own supporters and for the wrongness of their opponents based on the evidence. Usually the argument is before the tribunal of general opinion, but if it comes to a court case it will be done in exactly the same way before the judge. Each also exercises considerable covert disciplinary power over its own supporters in order to deny the other any opportunity for legitimate criticism, and each threatens retaliation for injuries done by the other.

Even while factions are universally decried in South Asian public moralizing, they are universally celebrated in some of the most revered literature, covertly of course. Most of the descriptive detail in India's two greatest religious epics, the *Mahabharata* and the *Ramayana*, consists of step-by-step accounts of the efforts of their heroes to build up their support in factional conflict on a universal scale. Their purpose is to right the wrongs that have been done to them, and they use the same ideas, appeals, and strategies that one sees in modern villages. By the same token, in the Afghan war against the Taliban regime, it was the factional idea system that was enacted in the processes of negotiating (secretly) with the enemy leaders, even in the heat of battle, that unsettled American advisers and mystified the American press. Yet the process regularly resulted in the opposition suddenly ceasing fire, coming across, greeting the winners with smiles and embraces, and being allowed to take their weapons with them and either join up or go home. Why the smiles and embraces? Because that is the way you greet friends. Why did the victors not take the weapons? Because you do not treat friends that way, only enemies, and there is no in-between.

Idea systems with something like this binary definitional logic and zero-sum game theoretic implementation seem fairly common in small, relatively self-contained communities. Jeremy Boissevain (1966) described something very similar for Malta, as did Raul Pertierra (1988) for the Philippines. Boissevain's definition was "a loosely ordered group in conflict with a similar group over a particular issue," adding that "it is not a corporate group" (Boissevain 1966, 1276).

Translocal Organizations

Anthropologists have always recognized a difference between seemingly localized organizations such as families and factions and large-scale organizations such as the major religions, government, courts, universities, or the military that seem higher or to represent the larger society or civilization. I will call these latter translocal.

This is another of those differences that is easy to see but hard to characterize without a comprehensive theory. Empirically, it is clearly not accurate to say that families are localized and that courts and the like are not. Both are localized somewhere, and both are also very widely distributed. Nor are families really face-to-face in a way that courts and the rest are not. In fact, the differences lie in certain very specific features of the idea systems out of which translocal organizations are constructed coupled with a very specific way this feature is represented ceremonially.

First, translocal idea systems define all their positions with an idea of office that anyone who meets the recruitment criteria can occupy and that every occupant eventually leaves. Second, the idea systems define the organization as being able to act interstitially. The term "interstitially" comes from Ehrlich's (1975) analysis of the relationship between courts and the living law of ordinary associations. It means two things. First, courts have the specific power to take people who are related in some way in nonlegal organizations, change that relationship, and then return them to the nonlegal situation with the change. Paul Bohannan at one point described the same feature as "double institutionalization" (1968, 75).

In fact, being able to act interstitially is a characteristic of translocal organizations in general: organized religions, the professions, the military, education and higher education, and even businesses. Second, however, it is not actually a power or anything that mysterious. It is rather that they all utilize a very specific type of ceremony, which can be called an interstitial ceremony. Interstitial ceremonies have all the properties of ordinary ceremonies plus several others.

In addition to the usual attributes of ceremonies, interstitial ceremonies have two sets of roles of a very specific sort. One is for the officers who have a long-term identification with the translocal organization itself, while the other is for the public who come in, undergo the ceremony, and leave.

In a courtroom, the different positions are clearly marked by different physical props: the judge's bench, the jury box, the witness bench, the positions for plaintiff and defendant and their respective attorneys, and the benches for the public. The permanent people are the same case after case. The public takes their positions for one case and leaves. What makes this possible is that the duties of the permanent members include instructing the transitory members on what to do in their positions as they proceed. How does a store clerk who has been robbed know what to do as a witness in court? He is told what to expect by police or attorneys, sworn in and told to tell the truth and nothing but the truth, guided in what to say by the attorneys and the judge as he proceeds, and released after testimony is given. How does a wife in marriage know how to take the role of a defendant in a divorce proceeding? She is told by her lawyer, further instructed by the judge, sworn in if testimony is given, released when it is over, asked to stand to receive the decision, and told what to do thereafter on the basis of it, and so on.

The judge's bench has obvious parallels in the lectern and the church pulpit. The litigant's bench is paralleled in the confessional, the chair in front of the official's desk, and the doctor's examining table. In businesses, restaurants, and theaters there are places for staff as against the places for patrons or customers, and on and on. Interstitiality is not rare. It is a common design feature that most of us who live in the developed world encounter daily.

Each type of translocal organization is associated with a distinctive body of texts. Each of the religious traditions has its central or sacred works. Courts have their law books, armies and navies their manuals and codes of conduct, governments their laws and rules, and professions their manuals and research materials. The texts give them the ability to have far more complex and ramified systems of positions, behavior rules, and recruitment rules than the organizations that rely on idea systems conveyed primarily through nonliterary means.

Texts require interpretation. Insofar as it results in a consensus, this is not a simple process. Meanings do not simply exist on the page. They are constructed in a conceptually complex process that Michael Silverstein and Greg Urban (1996) describe as entextualization. When interpretations are used to provide the basis of organizations, this must include a way for an interpretation to become authoritative. This usually involves the creation of authoritative positions or groups within the overall organization whose personnel are held to speak for the tradition as a whole. The relation between the authoritative interpretations and the organizations is symbiotic. The organization provides the interpretation; the interpretation is the conceptual basis for the organization.

Translocal organizations will not be my major concern here. Face-to-face organizations have to come first. But to make clear how the analysis can include them, I will follow through with some comparisons with law.

Information Theory

Cultural information systems act as information sources as defined in Shannon and Weaver's mathematical theory of communication, after we slightly rethink the latter. Their basic model described a linear process in which the "source selects a desired message out of a set of possible messages" (Shannon and Weaver 1963, 7), which is then transmitted by the transmitter through the channel to a receiver, which then conveys it to the destination. The information potential of the information source is its entropy, the degree of randomness in its organization. The information potential of the message is the inverse of the probability of its selection: messages with low probability have high information potential. Noise is inputs that are random with respect to the message and therefore lower the probability of recognizing it. Shannon and Weaver connected the idea of whether the message was understood to the idea of feedback. The message is understood if the reaction is predictable from it.

Shannon and Weaver spoke of the information source as possibly a person or some automatic device such as a fire alarm but also sometimes as a written code or language. The message was the words spoken or the triggered signal, the transmitter was the telephone and auxiliary equipment that converted it for the channel, noise was any signal in the channel other than came from the source, the receiver was the device that reclaimed the original message, and the destination was the listener or device that finally got it.

The reason we cannot find a cultural counterpart to the concept of the information source lies in the way Shannon and Weaver tied the mathematical properties of messages directly to the mathematical and organizational properties of the information sources. Their underlying thinking is like textbook illustrations of probability theory in which the chance of drawing a ball of a given color from an urn is a direct function of how many balls of that and other colors the urn contains. The problem is that we cannot find anything in culture that is urnlike in this way.

The obvious empirical candidates for the role of information sources are cultural idea systems and shared knowledge of their instantiations, but as we have seen idea systems are not containers; they are generative logical structures. As such they do not have discrete parts to which we could assign unique probabilities of occurrence. The solution is to recognize that the probabilities of messages emerge not from the nature of the source itself but rather from the process of instantiating it purposively. This sets up an implicit dialogue in which the speakers and hearers ask and answer a sequence of questions. The number of possible questions and answers at each step in the conversation reflects the formal structure of the message sources, and in this context we can assign them clear and definite probabilities even though we cannot do so in the message source itself.

For example, if two people were speaking Punjabi, the first question for the hearer would be whether the idea systems that define social relations are rural or urban. If rural, then the main choices after that will be one of the four main message sources that define almost all village organizations: kinship, religion, factions, or management units. So the probabilities are roughly one in four. If the factional model is indicated, then in terms of the factional ideas the next question has to be whether the model is being applied or only discussed: "Am I being taken as being in the factional conflict or not?" The odds are one in two. If the answer is that you are in the conflict, the next choice has to be whether the hearer was being placed in the same faction as the speaker-sender or the opposite. Finally, the last question would be what specific action was being asked for: attend a court hearing, show up for a physical confrontation, attend a meeting, and so on. Lyon's (2002) paper documents exactly this type of sequence. There may be some additional nuances, but on the whole the list is clearly predictable and makes straightforward sense both in terms of theory and the levels of subjective uncertainty that we actually do experience.

Figure 10 is Shannon and Weaver's model as corrected to describe naturally occurring communication without electronic mediation. Recognizing feedback, it is cyclical. Dropping the transmitter and receiver leaves the speaker and the hearer. Information sources, which are multiple (1 through n), then become the cultural idea systems that the speaker invokes and that the hearer must share. The process of constructing and sending a communication only ends when the sender recognizes the response as expected or unexpected, hence probable or improbable, in order to formulate the next transmission. The response may be a return communication, observable behavior, or both.

Message sources also define the channel. In unmediated communications of this sort, a channel appears whenever someone simply invokes an idea system without conveying an expectation of what it is to be used for. Once the speaker

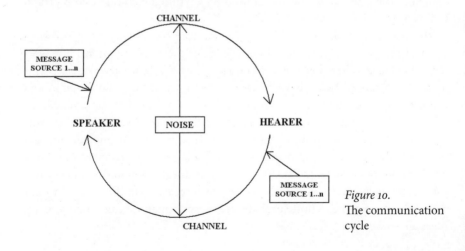

Figure 10.
The communication cycle

does convey what it is being used for—a purpose—then the message source is also the basis of the message. For an extended description see Leaf (2004).

Conclusion

Social idea systems are ultimate organizational premises. A few such systems have been previously analyzed by those particularly concerned with them—such as the idea systems of law, government, and many of the major religions. But the general comparative analysis of all such systems, recognized for what they are, is only now beginning. As we pay more attention to the formal structures of systems of role definitions and their semantic consequence, we will doubtless find more types and better understand how such systems evolve. But my bet is that the broad types described here will continue to be the most widely and frequently encountered. We do not have all the variations, but we probably have the main themes and main types of formal structures.

CHAPTER 5

Technical Information Systems

Social information systems provide the ideas needed to enable people to agree on who will do the work. Technical idea systems define how to do it. Familiar systems of this sort in developed societies include Euclidian geometry and linear programming, the established theories of the sciences, the conceptual techniques of the various branches of engineering, and the equipment and associated working knowledge that distinguishes, for example, a farm from a barber shop.

In the last twenty years, writers concerned with development policy have come to stress the importance of incorporating or being responsive to local knowledge (Timberlake 1985), time and place knowledge (Ostrom, Shroeder, and Wynne 1993), and indigenous knowledge systems (Warren, Slikkerveer, and Brokensha 1995). University-trained engineers, agricultural scientists, and the like, however, often find it difficult to take local knowledge seriously. Surely, they argue, you do not mean that we should consider all their beliefs about agriculture, water flows, pests, and diseases to be as well founded as our own? If local people think that fungus attacks are effects of the evil eye and that a broken pot on a stick will protect a haystack from the effects of the evil eye, should we really seek to limit fungus attacks with broken pots? Such objections are partly right and pose a serious challenge to proponents of this perspective. In any community there is sound technical knowledge, tested by use over long periods, and there is fantasy, and it is often very hard for an outsider to tell them apart. The challenge, therefore, is to distinguish which is which. How do we delineate the real technical idea systems?

Observing the Systems

Like social idea systems, technical idea systems depend on images. When Galison (1997) describes scientific logic as based on the imagery of certain key experiments, he is referring to the same feature. The image (not statements or propositions) is the vehicle of the embeddedness of the technical idea system in what it represents. It is the representation of the thing in imagination that controls the logic, the way the semantics of the individual terms and concepts is controlled by the thing that they refer to.

As noted, the simplest and most distinctive difference between technical and social idea systems is that technical idea systems are not founded on an idea of reciprocity that reflexively includes their users. They are about "it" and "them," not "I and thou."

A further distinguishing semantic property of technical idea systems is their embeddedness. Ideas are closely identified with the things and operations they refer to, and these meanings are readily adjusted or renegotiated in light of the behavior of those things. There was a time when the proposition "All swans are white" was considered to be true by definition. After black swans were discovered, this was no longer the case. To show someone what a wrench is, you show them a wrench; you cannot do that to show them what a father is. To show somewhat what a differential equation is, you show them differential equations and how to solve them.

Since technical idea systems are usually far more closely tied to and dependent on the things they appear to describe than are social information systems, in that sense technical idea systems are actually far more genuinely normative. They are not pseudonormative, as the social idea systems are. This is true even with respect to such highly abstract and definitional systems as those of mathematics. Everybody who learns geometry knows that there is no such thing as a perfect triangle in nature, just as anyone who knows a set of kinship ideas might say that there is no perfect son. But no one who encounters an imperfect triangle feels constrained to have a discussion with it on the need for self-improvement. People act quite differently when they encounter imperfect sons. These semantic differences in the individual ideas directly reflect, and transmit, formal and informational differences in the structure of the two types of systems in which they are defined.

Similarly, disagreements over technical systems, or variant versions of them, are not taken as posing moral or ethical problems for an organization or a community. Technical idea systems affect the way we organize our work but are not constitutive of organizational relationships as such, and as users we habitually recognize this.

Since the expansion of interest in cultural ecology, the ethnographic documentation of indigenous technological systems has increased enormously both in conventional publications and in ethnographic films. The films have been particularly important in showing their embeddedness, which is difficult to convey with words alone. Two films that especially stand out as genuine experimental records are John Marshall's *The Hunters* (1958) for the Kalahari Bushmen and Andre Singer and Stephen Lansing's *The Goddess and the Computer* (1998).

In *The Hunters*, Marshall used the camera to re-create the position of the ethnologist as participant observer. The dialogue is sparse and avoids generalization.

The narrator does not speak about the Bushmen or even this band in general. He introduces this person and that person and talks a bit about the differences between boys and girls and women's work and men's work as we come upon them and then rather quickly goes into the very long sequence on the hunt that results in the wounding, tracking, killing, butchering, and eating of an adult female giraffe. The camera accompanies the action just as an ethnographer would, and the narrator reports the discussions among the participants as an ethnographer would have heard them. The viewers thus hear what is said, see what is done, and can observe for themselves how the two are related. It is impossible to imagine that anyone, having done so, could come away with the conclusion that culture was a matter of following rules rather than accomplishing purposes or that all the ideas needed to guide a purposive process had to be the same as our own.

A central theme in the film is the way the men of the hunting party work to construct an understanding of the giraffe's individual attitudes, feelings, and intentions. It seems at first odd to us as Westerners (and nonhunters), but gradually we come to see that it is necessary. They are tracking a single wounded animal. She was hit by just one poisoned arrow. They must wait for her to die, and they must stay close. They cannot kill her with brute force because she is too big and too strong, but if she dies and they do not find her quickly, the meat and their effort may be entirely lost. They know when they start that they cannot predict how many days it will take for the poison to work. During that time, they will be at increasingly greater personal risk due to lack of food, water, and shelter. She can outpace them until the poison gradually takes effect. She can see them from great distances. She will cross many tracks of other giraffes on hard, dry ground. If the hunters mistake her tracks for any of the other animals' tracks they will spend days following a healthy animal that they will never catch. They must be able to pick her out, and in order to do this they need every kind of information about her they can develop. Looking for some specific mark on a hoof or two would not be nearly enough. They must form an idea of the animal as a whole, with as many aspects as possible. So this is what they try to do; they must come to understand her, and therefore also they must respect her. It makes perfect sense, although in our society and given our food-procurement technologies it may make equal sense to do exactly the opposite, not to personalize the animals we consume but rather to radically depersonalize them.

Singer and Lansing's monograph (1998) and film *The Goddess and the Computer* demonstrate the same kind of coherence and embeddedness but in a different way. The analytic framework of the monograph was developmental and historical, focused more on matters of efficacy than embeddedness as such. It covered a sequence of events in which organizational and technical ideas could readily be seen to be varying independently.

Traditionally, Balinese rice farmers organized their farming operations through a hierarchy of water temples closely associated with their hydraulic hierarchy of dams and watercourses. When Green Revolution technologies became available, the Indonesian government assigned authority over the irrigation systems to the government irrigation and agriculture departments, whose staffs were supposedly better trained in modern scientific methods. This was done with no regard for the past record of the water temples and without consulting them. One of the government requirements as a concomitant of introducing the new seed and inputs was that the farmers would plant all the land in rice simultaneously instead of leaving large sections bare in alternating seasons. The farmers said that they did this for pest control. The government experts thought that relying on insecticides would be better.

As the new technologies were adopted, yields rose but also became unstable, mainly because of dramatically increasing damage from pests. A sequence of different chemical pesticides was increasingly ineffective. The pests quickly adapted, one being replaced by another. It was becoming increasingly clear that it was only a matter of time before the farmers would run out of options. Finally, the government returned authority over cropping to the water temples. The farmers continued to use the new varieties but returned to the methods of pest control that had been integral to the traditional system of water management. Productivity was retained, and stability was restored.

Clearly, the water temples had been doing something right, and the government managers had been doing something wrong. The problem was to find out what it was. This mainly concerned the size of groups of farmers that the two different systems required to work as farming units.

The traditional method of pest control was the simultaneous fallowing of large areas of adjacent fields. If pests have no hosts, they die. The larger the area devoid of pests, the harder it is for pests to cross it and the longer it takes for the pest population to rebuild. On the other hand, however, the larger the area that had to be irrigated, the more difficult it was to fill at a single time. Since fields that were fallowed as a block had to be planted and harvested as a block, this meant that the system of planning for pest control was also the system of planning for water control and cropping. Everything had to be done together in a block of adjacent fields. Accordingly, the key question was what the optimal block size was and which management system most closely approximated it. To get the answer, Lansing worked with a plant biologist and developed a multiagent computer simulation that allowed them to try different block sizes and estimate the effects on pest buildup and consequent crop loss, which they could compare with what had actually happened. The conclusion was that the traditional block sizes associated with the water temples were about as close to the optimal block size as possible. It followed that the traditional way of negotiating water rights was also, in fact, an optimal way of organizing crop and water management unit sizes.

In the film, Singer and Lansing took the logical next step. If the computer simulation really were articulating embedded local knowledge, then we would expect local people to recognize this knowledge when it was presented to them. Furthermore, since the program provided the filmmakers with a way to manipulate this knowledge for exploring different management possibilities, it should provide the same opportunity for those whose knowledge it was. If so, this should also enable the different stakeholders in the organizational problem to develop more respect for each other's positions and work out a more effective mode of cooperation. This is the idea that Lansing tested in the return visit to the area, and this test is what the film documents. The film records his conversations with the irrigation officials, the temple priests, and farmers, their respective reactions, his broaching the possibility of using the knowledge to cooperate more effectively, and the spontaneous beginning of a working consensus among those people concerned. The prediction is made and is fulfilled, on the record.

To be teachable, information must be organized so that one can move through it in small doses. The doses must be interconnected, and they must be memorable. This is what tracing them out as idea systems lets us see. Technical idea systems have three major features, all reflecting the fact that they have the formal properties of information sources with high information potential: many elements loosely interrelated. First, as has already been noted, the systems are discrete. Water management can be learned independently from crop growing. Rice cropping can be readily separated from knowledge of growing barley or pulses, but also knowledge of one operation in rice farming can be readily separated from knowledge of another. They can therefore readily be divided into manageable packages to be spread among different people and groups. In rice production, weeding and keeping channels in repair is usually men's work. Transplanting is usually done by teams of women.

Second, since the ideas are closely tied to material devices and practical techniques, the formal interrelations among the elements of systems are not so much definitional as what we recognize as practical or causal. Water flowing down a channel acts in a certain way because it is water and because of the way channels work. Ideas used to control that water have to reflect these properties. Of course, there can be special cultural mnemonics such as methods of counting and culturally distinctive artifacts such as types of gates, but the underlying logic that holds these together and makes them work has to come from the water and the channel as such. The same is true for everything else, from raising chickens to building rockets.

Third, since ideas are organized into practical complexes in this way, there is generally not a clear separation between the boundaries of the technical idea systems in a logical sense and the boundaries separating the groups of people who use them. One is usually a good indicator of the other. For example, in large irrigation systems, the problems of maintaining major channels and managing large flows of water are very different from the problems of managing water at the farm level, and almost always these problems wind up being allocated to distinct groups of people with distinct organizations. Agriculture is full of little specializations that a farm manager, as the person with the most inclusive view of the farm system, has to bring together: channel building, plowing, sowing seeds, transplanting rice, weeding, harvesting, threshing, medicating animals, or making tools. This underlying embeddedness is exactly why it is much easier to provide a solid survey of agricultural systems than of kinship systems around the world. Schusky's *Culture and Agriculture* (1989) makes the point perfectly: the embeddedness is his central organizing theme as he applies a post-Boserup caloric-efficiency perspective to the development of the main forms of agricultural technology and management from the Neolithic to the present.

Since there does not seem to be the same kind of entrenched resistance to recognizing the multiplicity of technical idea systems that we encounter in relation to social idea systems, there is no need here to try to anatomize the major types. We will, however, return to the topic in discussing organizations.

Information Systems and Social Scale

There is an inverse relationship between the number of idea systems held in substantially universal consensus and community size. In general, it seems that the number of cultural information systems held in substantially universal consensus in small communities is consistently about seven. Very likely, this reflects constancies of human memory. As societies encompass larger and larger populations and geographical areas, however, the number of such systems that their members continue to agree on actually goes down, perhaps to just two in most nation-states: ideas of national government and economics. The ideas of technical and social systems held in the various cultural and occupational subpopulations, however, multiplies enormously. This is the basis of the common observation that small communities are more homogenous while large-scale societies are more specialized, the observation that Durkheim misstated as the difference between mechanical and organic solidarity.

Conclusion

Technical idea systems vary enormously in their specific form, but all have an objective and descriptive logic rather than reciprocal and relational logic, and none are used pseudonormatively the way social idea systems are. This fundamental difference holds up across the entire enormous range of cultural idea systems of both types.

CHAPTER 6

Organizations

It is important to characterize the relationship between the ideas in the idea systems and their use in building organizational charters and social relationships. This question has two main aspects: How are the images and conceptual relations defined in the idea systems transformed or transposed in forming agreed-upon conceptualizations of behavior, and how are the choices defined in the idea systems transformed or transposed to choices for individual and collective action?

Michael Fischer and his students (2002) have focused mainly on the latter problem in trying to formulate the way cultural ideas derived from textual analysis can be deployed in agent-based models of the way people use resources. To extract the ideas that make up cultural information systems from texts, Fischer has experimented with various applications of information theory. To model the use of ideas in behavior, he has used multiagent models. Although he may not see cultural information sources as being quite as definite and clearly delineated as I do (we are still discussing it), his basic observations of their relation to organized behavior have been the same. First, the ideas are both vague and flexible. Second, there are many more possible combinations and interpretations than are actually utilized or can be utilized. So there must be some process of selection. This being so, how do we characterize the process? Fischer's answer is that the logic cannot be determinate. You cannot use a logic that requires statements such as "If A then B" when the actual state of affairs is "If A then maybe B." In Fischer's view, the appropriate logics are more likely to be deontic (Fischer 2002, 370).

Deontic logic was originally developed in philosophy as a formalization of moral, rather than factual, assertions. It continues to be an area of dispute and analysis among philosophers; it is not something we can apply off the shelf. But since it does examine notions such as "oblige" and "permit" as well as the more usual "is" or "is in the class of," it does seem to be the sort of logic we need to simulate the process of going from cultural idea systems to ideas in use. This can be done with agent-based models, and Fischer and some of his students have done it (Lyon 2002; Bharwani, Fischer, and Ryan 2002; Bharwani 2006).

Read, on the other hand, has focused more on the problem of characterizing the way that the images and relations of the idea systems are transposed, and in this context he has employed the mathematical notion of instantiation, as I have. Instantiation is the process of transposing a set of defined elements from the form it takes in an abstract system to a form in which it is concretely applied (Read 2002). Here, it is the process by which the implications of an element defined in one or another of the cultural information systems takes on the shape it has in a social charter, the organization that that charter enables, and the contexts that take shape when that organization is enacted or evoked in communicative behavior.

The implication of describing ideas as instantiated in behavior is that there can be a precise mapping from a cultural information source to an organizational charter derived from it or from the charter to its uses in context. At the same time, however, when ideas are instantiated they respond to different constraints than they do in the idea systems by themselves. One of the main differences between the form an idea takes in its information system and the form it takes when instantiated is that instantiations are constrained by time. Further constraints come from the fact that the ideas must be represented by material symbols. As noted, a kinship terminology may represent generations as vertical ranks, one above another, but when this idea is represented in behavior, the verticality must be symbolized by something else: words, gestures, patterns of deference, or different locations in a single horizontal space.

In actuality, Fischer's and Read's analyses are complementary, or at least there is no absolutely sharp line between the transposition of images and the transposition of choices. The indeterminacy that Fischer describes pertains to the actor's problem of choosing one idea or another along with one purpose or another, while Read's contention that there is a regular and describable instantiative logic applies to the way the ideas work once they are chosen. What we find is that the instantiations we see in ceremonies, folk models, and the ongoing agreements that form organizations among people can properly be described as deontic mappings. That is, the relations between ideas in their message sources and those same ideas in behavior are mappings under deontic conditions. An important implication of this is that we cannot expect a direct correspondence between norms and behaviors in a positivistic sense; the idea of such a correspondence, when fully understood, is almost nonsense.

The analysis of instantiation has to proceed at three main levels: individual behavior, aggregate behavior, and emergent behavior. How does instantiation appear in communicative behavior and interaction as we observe individuals engage in it, and how does it appear in large-scale patterns of behavior? Chapter 9 will take up the further question of the relation between organizations and organized behavior and what is now generally described as emergent behavior, meaning further aggregate patterns resulting from the interactions of organizations that have not been directly organized in themselves and may not even be consciously recognized.

To understand how ideas, social and technical, are instantiated in organizational charters and organized behavior, the idea of purpose is pivotal. Purpose is defined in the idea systems and deployed in the organizational ideas, but in the process its role shifts. In the idea systems, purpose is not particularly prominent; it is implied in or framed by the other ideas. But in organizations, in being instantiated, it becomes the frame within which the other ideas are deployed. In addition to such constraints as having to be applied in time and in the physical world, the organizational purpose is the most general framing idea for an organizational charter. It is purpose that makes the connection between the individuals involved and the particular idea system. In Punjab if you want to have children, you would not think of ideas of faction; you would think of kinship. If you are a Navajo and want to raise some corn, you do not think of witchery; you think of outfits. In America if you need to obtain something you cannot make, you think of buying it. Once the purpose makes the general link, the organizational ideas associated with that purpose in the idea system can be drawn on to fill in the means to achieve it as needed in the practical situation. This generally happens in one of two ways: either someone innovates or they invoke stereotypes established in folklore, popular entertainment, ceremonial media, laws, or the many kinds of common knowledge. The latter is far more usual. The process is a pragmatic filling in or building up of specifications until enough is specified to do whatever is needed to move ahead toward whatever the purpose is.

Here we look at the primary notion of purpose and its relation to recruiting and retaining organizational members. In the next chapter, we focus on the way the rest of the details of charters are filled in and maintained in organizational strategies. This will finally get us to a full analysis of our initial problem of where the idea or sense of institutions comes from, from which can move on to the final question of how organization is related to ecological adaptation.

Productive and Regulatory Purposes

Pursuing organizational purposes involves choices. Cooperation involves choosing to engage in some possible behaviors rather than others, use some ideas rather than others, and make some commitments rather than others. Such choices cannot be made randomly or idiosyncratically and still result in coordinated action. There are far too many logical possibilities. The basis for these selections, the criterion that makes one choice obligatory and another wrong, has to be some future state that defines the end for which the specific choices are the means. Thought does not just bubble up, it looks ahead.

The purpose of an organization is directly related to the way it can recruit and hold members. In the long run and on the whole, people must get some kind of return for their efforts simply because being alive creates ongoing needs. Different types of organizational goals are logically related to different types of members' incentives. An organization that makes no money cannot pay its workers; a farm has very different resources to share than a bank has. The incentives to join an artists' cooperative are very different from those to seek public office.

From the perspective of the rewards or benefits available to distribute to members in return for their efforts, organizations are of two main types: productive and adjudicative. Productive organizations are those that create a product that provides a return to the people who make it up that they can then divide. In such organizations, the most basic force that holds members together is the difference between what the members can provide for themselves alone as opposed to what they can obtain by accepting the obligations of membership. Organizations of this type must therefore operate by some version of a calculus of benefit to members against cost to members. Adjudicative or regulatory organizations, by contrast, provide few or no benefits that the members can capture and divide among themselves. Their concern is with avoiding self-destructive relations among productive groups. The benefits they produce are broadly captured by nonmembers and members alike. Cohesion therefore depends on the members being able to provide enough general benefit to make the cost of participation negligible. Although it is not difficult to think of actual organizations that have aspects of both functions and draw on both types of strategies to produce cohesion, such as American political parties, the strategies themselves nevertheless remain distinct.

Productive organizations and regulatory organizations are mutually complementary. So-called neoliberal economic and political theories suggest that all regulation is fundamentally suppressive; it adds nothing to production, and everyone would be better off if it were removed and the market were allowed to operate unfettered with minimal friction. This illustrates the danger of incomplete theory. In fact, once we understand what productive organizations are, it is easy to see that regulatory organizations are both an essential support for them and a natural outgrowth of their activities.

Organizational Charters

To accomplish its purpose—whatever the purpose may be—an organization must be recognized by both its members and its nonmembers. Its organizational charter is what allows this to happen or assures that it will happen. As such, organizational charters are necessarily symbolic. But they cannot be only this; they also have to be tied to specific actual individuals with some level of binding force. There are, broadly, two ways to do this that are not in any way opposed to one another and often occur together. One is to use ready-made cultural mnemonics, such as ceremonies, to tie the necessary organizational ideas to specific people. Another is to make explicit contractlike agreements, including written agreements.

In the strictest and clearest sense, all organizational charters are explicit. An organization is a set of interlocking agreements of the form "you do this and I will do that," and people cannot arrive at such understandings without public expressions of what they are and who accepts them. These agreements may be very simple and ephemeral, as when two people come together at the scene of an accident, see an object that has to be lifted off an injured person, and one says to the other "You lift that end" and the other does so. Or they may be very elaborate.

Written charters are as old as writing and were evidently a major reason why writing was developed and spread. Examples of written charters are political constitutions, city charters, corporate charters, business licenses, marriage contracts, college and university governance documents, college catalogs, military regulations, and business contracts. Even a bill of sale is an organizational charter; the organization it establishes is the relation between buyer and seller. This disappears after the transaction, but the receipt attests to the fact that it did exist and did accomplish its purpose, transferring the property rights that it describes.

Written and ceremonial charters are often interconnected. Ceremonies are built around the creation of written charters; written charters serve as records of ceremonies. A marriage contract is commonly signed in the course of the marriage ceremony, a graduation certificate is awarded (symbolically) in a graduation ceremony, and a receipt is created in the process of a sale ceremony. Where there are systems of laws, the contents of major charters are often specified in those laws rather than in specific agreements arrived at in each organization individually. If a couple marries in Texas, their property acquired in the marriage is held in common. If they marry in a state that does not have community property, come to Texas, and get a divorce, their marriage is still treated as though it had been formed under Texas law. In a business contract, if part of what has been agreed to is not legal it will not be enforced by the court. This may mean that the entire contract will not be enforced, which may in turn mean that the relationship (organization) that the contract established will not be enforced.

Charters need not be expressed only at the point in time when an organization is initiated. What will be done depends on the logic of the organization itself. If the organization is considered to consist of specific individuals only and to be coterminal with their membership, as in a marriage, then of course it makes sense to say what they are agreeing to when the relationship begins. But if the organization is considered to endure independently of any specific individuals who make it up, such as an army, then expressing the charter only at its inception would be logically self-nullifying. To be self-consistent in this case, the charter has to be expressed in recurrent ceremonies such as oaths of enlistment, parades, ceremonies of assembly and disassembly, and awards of decorations and honors. All ceremonies of recruitment must be consistent with, and therefore express, the charter of the organization to which the person is being recruited in order to indicate their place within it: letters of acceptance to universities, the issuing of birth certificates, military oaths of enlistment, ceremonies of initiation, and so on. It would hardly make sense to tell someone that he or she had been accepted without saying what the person had been accepted into and what it meant.

Of course, establishing a charter in this strict sense is not all there is to creating an organization. The charter is only a talking point. The organization itself has to be an ongoing creation of its members, and no one with organizational skill would say that in this process the charter is the only important point of reference.

From the point of view of building a sound organizational theory, this is where the puzzle gets really interesting. Given what a charter is in a strict sense, and given that the charter is not itself causative of the organization but only a resource used in creating it, how do those in the organization know what to do? The answer is complex but again has two main components. First, there are many more examples of social charters that members can draw on besides the charter for their own organization. Charters for any major type of organization are embedded in all sorts of cultural media, and people in any individual organization draw upon this broader set of cultural resources in their ongoing dealings with one another. Second, the way that any ideas of social relations are used in creating actual relations also depends to a very great extent on practical constraints arising from what the organization is trying to do and the material means available to do it.

Charters, Myth, and Movies

Why does every society have traditions of fictional and artistic representation? Of course it is because they are entertaining, but what makes them entertaining? Why do we get, for example, a sense of reassurance or reaffirmation from a novel or film? Why do we care what happens to a fictional character? Why is *Casablanca* (1942) a great American film while *Thunder Over Arizona*[1] (1956) is a routine potboiler? Why do so many people find fiction in general more discussable than what they experience in real life?

The major part of the answer is that it is much easier to illustrate how to derive organizational charters from social idea systems in fiction than in ongoing actual behavior. It is easy to construct a story around one single set of organizational ideas, one social charter. It is almost impossible to construct a day this way. In stories, the key characters usually stay in the same social framework, the same set of relevant relations, from beginning to end. In the course of a day, we move from one different situation to another like actors in a traveling variety show. Accordingly, while social idea systems and the organizational charters constructed with them really live in working consensus, it is in fiction and art that they are more readily displayed for public comment and assent. Of course, in such fictional presentations the formal definitions are not described as formal definitions. That would call into question precisely what makes them most important, the stipulation that they are the unquestioned ground of the relationships portrayed.

Generally, different story genres represent different social idea systems and usually different organizational charters. Epic poetry is the most enduring genre of fiction. An interesting feature of it in comparison to other forms is that it is rhetorically monolithic but organizationally pluralistic. An epic is always many stories in one. Meters, rhymes, and other mnemonics are generally consistent to assist memorization and recitation, but the stories place the characters in multiple types of settings, each associated with a distinctive set of organizational relations, juxtaposed to each other and typically in tension or conflict with one another.

For example, the action of the *Iliad* and *Odyssey* of Homer is framed in terms of five distinct organizational charters. Each is associated with a distinctive type of place: the abode of Gods, the palaces of Agamemnon and Priam, the ships, the plain before the walls of Troy, and Odysseus's house.

The gods in Olympus are the family of Zeus in his household together with all his more distant relations. What are the characteristics of their relationships? Among them there are friendships and enmities, support, betrayal, and bitter jealousies. In many ways, they are a thoroughly unpleasant, unreliable, mean-spirited lot. They even conspire to thwart the will of Zeus himself. Yet no one is driven out, and no one leaves. Why? What would have made this reasonable to its intended audience? Obviously, it could not be something about Gods; Greeks twenty-eight hundred years ago did not encounter the gods any more than we do. But they did encounter families, and these are familial relationships. They are not, for example, political relationships, relationships to the polis. Betray your city and you would be exiled or executed. But family is different. Family relations are permanent. Since the gods were immortal, transposing such relationships to them is a clear way of saying that such relationships were immortal as well. You can choose your friends, but you cannot choose your relatives; live with it.

By contrast, the family relationships portrayed in scenes set in the palaces and war conferences of the rulers, Agamemnon and Priam, do not have this quality of enduring no matter what. They are clearly fragile. They can be broken or altered at a whim. Suspicions of disloyalty and possible betrayal are constant, and it is often not clear who is loyal to whom. They depend not only on who is what kin relation to whom but very importantly on who has the power and prerogative of the king and how that power is used, who is materially rewarded and why, and who is slighted and why. These are clearly not ideas of family relationships revolving around an ordinary household that we find represented by the relations among the Gods. They are the relations of the interest-based kinship alliances in aristocratic households, where family power and wealth cannot be separated from power to rule in the city-state. It is an idea system for government in a familial society, not kinship as such, and members join and leave on provocations that are microscopic compared to what the gods offer one another. Joining and leaving, fighting for and fighting against, and rewards and wealth are what the discussion and action in these settings are about.

The definitional relationships in the stories of combat before the walls of Troy are also different and represent the relationship between the aristocratic leadership (claiming partial divine ancestry) and the commoners. The same ideas are represented in Odysseus's voyage. Here, the themes are leadership and followership, discipline and indiscipline.

And, finally, Odysseus's relationship to his wife and her would-be suitors once the voyage is over is framed by the conflict between the values and rules of aristocratic marriage and inheritance in the family-based political systems and the values and purely kinship ideas of conjugal fidelity, love, and honor. Odysseus's problem in this substory is to reestablish himself simultaneously as both a king in the palace and as a husband in his family house, not just one at the expense of the other.

The adventures with the Cyclops, the Sirens, and Circe in their respective places are sideshows: the charter is the same as on the ships, but the circumstances bring out different underlying issues. What is the recognizable truth of the story of Circe, for instance, if it is not that a beautiful woman has the ability to make good men long at sea act like pigs and not want to return to the boat?

In America, film takes the place of epic poetry. Films are recognized as having formulas. Formulas are not scripts, such as ceremonies adhere to, but are basic lists of characters and relations that the scripts are expected to involve. For example, the main elements of the formula of a conventional Western such as *Thunder Over Arizona* are easy to elicit using the same method as for idea systems; I have regularly done so in undergraduate classes. It is not necessary to name any particular film. The main characters are the hero, heroine, villain, sidekick of the hero, gang of the villain, parent or parents of heroine, and townspeople. The action occurs not long ago in the West. The hero is just a cowboy and not attached to the region. He is just passing through. The heroine, however, has property, usually a ranch. She may have relatives in the film. Most often, it is an elderly male who cannot protect the property on his own. The hero seeks to protect it for her. Their mutual relation is love without lust, usually from the outset or instantaneously, and unwaveringly. The villain's relation to the heroine is lust without love, and he seeks to obtain her property rather than to protect her possession of it. The townspeople are initially either unaware of what the villain is up to or are insufficiently firm in their recognition to do anything about it. The plot is that the hero recognizes the heroine's problem and comes to her rescue by finding a legal way to expose the villain and secure the support of the townspeople. The contrast between the bumbling and genial sidekick of the hero and the menacing and secretive gang of the villain emphasizes the contrast between the openness and kindness of the former and the secrecy and meanness of the latter.

The Western is stereotypically expected to convey a kind of reassuring nostalgia. Critics and others express disappointment if it does not. The question, therefore, is how do we know all this? How do we know what to expect and what to feel? Since the answer can only rest on something in our experience, the way to answer the question is to transform it to one about that experience: Where do we encounter such relations? Where, or for whom, do we encounter men with the properties of the hero, women with the properties of the heroine, and so on? The interpretive key is to restate the description of the action at a just slightly higher level of generality than what the film actually portrays. Instead of "not long ago in the West," restate the locale as "the real recent past." Instead of "just a cowboy," note simply that you do not see any actual work. The hero is intelligent and active, loves the heroine, and has a plan to protect her. The heroine is a person with family property who needs protection. They love each other, but there is no overt sex. The love also has no observable beginning and no observable end. Once you see through the deliberately thin disguises, it is obvious that the plot enacts the stereotyped relationship between a father and mother as it should be seen from the perspective of a child. The classic American Western movie represents the organizational charter of the American family as seen from the perspective of a child in such a family. We go to them to feel what we think we should feel, or should have felt, in such a position.

In the complementary adult Western the organizational charter is the same, but the point of view is that of the adults. This is accomplished mainly by devices that call the elements of the initial formula into question, particularly the sharp love-lust and good-bad contrast between hero and villain. In *Shane* (1953), widely recognized as one of the first of the genre, the heroine was married and had a living husband, while the hero was someone she had apparently loved previously. This left the love between hero and heroine now (the time in which the film is set) and therefore the hero's motivation clouded and ambiguous. The townspeople knew that the villain was evil from the outset but were ineffective, and the characters included the heroine's annoying son of about six years old whose admiration for the hero was far more apparent than his admiration for his actual father, the heroine's husband, explicitly occupying the social position that previous Westerns had left for the viewer.

Specific film genres regularly become vehicles for enacting specific systems of organizational ideas for fairly long periods and then pass it on to another. The traditional war film (and novel) of the 1940s and 1950s dramatized ideas of teamwork and the separation of political unity from ideological, ethnic, or religious unity. Subsequently, this was picked up by much of the science fiction of the 1960s and 1970s. The ethnically mixed, dedicated, and at bottom good-hearted men of the infantry squad became the ethnically mixed, dedicated, and at bottom good-hearted men of the space ship crew.

The *Star Wars* (1977) genre picked up the plot structure of the Westerns, over-laid it with the imagery of the conflict between the ideals of the Roman republic and the Roman Empire, added a further overlay of religious conceptions of a final conflict between absolute good and absolute evil, and dramatically expanded the temporal and spatial scale. It occurs "a long time ago in a galaxy far, far away," not in the future like previous films involving ideas of space travel but an enlarged version of the Western's real recent past. For the rest, hero and heroine are the same; the republic replaces the heroine's ranch, and the galaxy replaces the town. The emperor is of course the villain, with Darth Vader as his assistant and symbol of the rest of the gang. The social relations of the first of the series were those of the classic Western, and the relational confusions among the principal characters of the first and second sequel are the complications of the adult Westerns.

The *Matrix* (1999) is substantially the same thing with a more particularly New Testament eschatology in which the Western hero is also the Messiah. But in this case, like the Western hero, he ultimately gets the girl. This is placed in the future, which is logically consistent with its theme of the Second Coming.

The ideas that appear in fictional genres also appear in ceremonies that establish actual relationships. The ideas of the classic American Western are substantially the same as the ideas of the stereotypic American wedding. The bride is the heroine, of course; the bride's father is in the picture. The groom is not associated with any relative but has to be supported by his best man. The guests who are separate before the ceremony and come together at the end parallel the townspeople. The villain is not present, but the basic threats are: to love, honor, and obey in sickness and in health until death do you part. This should not be surprising. It ought to be quite predictable that two descriptions of the same organization should have the same basic cast of characters. The same applies to the ideal of Indian marriages in the epics and Indian marriage ceremonies. Fictional genres are an embodiment of organizational folk models; ceremonies embody many of the same models, and actual organizations do as well. Because of the way information-theoretic constraints combine with our limited mental capacities, there can only be a relatively small number of basic idea systems held in wide and consistent consensus. Most of what we take to be creativity is not a matter of inventing things wholly new but of finding ways to refresh and reaffirm the deeply familiar.

For most people most of the time in most communities, such things are the formulas for their own relationships. Hearing or seeing such stories attests to their general acceptance. Discussing them relates that general acceptance to oneself and those around one. In short, the social charters in a community do not draw their meaning from arcane codes to be found by obscure hermeneutics. They use what everyone knows. They are not beneath the surface of things. They are the surface of things.

Productive Organizations

Wherever you have a productive purpose and resources to deploy in attaining it, you have the basis for a productive strategy to pull them together. Very often where purposes and resources are complex, there are not only strategies but also well-developed cultural algorithms that represent them. Although indigenous rationality and local knowledge are now widely recognized in principle, most of the efforts to establish them have involved showing that *our* models, such as game theory, decision theory, and optimal foraging strategy, can predict *their* action. This makes sense when the constraints being considered are of the sort we can reasonably expect any cultural system to take into account, such as economies of time and space, but such considerations are relatively crude. For more nuanced and more accurate prediction, we need to locate and understand the indigenous algorithms in which such rationality and local knowledge are embodied. But this is one of the most difficult areas to find ethnographic accounts for. I will focus on two, which stand at something like opposite ends of the scale of importance to human survival: peasant farming and bartending.

Peasant Farming

Table 4 is an indigenous South Asian algorithm for planning farm operations that I call the physical farm budget. It too was elicited as part of my activity on the Irrigation and Water Management Training Project after the crop costs in table 3 and figure 8. I had discovered the basic algorithm a few months earlier and by this time had collected several versions in different parts of India. The interviews were conducted with the action research director acting as translator using a portable laptop and entering the information shown as we proceeded. Those interviewed were groups of farmers he asked to meet us in public buildings in each of the four villages.

Eighteen budgets were collected from farms that ranged in scale from 4.2 to 33 acres and also ranged from very poor to intensively capitalized. This farm is about in the middle of the range. It is a farm of 17 acres in a village in about the middle of the irrigation command. I have previously published two other budgets from this same area as Excel spreadsheets that can be downloaded with a more detailed description of how the model is constructed (Leaf 2000).[2]

The language of the area is Marathi. I speak some Punjabi and Hindustani. These are not close enough to Marathi to conduct an interview, but this was not the only reason for using translators. My purpose was not just to find the models but to demonstrate what they were to the irrigation staff and then put them on

Table 4. Medium-scale farm, Pus Project, India

Food Crop	Gram/Meal/Man	Number Men	Number Women	Number Children	Yield Quintals/Acre	Price/Kilogram	Meals/Year	Acres Required	Acres Sown	Percent MNSA	Rupees +/-
Jowar	300	4	3	7	8.4	1.25	130	0.52	10	0.03	9954.00
Bajra	300	4	3	7	5.5	1.56	0	0.00	0	0.00	0.00
Wheat	200	4	3	7	8	2.8	600	1.68	2	0.09	716.80
Rice	50	4	3	7	20	4.75	0	0.00	0	0.00	0.00
Tur	55	4	3	7	1.75	7.5	200	0.70	1	0.04	388.50
Mung/Urid	55	4	3	7	0.172	4.5	165	5.91	10	0.32	316.62
Vegetable	80	4	3	7	30	3	365	0.11	0	0.01	-981.12
Oil	12.5	4	3	7	4.5	23	730	0.23	0	0.01	-2350.60
Sugar	27	4	3	7	12	5.7	730	0.18	0	0.01	-1258.29
Chilis	3	4	3	7	10	30	730	0.02	0	0.00	-735.84
Total								9.36	13.00	0.51	6050.07

Fodder Crop	Bundles/Day Pair	Ox	Buffalo Jersey	Cow	Yield Bundles/Hectare	Rupees/Bundle	Days/Year	Acres Required	Acres Sown	Percent MNSA	Rupees +/-
Jow dry	10	3	2	3	800	0.75	150	9.38	10	0.51	375.00
Jow wet	10	3	2	3	800	0.75	0	0.00	0	0.00	0.00
Groundnut	2.5	3	2	3	300	1	0	0.00	0	0.00	0.00
Lucerne	1	0	0	0	1000	0	0	0.00	0	0.00	0.00
Oil cake, kilogram	2	0	1	1	0	2.5	220				-1375.00
Total								9.38	10.00		375.00

Maximum net subsistence area 18.21   Actual subsistence area 13

(continued)

Table 4. (Continued)

Commercial Crops	Yield	Area	Price	Cost	Net
Cane	125	5	48	7000	23000.00
Cotton	2	0	0	0	0.00
Kharif sunflower	0.24	1	681	75	88.44
Sunflower	2.4	5.5	681	300	8689.20
	Total	11.5		Gain	31777.64
	Commercial + Subsistence Value				38202.71
	Total land farmed				17.00

Data is for Bhojala Shiv, 1987–88 *kharif rabi* (summer, winter).
All land on canal. Value/acre 2247.22. Urid and Mung were sown with jowar. Fodder consumption given at 30 bundles/day for all: 2 bullocks, 4 bullock calves, 2 buffalo, 3 cows for 5 months. May gives some surplus. Wheat yield not given. Consumption not given.

Note: Actual subsistence area is actual area under subsistence crops. Max net subsistence area is area required without overlap. Actual subsistence area is area sown in subsistence crops, less overlap.

the training institute computers for use in instruction. This was one of those rare instances when ethnographic field experiments actually could be done for an audience.

In farm households, the budget model is attached to the ideas that define the management organization just in the way that ideas of inheritance are attached to the ideas of kinship. I have elicited it all over India and Bangladesh, and there are many reasons to believe that something similar exists wherever there is household farming. Without such a system for conscious planning, it is very difficult to account for the energy efficiency of indigenous farming efficiency that has now been so consistently and universally documented (Turner and Brush 1987; Bayless-Smith 1982).

The most important point to notice is that this is not simply a way to decide what crops to grow. It is a way to decide what crops *this family* should grow in order to provide everyone with their requirements. The purpose frames the choices, and the purpose is clear. Indian agronomists summarize what farm households require as the Four Fs: food, fodder, fuel, and funds. The purpose is to obtain the most possible with the resources available.

The model allows what-if trials to be calculated and compared. It appears to exist only as an oral tradition. I could not find it in an indigenous written or symbolic form. However, farmers who could read English readily understood it once they saw it on my laptop even though none of them had ever seen a computer before.

The rows are the food and fodder requirements. The first column gives the commodity. The second column is the amount normally eaten by an adult male per meal. The next three columns are the counts of men, women, and children eating that food. The yield in quintals per acre is as reported by that family. The price per kilogram is the market price expected in the area. Villagers generally buy from each other at the price that would be paid in the nearby markets. The number of meals per year is the total number with that food per year for that family. Since there are normally two preparations a day and every meal involves some food grain, the first check for internal consistency is that under "Meals/Year" the total number of meals using food grains, rice, or breads should aggregate to 730 meals per year per person. Pulses together with vegetables should also aggregate to at least 730 but could be more since sometimes more than one vegetable or pulse is used to accompany the grain. Acres required is calculated by the model from the annual consumption and yield. Acres sown is what the farmer says he actually planted. "Percent MNSA" is the percentage of the mean net subsistence area, which is the total acreage this farmer needs for subsistence as computed by the spreadsheet. And finally, "Rupees +/–" is the surplus or deficit computed from his yield, acreage sown, acreage required, and market price. For cash crops, out-of-pocket expenses are included because they affected the decision on what crop to grow. For crops to be consumed on the farm, they usually did not. There are several reasons for this. The most important was that the gap between production cost and market price on commercial crops was usually much narrower than for food and fodder.

In this area, sorghum millet (jowar in the table) is both the main food grain and the most important fodder. It is hardy and drought resistant. People usually eat it as a *chapatti* with an accompanying pulse or vegetable curry. Animals get the chopped mature stalks, either green or dry. The main cropping season is *kharif* (summer), the time of the monsoons.

The monsoon rains that year had been lighter than usual but sufficient for sorghum. But there had been heavy whitefly infestations in cotton and other crops, as there had been through most of the state. As a result, cotton yields were no better than a third of normal and often were nothing. The winter rains had failed completely. Since the irrigation reservoir had filled to only 35 percent of capacity, each user was allowed 35 percent of the normal water. Since there was not enough water for both the winter and the following hot season (May–June), all the water was to be allocated for winter. This farmer received irrigation permits for five acres of sugarcane, five and a half acres of sunflower, and two acres of wheat.[3]

Reading down, the three sections of the model describe the provisions for food, fodder, and funds. Fuel is not forgotten, but many different things can be used.

The first food row is sorghum. To meet his food consumption requirements, this farmer only needed .52 acre. He actually planted 10 acres. This is the sort of decision government agronomists regard as irrational. Why plant so much of a traditional, low-value crop? The main answer is that he had needed 9.38 acres to meet his fodder requirement. So evidently he had given himself a little margin of safety. Another part of the answer is that this crop does not require irrigation.

The row for wheat is constructed in the same way as for sorghum, as are all subsequent rows. Either wheat or sorghum will be eaten at every meal. The spreadsheet indicates that 1.68 acres would have provided the wheat that his family consumed. He actually planted 2 acres. Since costs and risks for wheat are high compared to sorghum, the usual practice is to hold all of one's sorghum harvest until after the following wheat harvest. If the wheat harvest is good, the farmer will retain it and sell an equivalent amount of sorghum. Farmers said that sorghum can be stored for about a year, but by that time two quintals out of thirty-two has to be discarded, and the rest deteriorates rapidly thereafter. Wheat can be stored for several years.

The rows for tur and mung/urid are complementary. All three are used as dal. Pulses are the major protein source in the diet. The reason that the model shows ten acres for mung and urid (but at a very low yield per acre) is that the farmer interplanted them with the sorghum. They are nitrogen fixing, and their dry stems and husks are high-protein fodders. The one acre of tur was grown in a solid stand. Tur also produces some fodder, and its long fibrous stems are used for baskets and wickerwork. The green pods are used as a vegetable. The strategy was to plant several pulses in sufficient quantity to exceed the family's minimal requirements. He has a surplus in all three.

The remaining diet items, showing negative balances, are purchased. According to USDA analyses, such a diet would be quite adequate and is therefore consistent on biological grounds.

The fodder analysis is constructed the same way. The allowance is in kilos per pair per day. These are rules of thumb for the area. A pair is a standard planning unit all over South Asia and consists generally of two oxen or cows. These are the equivalent of one buffalo, one jersey (actually a Jersey Bos indica hybrid), one camel, or four donkeys. In this area, however, oxen are relatively small while buffalo are full size. So since oxen and cows are .5 pair each, we rated buffalo at 1.3 pair.

Fodder, in this area, meant only crops specifically grown for such use, prepared in the home. This was mainly sorghum. Wheat straw was not fodder, although it was fed to animals. Neither was browse found on open land. Fodder is fed only to animals that are working. For oxen, the annual working period was given as four months. For milk animals, it is the period of lactation. At other times, the animals are taken by paid herdsmen wherever there might be some browse. In their nonworking periods, they still provide manure. This is dried for fuel, used in making household adobe, or composted.

The local unit of measure for fodder is a bundle. A bundle is a set of stalks tied with a standard-length cord of twisted sorghum leaves. The weight was given as two to three kilos, depending on volume and moisture. The price was around three-fourths of a rupee per bundle at the time of the interview but would go up to one rupee before the next harvest. The farmer said that he had enough fodder. The calculation agreed. Oil cake, which is purchased, is only for animals that are lactating. This farmer has two, one buffalo and one cow, for his children. Goats do not get fodder.

Finally, there are the cash crops. For the summer crop, this farmer grew 5 acres of sugarcane and 1 of sunflower alongside his sorghum and tur, thus bringing the total land farmed to 17 acres, which is again internally consistent. The sunflower was an experiment to use a patch of land with shallow soils. It did not work, and he will not do it again. For the winter he followed the sorghum with 5.5 acres of sunflower and 2 acres of wheat on canal water. Four acres of sugarcane was carried over as a ratoon crop, and 1 acre was removed because of irrigation limits.

The deficit/surplus column (Rupees +/–) shows a surplus in all categories: food, fodder, and funds. Is the farm then commercial, or is it subsistence? At this level of precision, it becomes clear that the question is naive. Commercial calculations are integral to his strategy for meeting his subsistence needs.

Was this optimal? Could different crops have been grown? He could not grow more cane because he could not get more irrigation for it. Vegetables are usually grown only in small plots by wells and are sold locally in small quantities.

Could the proportions have been changed? The extreme form of changing proportions would be to eliminate one or more crops and expand the others into the land they would use. Since the farmer grows three main crop rotations but one (cane) cannot be increased because of water limitations, there is really only one other alternative: to replace the sorghum with cotton, which is considered a major cash crop.

If the model is reset with ten acres of cotton and no sorghum, which means that he would be eating wheat at market prices and buying fodder, and if the yield is assumed to be there quintals an acre, which would have been high this year, the total return goes up only to 41,284 rupees. If the cotton yield were one quintal an acre, which was common, total return would go down to 25,903 rupees. In better years, the cotton yield is expected to be ten quintals an acre, although in general this is only obtained about half the time. So if the budget is reset for a cotton yield of five quintals, the expected annual return would be 55,778 rupees, unless the fodder price goes up to 1 rupee, in which case it would be 53,903 rupees. But with cotton instead of sorghum, the risk would be much higher, and he would have to seek fodder to buy and bring every day.

Since all other possible combinations would be between these and what the farmer presently grows, it follows that the question of whether the farmer is optimizing boils down to a question of how much risk it is reasonable for him to assume. How much loss can he risk in bad years for a 46 percent gain in good years?

Institutional credit was closely tied to irrigation and irrigated crops and was not available for other kinds of expenses. Noninstitutional interest rates were so high that people took loans only for the most extreme emergencies. His seven children were also probably an important part of his reasoning.

The farmer I interviewed just before this one provides an instructive comparison. His was the most intensively mechanized and capitalized farm in the group.[4] He was well educated, spoke good English, and was a political leader. He too had 17 acres, although only 14.5 was cultivated. The rest was work area and wasteland, but it contained a well that could water 7–8 acres. His household was five adults and no children. They ate wheat and rice from the market and grew only two acres of sorghum, which he said he used to pay servants and for fodder. His summer crops were 6 acres of cane, 6 of cotton intercropped with tur, 1 of sunflower, 1 of jute, and a half acre of eucalyptus. With the addition of some catch crops after these, his total return for the year was 38,622 rupees, just 400 more than the first farmer. His cotton yield had been .33 quintal per acre. The reason was that he was especially reliant on chemical fertilizer and pesticides. The normal pesticide that would have been used for whitefly was not available. In its place, the Agriculture Department distributed rotenone. But if rotenone is used in sufficient concentration to kill whitefly, it will also kill cotton. The dose has to be just enough to control the whitefly but not enough to kill it. The agricultural officers had been very careful about supplying the right information and the right concentrations, but farmers had no way of knowing this. So he had made the usual allowance for adulteration, which was 50 percent.

We talked at some length after the more formal interview was over, and he explained more of his situation. He was deeply in debt, and his credit was exhausted. He asked if the computer analysis could help. I explained that it was only descriptive and reloaded his spreadsheet. Then, on the principle of attacking the greatest deficit first, I reset the crops to put all his land under sorghum except what he was using for groundnut and sunflower, cutting out cane and cotton. (It would have been better to keep the cane, but I did not think of it at the time.) Had he done just this, his total return would have been 55,763 rupees rather than the 38,621 rupees that he actually earned. His response was that he could not do it; it would not let him pay off his debts. He had to find a way to use the equipment he had bought. He had to find a new crop. The problem was that there was none.

Notice that the 55,763 rupees that is insufficient to allow this highly capitalized farmer to pay his debts is very close to the maximum possible that the first farmer could expect by shifting to a comparable strategy. While we could argue over whether the first farmer's solution was absolutely optimal in a strict sense, he clearly was better off this year and probably in the long run.

Wider Applications of the Farming Model

The household model can also be used for aggregate prediction, essentially as a system model. Since it is held and used uniformly among all households and since the input values for consumption, yield, and prices are largely uniform from household to household, in principle it should predict the aggregate cropping strategy of all the households that use it or any geographical subset. In fact, it enabled me to predict the cropping behavior of the entire irrigation command from which the information was elicited.

The Maharashtra Irrigation Department was serious in its interest in improving the efficiency and spreading the benefits of irrigation. Irrigation projects around the state were consistently underperforming, and revenues from irrigation were insufficient to provide adequate maintenance. Irrigated crop yields were low, and water was often underutilized. Projects were designed for an average intensity of 114 percent. Intensity is the measure of total land irrigated in two seasons to total land available in two seasons. Thus 114 percent meant that the water should be available for 100 percent of the land under command in one season plus 14 percent in a second season, or some other combination with the same total. Actual intensity around the state and in the Pus project was 49 percent. They were trying to understand why.

The administrative rule was that farmers only paid for irrigation on fields that actually received irrigation water. Farmers had to apply for water field by field, specifying the crop. Once they applied, they were charged for an entire season. This would normally be three or four waterings, but they would be charged the same if they only received one. Such shortfalls were common. Farmers therefore tried to get by on rain alone and waited to apply until they were absolutely certain that they could not do so. The effect was that irrigation served simply as an emergency backup for rain. Farmers continued to grow their traditional drought-tolerant but often low-value rainfed crops instead of higher-yielding irrigation crops.

Following the recommendations of the state irrigation department and a former World Bank officer (also an irrigation engineer) who had been in charge of this aspect of the project for more than a year before I arrived, the action research program was trying to organize farmers to allocate water more effectively. They were also encouraging farmers to grow sunflower as a water-saving commercial crop that would encourage more farmers to use irrigation and spread its benefits more widely.

The department was especially interested in having the sunflower replace groundnut (peanut) and gave two main reasons. First, it used less water per unit area than groundnut and gave a higher economic return per unit of water, although it gave a lower economic return per unit of land. The irrigation staff reasoned that those who grew groundnut were in a sense being selfish. The benefits of irrigation were being concentrated in fewer hands; if everyone grew sunflower, the benefits of irrigation would be spread more widely. Second, sunflower grows in the winter season when irrigation water is not fully utilized. Groundnut grows in the spring and the hot season (May–June) when demand is increasing. In addition, it seems to have been important that groundnut had not been part of the original cropping recommendation by irrigation department agronomists. It had been discovered by the farmers themselves.

The first year I worked with the Pus project was the second year of the drought. No permits were being issued for groundnut, and sugar permits were restricted to fields near the reservoir in order to eliminate the channel losses that would occur in sending the water to fields that are more distant.[5] So in a large part of the command, sunflower was the only crop the department would allow water for. For anything else, if farmers wanted to irrigate they had to use their own wells. Since farmers were accepting this, the irrigation department staff took it as a vindication of their reasoning and were preparing for sunflower to be much more widely adopted. To me it seemed very unlikely that irrigation engineers would be better than farmers themselves at identifying a genuine farming opportunity. The real constraints were elsewhere. My problem was to lead the engineers to see them.

The first step was to use the physical farm budget model and the project data on land areas, yields, population, and cattle to calculate a general crop pattern for each of the four action research villages. Table 5 is the model for the village that the farm of table 4 was in.

Table 5. Diet Budget Projection for Bojala Village, Maharashtra, 1987

Crop	Grams/Day Max.	Number Men	Number Women	Number Child	Yield Quintals/Hectare	Days/Year	Hectares Needed	% NCA Needed
Jowar*	400	645	615	1261	20	365	147.21	0.15
Wheat	250	645	615	1261	17	365	108.24	0.11
Tur w/Cot*	55	645	615	1261	1.75	365	231.33	0.23
Vegetables	80	645	615	1261	30	365	19.63	0.02
Oil/sunflower	25	645	615	1261	5	365	36.80	0.04
Sugar*	55	645	615	1261	56	365	7.23	0.01
Chilis	15	645	615	1261	10	365	11.04	0.01
Meat	0	645	615	1261	0	0	0.00	0.00
Total							561.49	0.57

Fodder

Crop	Bundles/Day Pair	Days Fed Oxen 221	Buffalo 101	Cow 101	Goat 85	Yield	Price/Unit	Hectares Needed	% NCA Needed
Jowar dry*	8	70	180	180	0	1000	0.8	323.67	0.33
Jowar wet	6	0	0	0	0	1000	0.8	0.00	0.00
Groundnut	2.5	120	120	120	0	800		105.83	0.11
Lucerne	1	0	90	90	0	3200		4.83	0.00
Oil cake, kilograms	2	0	180	120	0	0	0.6	0.00	0.00

Total 434.33

Annual subsistence area required: 848.60

Actual areas:

Geographical area 1104.00 GCA = 1154.00 NCA: 986.00 *kharif* 385.774

Cropped more than once: 167.00 (From notes at Water and Land Management Institute) *rabi:* 193.317

Hectares: CCA = 986 ICA = 273 (From Index map, 1985)

Average holding: 2.2 Number of holdings 169 (Index map)

* *Kharif* or perennial crop.

ICA = irrigated command area, CCA = cultivated command area, GCA = gross cultivable area, NCA = net cultivable area.

Fodder section restructured October 14, 1993. Data in notes of September 16, 1987. 1 bundle = 2 kilograms. Cattle data from socioeconomic survey, Action Research. Buffalo and cow are in milk. Net totals are 155 buffalo and 317 cows. Updated October 9, 1994, reducing excess days for fodder consumption but increasing buffalo allowance to 1.2 pair.

The general layout is the same as for the farm-level budget, but in this case I set the spreadsheet to calculate the area needed for each crop as a percentage of the net cultivable area (% NCA) for the entire village. A critical point immediately became obvious that the irrigation staff, focusing only on crop economics, had not been able to see. Out of the net cultivated area of 986 hectares, the net annual subsistence area was 848.6 hectares. That is, 86 percent of the land was needed for food and fodder for local consumption. This set an immediate upper limit on the amount of land available for cash crops such as sunflower that produced neither. Not growing the food and fodder locally was not a real option. The margin between cost and gain on the commercial crops was too narrow to overcome the food and fodder losses. Although groundnut was also a cash crop, its crop residues provided an important portion of the fodder requirements.

Fodder was the main consumption constraint. To meet its fodder requirements, as the model shows, required growing 324 hectares of jowar, 106 hectares of groundnut, and about 5 hectares of lucerne. It immediately followed that if sunflower replaced groundnut, the loss in groundnut fodder would have to be made up with much more of some other fodder crop. Second, since none of the unfarmed land was cultivable, this would mean that some other nonfodder or low-fodder crop would have to be reduced. The only major candidate for a fodder crop to increase was jowar, and the only major candidate for a crop to reduce was cotton grown with tur.

So the second step was to take each village projection and ask what would happen if sunflower replaced groundnut while making these further adjustments to meet the food and fodder needs. The third step was to combine all four villages together and take their aggregate cropping pattern as representing the command as a whole. The fourth step was to use this aggregated budget to simulate what the crop production and income would be for the entire irrigation command by replacing the village totals of population, cattle, and land with command totals. And the fifth step was to use this model to estimate the effects of the different crop patterns in bad and good years. Table 6 is an estimate for normal conditions.

I made several different versions of this estimate, but this is enough to show the strategy. It summarizes the aggregate returns to three different crop patterns. The first was the present crops as estimated by the model (there were no actual figures). The second simply replaced groundnut with sunflower with no further adjustments, which was the irrigation staff's minimum target. This made sunflower 11 percent of total cropped area and would have left a substantial shortfall in fodder. The third increased sunflower to 20 percent of the cultivated command area, reduced cotton and tur from 43 percent to 34 percent to provide the space for it, increased sorghum to 45 percent to compensate for the loss of groundnut as fodder, and increased the area under mung from 2 percent to 3 percent to make up for the loss of tur.

Table 6. Pus income projection, 1987

Crop	Quintal/Hectare	Price/Quintal	Current Crops			Replace Groundnut with Sunflower			Replace Groundnut with Sunflower and Adjust		
			Percent CCA	Hectares grown	Value	Percent CCA	Hectares grown	Value	Percent CCA	Hectares grown	Value
Jowar	25.00	125	0.36	4,924.80	15,390,000	0.36	4,924.80	15,390,000	0.45	6,156.00	19,237,500.00
Wheat	15.00	225	0.13	1,778.40	6,002,100	0.13	1,778.40	6,002,100	0.13	1,778.40	6,002,100.00
Rice	37.00	475	0.00	0.00	0	0.00	0.00	0	0.00	0.00	0.00
Tur (with cotton)	4.50	750	0.43	5,882.40	19,853,100	0.43	5,882.40	19,853,100	0.34	4,651.20	15,697,800.00
Mung	12.00	400	0.02	273.60	1,313,280	0.02	273.60	1,313,280	0.03	410.40	1,969,920.00
Vegetable	75.00	300	0.02	273.60	6,156,000	0.02	273.60	6,156,000	0.02	273.60	6,156,000.00
Oil	0.00	2,300	0.01	136.80	0	0.01	136.80	0	0.01	136.80	.00
Sugarcane	720.00	23	0.01	136.80	2,265,408	0.01	136.80	2,265,403	0.01	136.80	2,265,408.00
Chilis	0.00	3,000	0.00	0.00	0	0.00	0.00	0	0.00	0.00	0.00
Groundnut	10.00	700	0.11	1,504.80	10,533,600	0.00	0.00	0	0.00	0.00	0.00
Sunflower	5.00	650	0.00	0.00	0	0.11	1,504.80	4,890,600	0.20	2,736.00	8,892,000.00
Cotton (with tur)	10.00	700	0.43	5,882.40	41,176,800	0.43	5,882.40	41,176,800	0.34	4,651.20	32,558,400.00
Total			1.09	14,911.20	102,690,288	1.09	14,911.20	97,047,288	1.19	16,279.20	92,779,128.00

This is to estimate effect of changes in value of crop production of adoption of sunflower. CCA = cultivated command area.

The result was that under drought conditions (not shown in table 6) the income for the command as a whole was about the same with and without sunflower, but under the normal conditions that table 6 assumes, total income without sunflower came out at 102.7 million rupees. Replacing groundnut with sunflower reduced the income to 97 million rupees, and raising sunflower to 20 percent reduced it still further to 92.8 million rupees. Contrary to the irrigation department's reasoning, if everyone grew sunflower they would not be better off; they would be worse off.

On this basis, in a project seminar in New Delhi shortly after the field interviews, I presented a paper that flatly said that sunflower could not solve the water scarcity problems and would never rise above 10 percent of the cropped area. Farmers would stick with groundnuts. The training institute director and the action research director were present, and the director disagreed forcefully. He restated the equity arguments and declared that their efforts would continue. No sunflower had been grown three years before, he said. Two years before it was 5 percent. This year it had gone up again (admittedly in part because water permits had been allowed for it and not for groundnut). He expected the trend to continue. Ultimately, sunflower should occupy more than half the command area (see Leaf 1998, 55–81).

The next year, 1988–89, had normal rainfall in the monsoon season. By the following winter harvest, my prediction based on the farmers' models had proven correct. The percentage of cropped area under sunflower that had reached about 10 percent in some villages had begun to fall back. The director of the training institute and the director of the Action Research Program then both said publicly and plainly on several occasions that the sunflower program was a failure. It was both honest and gracious of them; they considered themselves scientists, and they acted as such. But the important point is that it was a failure of theory, not of good intention or administrative execution. Most fundamentally, it was the failure to recognize that choices reflect organizational purposes. Ignoring this or trying to impose a purpose inconsistent with the definition of the organization was bound to lead to predictions that the organizations would not fulfill.

A productive organization needs to assure its members that they are better off staying in it than leaving. To do this it needs to use its resources efficiently enough to compete with other comparable organizations and also assure that each member gets what they will regard as a fair share.[6] The physical farm budget provides its users with an explicit assurance of optimality and at least an implicit assurance of fairness. Indigenous models can be very powerful.

Bartending

John Gatewood teaches cognitive anthropology at Lehigh University. He has also been a professional bartender. This provides the kind of detailed experience needed to allow him to describe the way that what bartenders learn in bartender school is instantiated in what bartenders actually do in tending bar, transposing the logical order of the ideas as abstract systems to the purposive-strategic order of the action based on it. Although none of these analyses has thus far been published in print, several are available on his Web site.

The central technical idea system instantiated in bartending is the nomenclature for different kinds of drinks: beers, distilled liquors, wines, and mixed drinks. At first blush, these might seem to be simply taxonomies or even "shallow" taxonomies, as Gatewood says. But they are not that univocal. One of the points that he makes very forcefully is that they do not have the same kinds of meaning in a pragmatic sense for all of those who use them. For customers they may seem to be simply sets of labels that designate sets of objects, but for the bartender each term is not so much the name of a thing as a mnemonic for a specific recipe. Bartenders organize these mnemonics into hierarchical groups in terms of the ingredients and the ways they are processed, up to a final presentation. And from the point of view of the interaction between the customer and the bartender, the terminology is a means to facilitate ordering: "The primary function of drink names, independent of their linguistic form, is to establish an unambiguous, 1-to-1 referential relation—a publicly-known semiotic code— whereby customers can ask for a particular potent potable and be reasonably assured of getting what they asked for" (Gatewood 1994).

Finally, what sets the framework for the way the bartender uses all this information is the fact that bartending is work. Bars are places of business, and there is a social idea system that defines such places. In addition to knowing the recipes (a technical role), the bartender is an employee who has to earn his salary and tips (an employee role). To do this, his aim has to be to move as much money into the cash register per hour as possible. This involves much more than just making the drinks according to the standard recipes and presenting them properly. It has repercussions for the way the bartender sets up the bar as a place to work, organizes the steps he takes in making the drinks and maintaining the area, cooperates with other bartenders, and responds to customers on a move-by-move, moment-to-moment basis that Gatewood characterizes as "active knowledge." Such active knowledge "interlinks with" what he calls "public culture" in the sense of common knowledge or what everyone knows (such as the drink nomenclature) but is not the same as public culture (Gatewood 2001).

Regulatory Organizations

The kinds of incentives that allow productive organizations to hold their members to their tasks are not available in regulatory organizations. The material benefits produced by regulatory organizations are usually not captured by the members, and there is little possibility of calculating productive efficiency in their use of resources. Members often are not compensated in any direct way at all. Yet they do it.

Courts are only one small subset of regulatory organizations. Other regulatory organizations sometimes solve disputes in the way courts do, but more often work like planning and zoning boards or city councils. They make rules and rulings that limit people's rights to claim resources. They prohibit some occupations and attempt to encourage others. They designate areas for specific purposes such as saying where an organized hunt should take place, distinguish housing areas from farming areas, or assign land or house sites to specific groups. They set standards and provide for common facilities such as common grazing lands, garbage dumps, roads, canals, and public wells. In short, they set the ground rules for productive competition and cooperation and resolve the problems that inevitably arise when such competition threatens to be destructive of general welfare. This is why Bates argues that cultural ecology always includes political ecology, in the sense of "the study of how people compete to gain access to, maintain control of, and utilize natural resources" (2001, 42).

Regulatory organizations generally have three distinctive characteristics: (1) They are separate from productive organizations, (2) they draw on the productive organizations for membership in a systematic way, and (3) they exercise very substantial authority although in traditional, small-scale societies they have little or nothing in the way of a dedicated police or enforcement apparatus. There are good reasons for all of this.

The Formal Problem of Occupational Choice

It is almost impossible for productive resources to be assigned to one person, organization, or group in a community without affecting what can be assigned to others. If one takes land, another cannot have it. If one uses his land for rice farming, others nearby will not be able to plant trees. If one wants to graze cattle, it will affect the ability of another to grow crops. If one has a smelter, it will affect the ability of others to have a house. A community would be extremely unwise to allow a few of its members to pursue an occupation that is destructive of the livelihoods or quality of life of most others. In the West, virtually every governmental jurisdiction has power to control such conflicts, from town planning and zoning boards to national regulatory commissions. Among the Hopi, access to land and property is a major concern of the associations of men who put on the annual ceremonial cycle, who also represent the landholding clans. In South Asia where national government does not allow local government the regulatory power that such problems require, it is a major concern of factions.

The basic problem of assigning the right to engage in productive activity is illustrated in figure 11. This represents the minimal case: a community consisting of two people or organized groups, each with a choice between two productive activities, A or B. Assume that both activities are equally beneficial to the

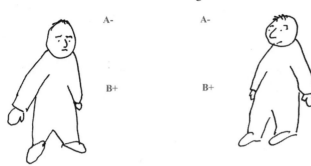

A-

A-

B+

B+

Figure 11. The logic of occupational choice

group who would engage in it and therefore equally likely to be chosen, but one activity will be harmful (–) to the interests of the other and one will be helpful (+). What are the possibilities?

If each person or group chooses independently, then the possible combinations are AA, AB, BA, and BB. The probability of each one is the same: it is 1 in 4, or 25 percent. It follows that there is only a 25 percent chance that the decisions made will be mutually beneficial (BB). Against this, there is a 25 percent chance that both will be injured by the choice of the other (AA) and a 50 percent chance that one will be benefited by the action of the other but that the other will be injured (AB plus BA). That is, whatever the conscious intent of those involved, there is a 25 percent chance that the result will be the same as that of mutual hostility, a 50 percent chance that it will be the same as that of betrayal, and only a 25 percent chance that it will be the same as mutual cooperation. Thus 75 percent of all outcomes will produce conflict and probably be organizationally nonsustainable (characterized by negative feedback). Only 25 percent will be sustainable (characterized by positive feedback). The proportions of outcomes that are good all around go down even more as the numbers of choices for each person or group go up. If we assume that community adaptation depends on stability and cooperation, this does not bode well.

From an adaptive point of view, it is essential to find a way to make the likely outcomes more favorable for the community while not making them worse for the individuals or organizations that make it up. This cannot be done simply by stipulating a rule, nor can it be done by authoritarian control. All possible combinations of productive activities that might be harmful cannot be specified in advance, and lack of a clear specification giving the power to limit such choices to one or a few individuals would amount to giving them the power to choose arbitrarily who will benefit from their action and who will not. Corruption, divisiveness, and self-destruction are sure to follow. What then? Very simple: require each person or organization to have the other's permission to make his choice. Then each person will prohibit the other from making the choice harmful to them, and this will provide prior assurance that the remaining system of choices will be mutually beneficial and sustainable. Only then can a mechanism such as the invisible hand of the market come into play constructively. This is the first half of the solution.

The Necessity of Collective Expression

Given that each person or organization requires the others' permission, the next step is to ask how they know they have it. How is this agreement to be expressed? Shall it be by private bilateral agreements or public decision? It must be clear, and it must be binding. The answer is that it must be public, and the reason lies in the mathematics of bilateral discussions.

As more organized groups and more activities are added, the probability of adverse combinations continues to be the mathematical product of the number of positive and negative choices and the likelihood of each. However, the need for a specifically designated public decision process managed by a formally constituted body increases exponentially. For the minimal case of two groups, there would of course be one bilateral discussion, which would be the same as a public decision. So in this case there is no issue. But for ten groups there are 45 paired relations that would require 45 simultaneous bilateral decisions. For twenty decision makers the number rises to 190.[7] Somewhere between these two points, a community is bound to find it advantageous to devise a public method for those involved to make such decisions together and all at once. That is, they would have to set up a specific type of meeting, specific notions of who would attend, a specific way of discussing the options, and a specific symbolic form for reaching and expressing a conclusion. It would not matter whether it was done under the aegis of religion, politics, kinship, magic, or pixies. What would matter is that it is public, and its decision would be recognized as that of the community as a whole. They would have to build a community-level regulatory organization.

The functions of regulatory organizations commonly overlap with responsibilities for infrastructure and reflect the same internal logic. Any physical facility such as a canal or a roadway will have differential benefits for different people. What these are and how they balance will depend on exactly where it will go and how it will be designed. How to decide? If only those who would benefit from any one design would be involved, the result is bound to be divisive. If everyone has the power to veto it, the design that emerges is bound to be the one that produces the most benefit and the least damage, and since in a large community this cannot be done by bilateral negotiation, the most obvious way to do it is with some sort of representative body.

Once we understand the relation between such regulatory organizations and the productive organizations they regulate, we can understand what holds them together in the absence of the kinds of material benefits that hold together the productive organizations themselves. First, substantially everyone recognizes that the benefit to everyone from such regulation is so great and the individual effort among the representatives who produce it is usually so small that there is ample personal benefit for the regulators even with no specific compensation. Second, if there were specific compensation, it would have to take the form of a transfer of usable resources from the producing organization and hence would reduce their gain from complying. Thus the larger the compensation was, the less useful the regulation would be. Honor alone, or nearly so, is not only sufficient but actually best.

In settings where those who serve on such bodies are full-time specialists and have no independent means of earning a livelihood, some arrangement must be made to associate membership with the provision of a livelihood. Full-time judges have to have some kind of salary. But to an even greater extent than with infrastructural bodies such as orchestras and universities, such a livelihood is virtually never directly attached to the decisions that such regulatory organizations produce.

Networks

In some cases, the use of organizational ideas leads to the formation of networks. Sometimes networks are very clearly a kind of organization in the sense that those who make them up have mutually adjusted behavior, a name, and a system for making conscious collective decisions. But sometimes the organizational character is tenuous. The action of one may only affect one or a few others, and the overall pattern may have no real social recognition or self-awareness. Families who exchange marriage partners make up networks. So do firms who exchange goods, and so do scientific or literary citations. Whether a network is important is a question of fact, but they exist wherever relations can be thought of as durable.

The best-developed general approach to describing networks is by simulation, using the network analysis of Douglas White and others (White 1999; Smith and White 1992; White and Johansen 2004) that draws on recent developments in graph theory.

A network is a set of definite, enduring relations of a specific kind among a set of nodes. The linking relations may be directional, bidirectional, or nondirectional. The important thing is that for one model they should be of one kind. The nodes may be individuals, organizations, or groups. This is one reason why we cannot equate networks with organizations as such. Another is that an organization might be in multiple networks or might include individuals in multiple networks. But there is always a connection in the sense that it is very difficult to think of a way we could have an organization that did not produce or involve at least one network of some kind, and different organizational charters will produce networks with different logical properties and shapes.

Data for assembling a network simulation could come from seeing who attends each other's weddings and court cases in any given period of time, such as a year. What we would find is that this pattern was largely instantiated except that some of the people in the opposed groups also maintained relations of mutual support in a subset of occasions other than those that were the focus of the main conflicts, and these often provided the pivots that led to changes of alignment.

A network formed on the basis of kinship ideas in the village would have an entirely different shape, and different individuals would be close or distant in terms of nodes. To begin with, it would involve everybody in the village, not just some, and would probably need several complementary types of linkages, such as marriage, descent, common ancestry, and adoption. Such linkages would connect different individuals in different families within castes but not across castes, so in this pattern caste would emerge as a salient boundary condition whereas it would not do so for the factional networks. A network of families (not individuals) connected by marriage would be different yet again and would link families in the village mainly to families in other villages. A network formed on the basis of long-term economic relations in farming would also have a very different character and would link families across caste lines and also to others outside the village. Communities always involve many networks of many types with many different logical properties.

Figure 12 is a Pajek analysis of the *meli* (marriage support group) relations of the three families that arranged the marriages of daughters that occurred during my first fieldwork. A central hypothesis for the research was that the marriage ceremonies were to be read as contracts, and thus we could predict who would support them by knowing who would have an interest in supporting that particular arrangement for those particular individuals. Interested persons would come and lend support; disinterested persons would not. The village or the caste does not attend village weddings, even though this is the way descriptions are usually stated. The hypothesis turned out to be correct, but at the time there was no really simple way to display the data that proved it. Now there is.

To construct figure 12, I did nothing by way of drawing the network itself. I only entered the names of those who attended each of the three ceremonies as part of the *meli* as a list of pairs. Each pair was the name of the person who attended and the name of the person whose *meli* it was. The program did the rest. Each starburst is the *meli* network of the person who is named as the central node. The central node is the person who organized the wedding in the capacity of father. This node is identified by the network algorithm. The top two central individuals support the same party (faction); the third central individual supported the opposite party.

With respect to my original research question, you have to know who the named individuals are to fully interpret the pattern, but the striking point is that their interests are very close to the principal person arranging the ceremony. They are either close kin who have ongoing interactions with the family of the

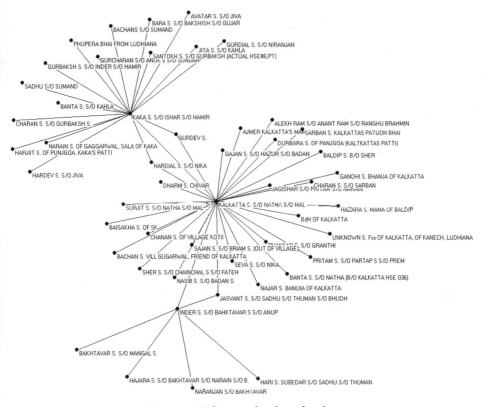

Figure 12. Meli networks, three families

girl, or they are individuals immediately involved in close cooperation as a matter of friendship or factional conflict.

With respect to the more general theoretical issues, this shows in yet another way how completely dissociated two different kinds of organizations can be. The Pajek analysis for participants in the party conflicts that were going on at the same time as the weddings shows this clearly: two entirely separate clusters, represented in figure 13.

In this case, each name was paired with my letter designating the party (A or B), so the letter becomes the central node. Note that no names recur in both party groups, although comparison with the *meli* networks will show that some of the names in the opposed parties appear in the same *meli*s, and names in different *meli*s appear in the same parties. Why? Again, it is because *meli*s and parties are different, not just in the way that the parties differ from each other or the *meli*s differ from each other but in kind. And it is because they are different in kind that parties cannot be thought of as composed of *meli*s by the villagers, nor can they be held to be composed of *meli*s objectively.

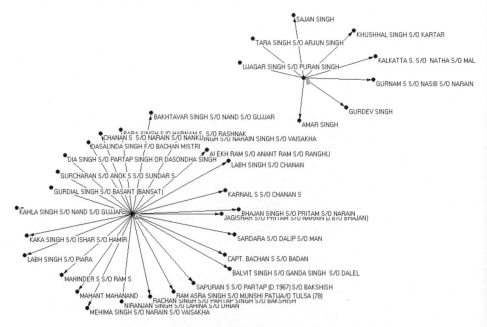

Figure 13. Pajek party network

We can also represent the network of who supports whom in specific conflicts, such as legal cases in which the supporters of each litigant are matters of record. There were about six cases I knew of during the time of my fieldwork that were party matters. The major conflicts in Sidhpur Kalan at the time for my first field study, for which I could get the identities of the participants, are represented in figure 14.

As with Kinship Algebra Expert System representation of kinship terms, I again stress that the diagrams are not my representation at some interpretive remove from the data. They are the data. The input is again two columns of names. In this case, they are the names of those involved in five of the six confrontations that occurred during the course of my fieldwork. (My information on the sixth case was only about those on one side.) Each pair consists of the name of one of the opposed litigants and one of their supporters.

The right-hand group corresponds to party A in figure 13, the left-hand group to party B. This is a one-mode network, meaning that it relates only one kind of object to other such objects. It is also a network of directed arcs, meaning that the relationships are unidirectional. The relationship in this case is "support in a conflict." Each node at which the arrows converge represents the person supported in one or more cases. The supporters are the nodes at which the arrows originate. The question is whether the patterns of alliances actually do converge in the way the factional model implies. The answer is that they do.

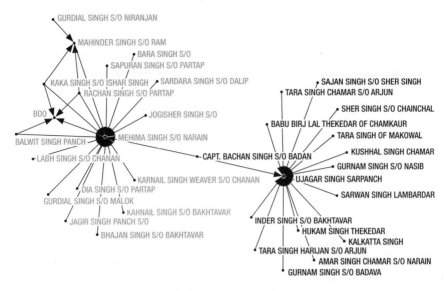

GURDIAL SINGH S/O NIRANJAN

MAHINDER SINGH S/O RAM
BARA SINGH S/O
SAPURAN SINGH S/O PARTAP
KAKA SINGH S/O ISHAR SINGH SARDARA SINGH S/O DALIP
RACHAN SINGH S/O PARTAP
BDO
JOGISHER SINGH S/O
BALWIT SINGH PANCH MEHIMA SINGH S/O NARAIN
LABH SINGH S/O CHANAN
KARNAIL SINGH WEAVER S/O CHANAN
DIA SINGH S/O PARTAP
GURDIAL SINGH S/O MALOK
KARNAIL SINGH S/O BAKHTAVAR
JAGIR SINGH PANCH S/O
BHAJAN SINGH S/O BAKHTAVAR

SAJAN SINGH S/O SHER SINGH
TARA SINGH CHAMAR S/O ARJUN
SHER SINGH S/O CHAINCHAL
BABU BIRJ LAL THEKEDAR OF CHAMKAUR
TARA SINGH OF MAKOWAL
KUSHHAL SINGH CHAMAR
CAPT. BACHAN SINGH S/O BADAN
GURNAM SINGH S/O NASIB
UJAGAR SINGH SARPANCH
SARWAN SINGH LAMBARDAR
INDER SINGH S/O BAKHTAVAR
HUKAM SINGH THEKEDAR
KALKATTA SINGH
TARA SINGH HARIJAN S/O ARJUN
AMAR SINGH CHAMAR S/O NARAIN
GURNAM SINGH S/O BADAVA

Figure 14. Village party network by cases

The two major nodes involve three main litigations. Two of these concerned land consolidation. This is a process in which the village lands are aggregated together and then redistributed in larger units to make for more efficient farm operations. The A group, led by Ujagar Singh Sarpanch, supported the redistribution plan, which included giving some land to Harijans. The B group, led by Mehima Singh, opposed it. Those in this group generally had better land nearer the village center. The third case revolved around the block development officer (BDO). This was a charge of sexual harassment (in our terms) brought by Ujagar Singh Sarpanch and several members of the A group. There are also two minor nodes associated with the B group at the far left. These involved other cases against members of the B group. The one centering on Mahinder Singh was a case brought by Inder Singh. Mahinder was supported, as the chart shows, by Kaka Singh, Dial Singh, and Rachan Singh. I do not know definitely who supported Inder Singh, so there is no separate node for him in the A network, although I suspect that he was supported by Kalkatta Singh and Sher Singh, son of Chainchal. The other case, represented by the node labeled BDO, represents those in party B who supported the BDO against the charges brought by Ujagar Singh and other members of the A party.

As the graph makes clear, the two party memberships are separate across the several different conflicts except for one person. Only Captain Bachan Singh supported people in both parties. Specifically, he supported the group led by Mehima Singh in one of the consolidation hearings in arguing against the specific redistribution of land that was proposed. But he supported the group led by Ujagar Singh Sarpanch in another consolidation hearing in which he favored the idea of giving surplus land to Harijans (which others in group B opposed). This, however, is not an exception to the general party model so much as an indication of some of its nuances.

A *sarpanch* is the elected head of the village *panchayat* (council). A member of the *panchayat* is called a *panch*. The *sarpanch* and *panches* have legal standing as official witnesses, and their expenses in attending court are paid by the state. Expenses for ordinary people are not. Mehima Singh was a *panch*. All members of the *panchayat* were active in legal cases; it is a major reason for seeking office. Ujagar Singh was a Harijan by caste and a committed political activist supporting the Communist Party of India. Harijans generally work as agricultural laborers and are poor. The land to be allocated to them would only have been enough for a garden plot. Captain Bachan Singh was neither communist nor procommunist but agreed with Ujagar Singh that they deserved it and considered this a matter of general ethics rather than party. The reason was that party matters are matters of defending one's personal interests. Other villagers did not necessarily accept this view of this issue, but when I probed for reactions to the notion that Bachan Singh's position therefore falsified the definition of party that I had been given, it was clear that if I had insisted on such a conclusion I would have been regarded as foolish.

Everyone recognizes the model as a model to be filled out in the process of constructing social relations. It is neither a simple description to be verified or rejected nor an absolute cultural norm to be obeyed. Everybody knows that all supporters of a party do not automatically join all the conflicts of everyone else in the same group. It would hardly make sense to try. Different individuals come together in different conflicts, and in the perspective of the general party these individual conflicts are then conceptually amalgamated to produce an inferential sense of a total pattern. The pattern of figure 12 is thus recognized as a composite of the alignments of the conflicts represented by figure 13, and others, that were going on at the time. It was an inferred pattern in the nature of the case, inferred both by me and by those I talked to about them (secretly, of course). Thus while *meli* alignments are matters of record, party alignments are ongoing guesses, but both types of instantiation are absolutely consistent with the cultural idea systems they instantiate.

Although White and his colleagues have not framed their analyses up to now in terms of cultural idea systems and their instantiations but rather the more usual language of cultural rules and the ongoing relations that correspond to them, the sense is generally the same. Network analysis as they represent it does not mix up observable social relations with cultural or social norms or rules, as earlier anthropological analyses consistently did. It rather provides a way to independently describe the logic of the rules and the logic of the relations in order to compare them. White has mobilized the mathematical techniques of graph theory to generate the networks that specific rules imply and, conversely, has used the same concepts to analyze actual networks to expose the rules or principles they embody. This provides a precise but in principle absolutely general way to describe and compare linkages formed on the basis of the organizational charters, leading to what they call the emergent groups as contrasted with the ethnographically named groups. White's emergent groups usually correspond to what I would describe as organizations, although they may also be larger-scale systems composed of sets of organizations working together without necessarily being aware of each other. White's analytic scheme also includes definite, formal ways to measure and characterize organizational cohesion.

White has described marriage relations in certain kinds of kinship systems (cf. White 1999), trade relationships in the world economy (Smith and White 1992), the emergence of school attachment out of cohesive subgroups in high school friendship networks (Moody and White 2003), and other types of relations. In addition, he has formulated definite ways to express the expectations for such patterns implicit in the stated organizational rules and compare them with the patterns in the networks (see White 1999). This generates the possibility of finding the often dynamic relationships between the networks and the stated organizational charters over time. And finally, multiple network analyses in a single community can be treated as overlays, which can let us see how the organizational consequences of such organizational rules interact, relating, for example, marriage networks to economic networks. For a demonstration of the way that a variety of these ideas and techniques can come together in a single ethnographic analysis, see White and Johansen's *Network Analysis and Ethnographic Problems: Process Models of a Turkish Nomad Clan* (2004).

While there are many kinds of social relationships that are not defined so as to be durable and definite enough to be thought of as forming networks, for those that are so defined this is another substantial advance.

Conclusion

Within productive organizations, sustainability requires dividing the product fairly. Of course cultural ideas of fairness can vary, but at a minimum in order for an organization to be sustainable it must assure that no one comes out worse off because of their contribution.

When many groups engage in similar productive activities, these similarities necessarily place them in competition for whatever scarce resources they all need. Competition can be dangerous. To avoid or control the dangers, such groups need to form mutual agreements. At the same time, the logic of communication requires that for any but a fairly small number of such groups, bilateral negotiations will not be a practical way to bring such agreements about. There must be public expressions of a general consensus, generally attained by setting up a second type of body that is regulatory or adjudicative. This too must have an organization, but for regulatory organizations, effective participation is obtained by assuring that the regulation is efficacious and, generally, that the regulators are subject to the consequences of their actions. If the regulators can create common benefits in which they share, the benefits can easily be so great that the question of whether one person's effort is more or less highly rewarded by any sort of direct compensation is trivial. Such regulatory bodies may also play a role in supporting the process of standardizing organizational ideas, but in a society of any scale they cannot dominate it.

Finally, what holds within organizations also holds between them. Organizations too form mutual adjustments of behavior, and these also hold together as long as they yield common benefits that they share. Such relationships can be represented as networks. Network models are particularly apt where the entities that serve as the nodes have no accepted organizational charter and no person or body who represents them as a recognized entity and where the effects on the individual units arise more as emergent properties than in response to an accepted agreement or plan.

CHAPTER 7

Groups and Institutions

Now we have the pieces needed to show where the perplexing sense of an institution comes from. First, attend more closely to the perplexity. When we try to explain how an institution is organized, exactly what does it feel like? There are many kinds of perplexity. What kind is this? The first observation is that we have encountered it before. The mind seems to seize up; we know we cannot answer it without being able to know why. It is like trying to answer a question such as "What is the sound of one hand clapping?" or "How do you square a circle?" The reason for the reaction, if we can bring it to the surface, is that the question contains a self-contradiction. Clapping is what two hands do, so the question actually amounts to "What is the sound of one hand making the noise of two hands coming together?" It is unanswerable because to answer it we would have to say two opposed things at once. Similarly, we know by definition that a circle has no straight edges, so we know that it cannot be squared. So it is for institutions. In this case if we can think it to the surface, what we know habitually is exactly what positivistic theorists did not want to recognize: that things such as the economy, the family, the legal system, or the legal profession contain multiple organizations that are mutually contradictory and incompatible. So asking "What is the organization of an institution?" is asking "What is the organization of a thing with many separate and incompatible organizations?" And this too is a self-contradiction.

But of course this only raises a further question: How do we know this? The answer is that while the idea of institution may not be part of everyone's folk vocabulary for dealing with social organizations, the idea of a group as I have defined it certainly is. This is the same as what we mean when we speak of a family group, a professional group, or a church group. This is all it takes. The idea of an institution as it has been formalized in social theory is nothing other than a reified and generalized version of this indigenous idea of a group. Since this occurs in all human communities, all of us know habitually that groups in this sense may have multiple organizations, but they cannot be multiple organizations. A group can have multiple organizations, but an organization must itself be singular. If it is not singular it is not an organization because it is not organized. So the important empirical question is not how we get our idea of an institution but how we get this idea of a group with multiple organizations.

Generating Underlying Groups

Promulgating organizational charters necessarily involves promulgating an idea of a group that is so organized. But if this is a universal process, why is it not common knowledge? Evidently, two things obscure it. The first is that most such very fundamental processes are ingrained at the level where we find things such as linguistic grammar. We think it without thinking about it. The second is that we regularly encounter many presentations of social charters that do not involve creating organizations, and these are often more conspicuous than the presentations that do create them. This is, for example, the difference between a constitutional convention, wedding, funeral, contract signing, recruitment ceremony, trial, or graduation in a film or play and a real wedding, trial, graduation, and so on. Which do we encounter more frequently?

There is a difference between a presentation of a social charter that is authoritative and creates an organization and a presentation that is not authoritative and does not create one. The difference exists even though the ideas are the same and even though nonauthoritative representations act as repositories of information for the authoritative representations. The difference is precisely what Goffman (1959) misses in his dramaturgical analysis of the presentation of self by treating the process as though it were only acting. It is also what is missed by the type of social constructionist analyses that Hacking (1999) criticizes and that Clifford and Marcus (1986) represent when they leap from recognizing the fact of social construction to the conclusion that nothing is actually real or that everything boils down to the assertion of competing subjective realities. Fiction exists, but so does nonfiction.

The difference is not anything about the text of the document or the content of the action. The real and the unreal can involve precisely identical actions, documents, and words. It is a difference in the purpose of the participants and in the associated sanctions. In the real thing, the parties are understood to be making a commitment and intend to hold each other to it. Otherwise, they are understood not to be making one. Obviously when someone makes a commitment, it is important to note just who that someone is. For authoritative ceremonies and other types of charters, designating the specific individuals taking the roles that are described or enacted is a necessary part of the instantiating process. Thus it is only the authoritative—the actual—application of charters in creating organizations that promulgates the idea of a group, but in these instantiations the idea of the group is absolutely essential. It is precisely what makes the difference between a real charter and a replica of a charter.

Once we see how projecting an organizational charter necessarily designates a group, we can see how the same process can generate the further idea that such a group may have additional organizations. The process is built up in a very specific way. To describe it, for simplicity it is best to focus only on the process of group creation in which the charters are expressed through ceremonies as opposed to written documents or other symbolic forms. Ceremonies make the process particularly clear.

Any one ceremony or other mnemonic has to be limited to just one set of organizational ideas. The reasons are the same as the reasons that a film or play is limited to only one plot and go to the fundamental nature of thought. As Kant recognized, thought requires consistent distinctions; it requires coherence. Something cannot be a mnemonic if it lacks this quality. A marriage ceremony has to convey just one idea of what a marriage is, not several and not a marriage plus something else. A graduation ought to convey just one idea of what graduation is, not several and not a graduation and something else. To participate in something, people have to be able to know what it is.

This being so, if you wanted to design a ceremony that created multiple organizations for the same group, how would you do it? It may seem logically impossible, but the answer is widely documented ethnographically, although the significance of this ethnographic record has not been recognized theoretically. The key is to realize that such terms as "wedding," "funeral," and "graduation" do not designate just one kind of ceremonial performance but two. They designate both one ceremony of a very specific type that occurs in one specific kind of setting and also a cluster of ceremonies that are very different from one another and occur in many settings. On the one hand, a Western wedding is what happens in a church, synagogue, or wedding chapel. Ask a culturally knowledgeable person to describe one without further qualification, and this is what you will get. Attend plays or films, and this is usually what you will see. But on the other hand, weddings also involve showers and receptions and other things that are very different and occur in other quite different places. Ask a person who is having one, and all of this is what they will be concerned with. Each of these individual ceremonies presents an organizational charter and constitutes an organization, just one with one membership. But the cluster and the set of people who move between them constitute the sense of the group that lies behind the organizations. In doing this they also, inescapably, lay the foundation for the perplexing sense of institution that social theorists have been so unwilling to give up but so unable to explain.

The main symbolic device that delivers the message that there is an underlying group is a specific kind of segmentation. Each ceremony in the cluster occurs in a clearly demarcated ceremonial space and time but is separated from the others by blocks of conventionally ordinary space and time. The different ceremonies are marked by conspicuous scene and costume changes that the ordinary space and time is used to create or, as in the ceremonies Turner (1969) described for the Ndembu by periods of conspicuous nakedness, waiting, and preparation, by periods of being betwixt and between statuses rather than in any status.

The most basic logical implication of these betwixt-and-between periods can only be that the segment following the break—whatever it is—is different. The ceremony before the break was not interrupted and later resumed; it was ended. What came next was something else. This makes it absolutely clear that the ceremonial segments are clustered but not merged. Separate charters are thus separately symbolized, but at the same time they are juxtaposed in such a way as to emphasize that while they are not the same organizational ideas they do apply to the same set of people. Hence, the deepest message of the whole complex is precisely that organizations are one thing, the group is another, and this group has multiple organizations. The sense that all these organizations somehow fit or come together, despite or beyond their differences, is what is reified into the sense of institution. The reason it is perplexing is that we really know habitually that they do not fit together conceptually. If they did, it would not have been necessary to represent them separately. They only utilize the same people.

To make this absolutely clear and concrete, I will describe how it is done in detail for two institutions commonly placed at opposite ends of an organizational continuum from traditional to modern and face-to-face or local versus higher or translocal: households and the legal profession. For households, the principal constitutive ceremony is the wedding. The ceremonies are from India and America. For law in general the definitive organizational ceremonies are court cases, and for the law as institution the cases of particular relevance are those that can be brought when a lawyer's various organizational roles, responsibilities, and opportunities come into conflict with one another.

The analysis of weddings is my own. The legal analysis is from the American Bar Association's *ABA Model Rules of Professional Conduct* (1983).

Households

My main experience in India is with weddings associated with the Sikh religion, mainly in rural villages and conducted in Punjabi. This is what I will mainly describe, but Hindu and Muslim weddings have the same general segments and draw their organizational ideas from the same social idea systems: kinship, party, management, and economics.

An Indian marriage, like a standard Euro-American marriage, requires one ceremony that is usually described as indispensable and many others described as inessential but important. The other ceremonies begin many months before the main ceremony. They occur in the villages of both the bride and the groom and mark all the steps in the creation of the marriage, which is considered to be a gradual process that develops over time rather than a bond created more or less instantaneously with a single crucial action. There are three main blocks: engagement, the central ceremony, and the transfer of the bride to her husband's village. Each is performed in such a way as to appear to be highly scripted. Each has clearly marked beginnings and ends, with distinct spaces of normal time and action in between. And each of these major segments also consists of several smaller segments in turn that are similarly marked by ceremonial actions performed as though they were highly scripted and are separated by segments of normal time in which people act as though what they were doing was not scripted.

Engagement occurs in the village of the bride. Like all the ceremonies, this is conducted under the guidance of a formal representative of each family. For upper-caste families, this will be a man of Barber caste who specializes in this type of work. The groom's family comes to the house of the bride's family, and with their Barbers as mediators they formally agree that their respective son and daughter (or sometimes two sons and two daughters) should marry. The prospective bride and groom do not meet, however. The prospective groom is present and the prospective bride may see him, but he cannot see her. She may then reject the match. He has no such option. The families set a date for marriage, gifts are given to the groom's family, and they return to their own village. In the interval between this and the central ceremony more gifts will be exchanged as tokens of respect, again involving the Barbers.

When I describe these ceremonies as seemingly highly scripted, I mean that they are enacted as if there were a detailed script that they were following. In observable fact, however, while everyone has a general sense of what should happen, the details are whatever is provided by the Barbers as they go along. Actions under their direction are presumed to be scripted and are therefore ceremonial. Actions not under their directions are presumed not to be scripted and are therefore nonceremonial.

The central ceremonies again occur in the village of the bride and are again part of a series of seemingly highly scripted actions in ceremonial time separated by nonscripted segments of ordinary time. In fact, the ordinary behavior is often what might be described as counterscripted. People act in ways consciously contrary to the modes of action in the scripts. In the scripts, for example, the men of the two groups act as though they do not know each other; they respect each other but are wary of each other. In actuality, however, many of them do know each other, and in the ordinary time of the breaks they visit and socialize in an often exaggeratedly friendly way. It would be considered a possible affront if someone in one group knew someone in the other and did not visit in this way unless they were clearly otherwise occupied. At these times the men engage in a substantial amount of drinking, traditionally of country liquor (homemade rum). In the hot season just before the rains—the agricultural slack season when most weddings are scheduled—this often can have devastating effects on the principal actors, particularly the groom. This would not normally be commendable behavior, but at weddings it is appropriate as a sign of happiness.

In Sikh weddings the indispensable ceremony is called *anand* (joy) and occurs during what would be a normal morning religious service, beginning with the usual initial prayer, the "Asa di War" (Song of Hope). In order to be present this early in the day, the custom is for the groom's party to arrive the previous evening. The ceremony of welcome will be described below. This arrival ceremony is followed by a break and then a formal dinner and another break. The wedding morning, before *anand,* begins with a formal tea and then another break.

The ceremony of *anand* occurs in a place that has been set up as a *gurdwara,* the normal Sikh place of worship. This may be in the bride's family's house, an actual *gurdwara* if there is one, or a public area arranged with tenting. It makes no difference. What matters is the presence of the Guru Granth Sahib, the principal Sikh compendium of liturgical poetry. The presence of the Guru Granth Sahib together with five (or more) Sikhs is what makes a place a *gurdwara,* and *gurdwara*s normally have morning and evening readings of the Guru Granth Sahib.

The script of the ceremony symbolically includes kinship ideas that are consistent with the ideas represented by a *gurdwara* and symbolically excludes those that are not. For example, Sikhism argues forthrightly for universal social equality as well as universal religious tolerance. God is in everyone, and all religions are only different ways to understand this. Accordingly, what is said and done in the ceremony includes representations of family unity and individual equality but excludes representations of caste and other invidious differences. In this ceremony as in all others, the Barbers serve as the general ceremonial representatives of the bride's and groom's families. But here they are never addressed or referred to as "Barber," which is a caste name. They are described and referred to as "Raja" (literally, king). Describing him by caste would be inconsistent with the religious ideas. Describing him by a noncaste term indicating respect is consistent. In the ceremonies that do not have a religious character he is described as "Barber." Sikh teachings also reject gender discrimination, emphasizing only the individual's relation to God, and accordingly the audience consists of both men and women. The seating usually has the men of the groom's group on one side of the room, the men of the bride's group on the other, and the women of both groups in the middle. This reflects the way that women, as sisters and wives, form links between households.

In principle, all Sikh religious ceremonies are instances of coming together for instruction. Morning is appropriate as a time of beginning, and also the first half of the day is considered auspicious. The term "Sikh" is from the verb *sikhnaa* (to learn or study). Although receiving instruction is considered to be fundamentally an individual activity, it is often taken in groups, and there is no inconsistency with recognizing the presence of a family. In religious terms, the ceremony enacts the idea that the bride and groom are coming for the Guru Granth Sahib's instruction and blessing at the start of their common undertaking. The marriage ceremony follows the usual order for this morning service.

After the morning ceremony has begun in the usual way and most people are seated, the groom comes in with his kin. He sits down before the reader and the Guru Granth Sahib, and his kin leave him to take their place with the rest of the assembly. In his right hand he holds a piece of cloth by one end. The girl's relatives then guide her in, seat her on his left side, and place the other end of the cloth in her right hand. (Right is auspicious.) After blessing the couple, they too take seats in the audience except for an elder sister who sits just behind the bride and to her left, as shown in figure 15.

From the beginning of the ceremony, the bride cannot see where she is going. She is wearing a wedding outfit with a large shawl, all of red cloth trimmed with gold. Red is a joyful color and is commonly associated in ceremonies with life and self-sacrifice. Gold symbolizes itself, indicative of good fortune. Over this, however, for this ceremonial segment only, the bride also wears a white mantel, usually a sheet. This completely covers her other garments and hangs down in front of her face. White is stereotypically worn by religious devotees and suggests austerity, passivity, and purity.

Figure 15. Bride and groom before the Guru Granth Sahib

The defining act that unites the couple occurs after they have thus sat and received blessings and advice from the person reading the Guru Granth Sahib and conducting the service. It is the circumambulation of the Guru Granth Sahib.[1] This is done four times as four customary verses are read. Each time the couple rises. The groom holds one end of the cloth and the bride the other as he leads her around the Guru Granth Sahib and the reader. As she walks behind him, she is held and supported by her elder sister. Her male relatives stand in a circle around them all and support and guide both the bride and the sister, as illustrated in figure 16. When they return to their starting point, the couple again is seated. The religiously enacted definition of the marriage relation is thus that the bride and groom are setting out through life together in the context of their relations to both their families, and they expect to form a fruitful and prosperous bond of mutual support between these families in their respective villages. They will seek their fortune in life together. She follows his lead but continues to be supported by her own family.

After completing the four circumambulations and ending the ceremony, the couple remains seated and is again blessed by those present, usually by circling money over their heads and then pinning it in garlands around them or putting it in their laps. Finally, the groom and bride are separately led away. This is followed by a substantial interval of normal time. Then there is a formal lunch for the men of both groups in which the groom's group is served first and more formally. Traditionally, order of service indicates order of rank. Women eat separately from the men, and both groups of women mix together much more casually.

In the managerial context, the household is defined in terms of property, its owners, and their dependents. Since only men have rights in the household's ancestral property, the managerial organization is defined as centering on a group of male coparceners and associated women, which is why the *parbaNDhak* is generally a senior male. Landowning households have occupational and social relations with households with other types of property; these are what are described in the ethnological literature as caste relations. These ideas are enacted and applied in a series of ceremonies for men that involve gifts given by the father of the bride to the various members of the groom's party and a parallel set of women's ceremonies that represent the woman's life cycle. The groom's role in the *anand* ceremony definitely does not suggest the idea of a *parbaNDhak*. In kinship terms the bride and groom may be starting a family, but in managerial terms the groom is a member of a family, and the bride is going to leave her family and join his.

The ceremonial gift giving by the father of the bride to the men of the groom's party is called *kaTH*. It occurs after the break following the lunch that follows *anand* and after three smaller ceremonies also involving gifts. The first of these latter is that the father of the bride or other person serving as the male head of the group sends gifts to the band, which has accompanied the groom's group.

Figure 16. Circumambulating the Guru Granth Sahib

These men are understood to be of low caste, usually Sweeper. The gifts may be sent through the Barber, or the band may come to collect them.

Then the father of the groom formally displays the gifts he is giving to the bride. This generally includes henna and other things for personal adornment, emphasizing that the relation is personal, appreciative, and attentive. The implication is that he is taking responsibility for her as he would for his own daughter.

Then the family of the bride displays all the gifts they have given her that she will take with her to her new home (figure 17). This is what is usually called a dowry. They are quite substantial and consist of things for the use of the house such as bedding, clothing, furniture, and a sewing machine. Although in Punjab no one would ever say how they decided how much to spend, because, as it is commonly said, "you cannot put a price on a daughter," in general it was about what her share would have been had she been a son.

For *kaTH*, an area is cleared for the men of the two groups to sit near the display of gifts for the bride. When all is ready, the men of the groom's group are sent for. They arrive and inspect the gifts given to the bride. Their manner, as usual, bespeaks caution and concern more than approval. Then they sit. The groom is in the center, his group behind him and the bride's group facing them. The father of the bride takes some cooked rice and turmeric from a tray that has been prepared, crushes them together in his fingers, and solemnly puts a mark (*tilak*) on the groom's forehead. From the same tray the father of the bride next places a sweet in the groom's mouth. Next, from a different tray, he offers a large

Figure 17. Display of the gifts to the bride

and auspicious sum of money (such as 101 rupees, 501 rupees, and so on)[2] to the father of the groom. The groom's father can accept this but does not. Instead, he takes one rupee and refuses the rest. The meaning is that he acknowledges the expression of respect.

Next, through the Barber acting as intermediary, the bride's father distributes one rupee each to all of the close relatives of the groom's group as their names and relationships are read out from a formal list that the two Barbers have prepared in advance. The basic idea is that the father of the bride is showing that his daughter is cherished and valued and that he is making a free gift of her to the groom and his family, taking absolutely nothing in exchange. But of course there must be reciprocity, and the logic of the gifts being all from the bride's family to the groom's family is that what the groom and his family owe in exchange will have to be given to the girl herself. She is to be cherished and respected by them just as she is by the family that is giving her up. The ceremony very clearly marks who the members of this receiving group are and what their relations are to each other, to the bride and groom, and to the giving group. The ceremony ends, and the groom's group again departs. This is followed by another interval of ordinary time that is used for visiting and preparations for the next major ceremonial segment.

Each major segment and each meal begins and ends with a formal procession to and from the place where it takes place. The processions are also ceremonies and instantiate ideas of management that portray the household as a unit in the village division of labor. The participants are always segregated by gender and marked by caste. The men of the groom's party come and go as one cohort and meet with the men of the bride's party. The women of the groom's party come and go separately from the men and meet with the women of the bride's party. The leading figures are the bride's and groom's fathers and mothers, respectively, and not the bride and groom themselves. The latter are prominent but passive. Within each group, nuances of clothing mark those in the father's or mother's family and caste, and clothing and more overt symbols mark those in other castes.

Three of the women's ceremonies are particularly prominent. The first is the arrival of the bride's mother's mother (the bride's *nana,* or grandmother) with the women of her family. They enter the village with each of the family's servants carrying an indication of their service: the sweeper a broom, the water carrier a pot of water, and the like (figure 18). These are the women of the household and village where the bride's mother was born and grew up.

The second ceremony is the arrival of the women of the groom's household, which is organized the same way. Like the centrality of the women's group in the seating for *anand,* these processions enact the way that the rule of village exogamy always links each family in a village to multiple families in others. But in this case each woman is also represented in terms of her position in the village occupational hierarchy.

Figure 18. Arrival of bride's *nana*

The third ceremony is the departure of the bride to the house of her husband, which is of course also the house of her husband's mother. This is the final women's procession. They start at the bride's house and go to the waiting vehicle, where the men of the bride's group are already assembled. The bride, wailing loudly and stumbling along in what usually appears to be genuine distress, is accompanied by, and usually physically supported by, her mother and elder sister. They are followed by her female relatives and her mother's female family servants. The mother is saying the equivalent of "there there, now now," and the trailing female relatives and servants are generally singing earthy folk songs.

The first time I heard the wailing it was thoroughly convincing; I had a moment of considerable alarm thinking that my instrumental and contractual understanding of the ceremony might be wrong and the more common irrationalist reading might be right. I expressed this concern for the bride to a villager standing beside me. His response, with a smile, was that she must wail this way. If she appeared to be happy to leave her home, it would suggest that there was something wrong in her relations with her family.

When they reach the vehicle in which the bride will depart, the bride enters. She is accompanied by the wife of the Barber as a chaperone. Then the entire group of the bride's relatives and servants, male and female, pushes the vehicle off. This signifies that they agree with her leaving and are letting her go willingly.

The organizational implications of the women's ceremonies are plain: the bride and the mother represent the start and the culmination of a married woman's career in managerial terms. The entourage represents the occupational system in which the bride will take her place, just as her mother represents what the bride in her turn will eventually become if all goes well. The journey from the house to the vehicle and thence to the husband's village represents the start of the journey that will move her from the position of a child of one house to the mistress of the other, where she will in turn play the part of the mother of young children, the mother of a girl leaving as a bride, and finally the mother-in-law of a girl coming in as one.

The next ceremony of the sequence occurs in the groom's village that night. It is a long series of something between teasing and party games in which the bride and groom meet in the company of friends and relations but do not get to meet each other alone. After this, the next day, the bride returns to her own village with the Barber's wife.

In the final ceremony, the groom comes alone to take the bride back to his village. She may go with him or stay at her option. The time interval between her return to her village and this visit to fetch her back to the groom's village is not fixed and mainly depends on the wishes of the bride and groom. If she refuses to go, her gifts must also come back. The gifts will also have to be returned if the marriage breaks up at a later date; they are her property, not the property of the groom's household. This journey of the bride with her groom to his family house, finally, represents them as a single pair of individuals, agreeing on their own and freely to form a couple.

Factional ideas too are ceremonially instantiated but covertly. Since factionalism is considered to underlie and undermine village solidarity, the logical place to symbolize it is in ceremonies that represent such solidarity. This is done particularly clearly in the very first ceremony of the entire sequence, the entry of the groom's party into the village of the bride. The name of the ceremony in Punjabi is *milni* (meeting).

Overtly, the nonceremonial organizations called upon for marriage ceremonies are the *meli* of the father of the bride and father of the groom. As already has been noted, the *meli* are kin and others who support the family in their activities. The term comes from the verb *melna*, which means both "to unite" and "to concur." In principle, one's *meli* attends all of one's family ceremonies, not just weddings. Those who attend a marriage ceremony make up the *brāt*, which is the wedding party in general, and in this particular ceremony of greeting the assembly of the men of the *brāt* is called the *panchayat*, implying judicial or judgmental responsibility.

To begin, the girl's *brāt* stands together outside the village gate or in front of her house with her father in a leading position, facing the direction from which the groom's party will arrive. The groom's *brāt* approaches formally. Although they may have arrived by bus or farm wagon and unpacked earlier, they will assemble and arrange themselves for the approach. Like a prince leading an army, the groom dresses regally and martially. He carries a sword and wears marking ornaments, such as a gold necklace. If the family can afford it he will ride a horse, always a mare. The younger brother of the groom is similarly dressed but without the sword or horse. He is called the *sir-walla* (head-person). It is said that if the groom is killed, the *sir-walla* will take his place.

As shown in figure 19, the groom is in the center wearing a necklace and carrying a cloth and sword. The *sir-walla* is to his far right, wearing the necklace. The father or whoever else is serving as the male household head is the commander of the *brāt*. He stands out prominently but is not dressed martially. In this case he is seven places to the groom's left, in the front row with the extra cloth on his right shoulder. The lower-caste associates of the family are usually represented by a band that walks ahead playing music. Among the higher castes, there will also usually be one or two Brahmins, distinguishable by dress and tonsure.[3] The imagery is therefore that of the village in its managerial aspect but this time with a warlike overlay.

Figure 19. Arrival of the groom's *brāt*

The groom's *brāt* comes forward to form a line directly in front of the bride's group, face-to-face a few meters apart. Their demeanor is stern, proud, and distant. Then the two fathers step out and embrace, each with their arms fully around the other. This turns into a wrestling contest in which each appears to try to lift the other from the ground. The father of the groom wins, and his *brāt* is then welcomed in.

The folk model associated with the ceremony is that the two *brāt*s are like two war parties. The groom's *brāt* is coming to capture the bride; the bride's *brāt* is defending her. Such ceremonies, and this explanation, were what J. F. McLennan (1865) interpreted as survivals of the very first form of human marriage, marriage by capture. In fact, the explanation is much less a cultural fossil than a quite functional legal myth. It is a real threat of possible future action dressed for the occasion as survival of an ancient practice in order to be enacted without rancor or implied accusation. The bride's *brāt* is always described explicitly as the men of her father's village. Secretly, however, it is recognized that they are the men of his village who are also of his faction. In this secret context, they are understood to be not only the father's public and symbolic supporters but also his actual supporters. The implication is that if there is a dispute about the terms of the marriage, each father will be supported in actuality by those who have attended the ceremony. If there is a court dispute, they will act as witnesses on his behalf. If there is a physical confrontation, they will back him up with physical force. If the marriage breaks up and the bride returns home, the bride's group will assist her father in recovering her property from the groom's house. The men of the groom's father's group have the same relation to the groom's father. Villagers explain that *meli* is not the same as party, but they are related.

Although there are still other ceremonies that enact yet other distinct sets of relationships (Leaf 1974, 133–55), this should suffice to demonstrate what is required. The ceremonies are separate in their times and staging because the organizations they portray are logically incompatible with one another and cannot be combined. The ceremonial separations instantiate the logical separations. They therefore also instantiate the fundamental fact that the marriage group has multiple organizations.

Euro-American weddings have the same kind of segmentation for the same reasons. In American ceremonial complexes, gifts are given to the bride at a bridal shower before the marriage, and very different gifts are given to the couple at the reception. Why? At the marriage ceremony proper, no gifts are given at all. Why not?

The short answer is that gifts at the main ceremony would be inappropriate, and the gifts given at other times are appropriate to the ideas being instantiated in those other ceremonies. What makes the gifts appropriate or inappropriate is the definition of the bride, groom, and bridal couple in each of these ceremonies. The gifts are different because these ideas are different, and the gifts instantiate the ideas. The gifts at the bridal shower are to the bride alone and generally are things that a woman would have in a luxurious house. They are not things for joint use, and they are not utilitarian. Hence they define the woman as an individual with distinct material interests, and by and large this interest is portrayed as living well in a nice house with nice feminine things that reflect high social status. The bachelor's party, similarly, describes the groom in terms of the stereotypically self-indulgent desires of an individual male.

The gifts at the reception are also things that convey a concern with material comfort and high social status, but they are things for joint use. One does not give functional glassware but crystal, not ordinary china but special china, such as may be used when having guests. The underlying imagery in this case is that the husband and wife face the outside as a couple, not each other as individuals.

The religious ceremony, with no material gifts at all, by contrast defines the couple as formed by the free gift of the bride herself, by her father to the groom, wherein the couple promises to love one another and raise a family according to moral principles without regard to fate or fortune, sickness or health, so long as they both shall live. It would be in extraordinarily bad taste for either or both of them to add a clause such as "as long as I attain material comfort and high social status." In short, the ideas enacted in the different ceremonies define the marriage relation in three entirely different and conflicting ways.

In both communities, a world apart, each distinct type of separate ceremonial segment enacts a social charter for a distinct type of organization. Each such charter provides for a reciprocal logic in the relations it defines, a consistent and noncontradictory set of reciprocal relations. But the segments are separated by space and time for a reason. They cannot be spatially and temporally combined because they cannot be logically combined. Moreover, the movement of the wedding groups from segment to segment enacts the movement of individuals in household groups from organized situation to situation, and the idea that these different segments are nevertheless part of a marriage ceremony in a larger sense enacts or expresses the idea that the household group is a group in a larger sense. Finally, the fact that each ceremony declares itself to be fundamentally like all other such ceremonies, regardless of details, recognizes that the group that underlies its various organizations is fundamentally like the groups that underlie the organizations created in all other such ceremonies. Each and every marriage ceremony, in the encompassing sense, thus directly projects the idea of marriage or the family as an institution in the encompassing but intrinsically unexplainable sense that social theorists speak of it.

The Legal Profession

The same analysis applies to the legal profession. The profession, as such, is an institution. It is, as lawyers speak of it, something beyond all organizations that lawyers take part in and something that unifies them. Exactly what this something is, however, is considered very difficult to explain. People often feel that they could explain it if they concentrated on it hard enough, but in observable fact they cannot.

There are many kinds of legal organizations and many legal groups. Each group has at least one organization, one set of specifically legal or law-related social relations that its members recognize among themselves: the relations of a court, of a law office, and so on. Usually they have more than one organization. Courts are also usually government offices. Law offices are usually also private businesses. Law schools are parts of universities, and so on.

Each organization is a set of expectations among a definite set of people. These expectations are built up through transactions undertaken, in Pound's phrase, "in title of" (1943, 2ff.) the organizational charters they utilize, which thereby constitute them. Some of these transactions are highly stereotyped. Their significance is well defined and publicly recognized in ceremonies. Some are idealized in folk models. The legal system or legal profession as an institution, as that which is thought to lie behind all of these together, is in actuality what is projected by all of them together.

The most important and prototypic legal ceremonies are trials. All trials are interstitial ceremonies, but different trials involve slightly different sets of roles and different scripts according to the type of case it is: whether there will be jury or not, what the roles of the attorneys will be, what kinds of arguments are allowed, and what kinds of decisions are allowed. The different sets of trials articulate, apply, and in turn preserve specific bodies of law that are not just statute but statute as interpreted by courts themselves. What a judge applies is not the law as such, which lawyers call black-letter law, but the human experience that has been accumulated in applying different sections of it to disputes of different kinds. It is the balance of considerations found in past trials, classified by their respective types of cases. As Holmes (1923) stresses, the phrase "reasonable man" does not have the same meaning in criminal matters as in civil, and in civil law it is not the same thing in cases dealing with personal liability as in civil liability. Similarly, standards of proof vary in different areas, and so do the ideas of a legal remedy, of what the law is trying to accomplish.

But trials are not the only ceremonies that lawyers engage in, and the other ceremonies also provide charters for one organization or another: graduation from law school, hiring and being hired in law firms, signing business contracts, being enrolled in a bar, the ceremonies of professional societies, disbarment, inter alia. Each of these is associated with a specific kind of legal organization and conveys a definition of what that organization is.

Lawyers are subject to law. All the statutes that apply to other professionals, businesspeople, and employees also apply to lawyers. Moreover, since lawyers are litigious, the organizations they belong to are particularly well defined in law, and as the organizations are different so are the rights and duties that membership in them imposes. In the United States, the implications of these often conflicting organizational definitions and statutes for lawyers have been codified in ongoing editions of the *Model Rules of Professional Conduct* of the American Bar Association. The stated purpose of the *Model Rules* is to provide "comprehensive and consistent guidance for resolving the increasingly complex ethical problems in the practice of law" (American Bar Association 1983, xiii). It is generally recognized, however, that while this is called legal ethics, no overriding set of what might be regarded as purely ethical rules—rather than legal rules—is ever stated.

Relevant statutes deal with such matters as misappropriation, theft, fraud, misrepresentation, conflict of interest, contractual and civil liability, and contempt of court. These are not, however, the divisions of the *Model Rules*. Rather, the *Model Rules* are divided according to the various kinds of relationships that a lawyer enters into. The headings are (1) Client-Lawyer Relationship, (2) Counselor, (3) Advocate, (4) Transactions with Persons Other Than Clients, (5) Law Firms and Associates, (6) Public Service, (7) Information about Legal Services, and (8) Maintaining the Integrity of the Profession. Each of these sections actually invokes a different organizational charter. The first two concern lawyers' relationships to their client: the lawyer as a hired professional and the lawyers as an adviser, respectively. The third concerns the obligations to client and court as an officer of the court, so the organizational charter is that of a court. The fourth concerns lawyers in relation to other people besides their client outside the court; the imagery is that of a body of professionals dealing with the public. The fifth concerns lawyers as members of business firms in relation to other members or members of other firms. The sixth concerns lawyers as citizens under a general obligation to serve the public interest. The seventh has to do with the lawyer as a businessman in competition with other lawyers. The last concerns lawyers as members of legal bar associations and subject to disciplinary action by them. Each section presents a distinct folk model—a clear image of a lawyer set in a specific organizational context—and each of these folk models is supported by and elaborated in a technical and legal literature and backed by sanctions.

The different social charters frame very different contexts within which seemingly uniform legal ideas such as agreement, contract, misrepresentation, fraud, or theft can have very different meanings. To avoid liability, the lawyer needs to know what they are and how to balance them. Consider the section concerned with the lawyer's role as advocate, which begins with a section headed "Meritorious Claims and Contentions": "A lawyer shall not bring or defend a proceeding, or assert or controvert an issue therein, unless there is a basis for doing so that is not frivolous, which includes a good faith argument for an extension, modification, or reversal of existing law. A lawyer for the defendant in a criminal proceeding, or the respondent in a proceeding that could result in incarceration, may nevertheless so defend the proceeding as to require that every element of the case be established" (American Bar Association 1983, 20).

In this case, the conflict is between the lawyer's role as an advocate for his client's interest and his role as an officer of the court. Courts have an interest in expeditious proceedings. Clients do not always share this interest, so the lawyer has to strike a balance. Yet the two sets of demands are not only mutually inconsistent, they are actually incommensurable. The professional-client relationship is simply unlike the court-officer relationship, as different as the husband-wife relationship defined as joint ownership of a community property and the husband-wife relationship defined as a union of two souls without regard for worldly fortune. The common element is putative only; their attribution is to the same individuals, each of whom will be subject to ethical and legal evaluation as a physical individual on the basis of action in any one of these separate spheres. This is why the balance must be struck afresh by each lawyer in each case, why it becomes so important to get the advice of other lawyers in striking it, and why the idea of the legal profession as an institution is not merely a kind of cultural fiction. It is a construction, but it is a construction with teeth, or more to the point with organizations (such as the American Bar Association) that are regarded as representing it and can be very helpful in coping with conflicting organizational demands that being part of the profession involves one in.

Conclusion

Institutions such as the family and the legal profession are inherently unintelligible projections or imputations, and such highly structured and unavoidable imputations are a marvelous cultural tool for creating ordered relations. Lacking attributes, they cannot be differentiated from one another. Since they cannot be differentiated, they make the various differently defined problems of their members appear to come together. Yet because they are inherently uncognizable the members cannot say how. The logical result is that those who accept the feeling that the organizations come together must also accept the burden of making the feeling come true, as best they can, for themselves and in their circumstances. The sense that we live in ordered surroundings, when combined with the fact that such ordered surroundings are not objectively observable, imposes an essential creative task. It leads us to act as though the underlying order or encompassing order exists, and this process of acting as though is the process of creating the order whose existence we assert. When we do it together we can create a collective agreement backed by many layers of organized force. The idea organizes the sanctions, the sanctions support the idea, and the whole is as durable and irresistible as it is ungraspable.

The idea of a group that the idea of an institution is founded on and extends has the same kind of unifying power at the level of individual organizations. It projects the idea of a single set of individuals behind multiple separate organizations in a way that allows the organizations to be kept conceptually distinct yet also to be interrelated. The reason they can be interrelated is that there is such a set of individuals, and it is they who establish the relations by balancing the purposes, interests, and strategies of each organization in which they participate against the others in which they participate.

CHAPTER 8

Adaptation

Given what organizations are and how they form, we can build our analysis of their relation to adaptation.

The new cultural ecological studies have reaffirmed the need to recognize individual rationality as an adaptive mechanism. But what produces rationality? The answer lies in the relationship between multiple organizations and the formation of a sense of self, a self-identification. The argument extends Kant's analysis of the self as a noumenal projection described in chapter 2. First, in order to have individual rationality, one must have a concept of an individual self to locate it in. Rationality implies purpose, and purpose requires a purposive subject. No one can act on a purpose defined in an organizational charter without making it their personal purpose as well, thinking of the group as another kind of "other" and thinking of themselves in its place. Multiple organizations (which are also noumenal projections) plus the idea of the reciprocity of self-other provide both the conceptual tools that let us define such selves and the compulsion to use them. Second, once we form such an individualized self, multiple organizations constitute alternative ways that self can obtain or employ resources. They therefore define the possibility of transferring resources from one such organizational context to another. Third, when people can transfer resources from one context to another, multiple organizations provide both the incentive to do so optimally and the conceptual tools needed to frame the task. Moreover, they do so both at the level of each organized group and at the level of collections of such groups up to and including whole communities and systems of communities.

Forming Individual Rationality

Because of organizational multiplicity, individuals from Papua New Guinea to Paris and from the Upper Paleolithic to the present have been faced with the same basic and inescapable problem. How are they to respond to all the distinct kinds of demands of all of their separate relationships? There are two main logical possibilities. They can respond to each demand separately without regard to the others, or they can respond in combination. The former is probably not possible in fact, either psychologically or practically. But to respond to the demands in combination, one must have some basis for balancing them against one another, some idea of a common focus that they all come to. This is what is provided by the idea of a social self that has a moral or conceptual unity, in the way that one's physical body has physical unity. Organizational charters postulate a group. The idea of a group implies the idea of an individual.

Forming a Self

The idea of an underlying role-taking self is what Mead discussed as the relation between the self as "I" and the self as "me" in which he argued that "an 'I' is a presupposition but never a presentation of conscious experience" (1913, 374). What Mead is describing is what these many different ideas imply as their supposed locus. It is the unseen "I" to which we attribute a consciousness, just as it is the "I" that "is" or acts as a teacher, soldier, husband, citizen, or buyer from time to time and situation to situation.

The self in this sense has been widely recognized. It is of course the soul or mind of Western Judeo-Christian religious traditions and nominally secular philosophy. It is described as *Atman* in Vedanta, the necessarily featureless basis of what one sees but that cannot itself be seen. It is what classic Buddhist thought identifies as something we impute into the successive moments of our physical existence, and it is at least arguably the idea of the Tao as the underlying formless basis of contrasting qualities and attributes represented by the yang and yin in the type of Taoism associated with the Han synthesis. All of these formulations point to the same inherent featurelessness, which is precisely what lets it serve as the supposed basis of all the more conscious identities we see it as taking on or manifesting. It does not matter what sorts of "me" this self is supposed to manifest or enact. The subjective self is a socially constructed conceptual void into which all mutually incompatible or contradictory definitions of objective selves can appear to be absorbed.

The logic of the formation of the self is the same as the logic of the formation of groups and institutions except that it is projected inwardly rather than outwardly. We attribute a self inwardly to bring order to our inner life just as we attribute such large-scale entities as groups, institutions, and society outwardly to bring a sense of order to our contexts. We impute the self to our physical bodies as underlying and unifying its many identities in the same way that we attribute institutions to sets of related organizations and in response to the same cultural cues.

Selves, Bodies, and Incentives

Although I know of no system of thought from any culture in which this subjective social self is considered to be identical with one's physical body, I also know of none that considers them completely separate. One way or another, the subjective self is associated with one's physical self. This association is logically important because it allows us to assign to our cognitive self a property that cognitive selves do not inherently have but that physical selves do: fungibility.

Our physical body is fungible in the sense that we can physically move it from one context to another, and the abilities and powers it attains in one context can be deployed in the other even though the two contexts themselves are not comparable or commensurable. If I save time in my office, I can spend it at home. If I undergo surgery as a patient, I will carry the results as I teach. If I learn something as a student, I can employ it as a worker. If I am killed as a soldier, I will be equally dead as a student, husband, anthropologist, or teacher.

Many physical objects that we obtain in our different organizational capacities are fungible in the same way. In general, if any physical thing has a definition in more than one cultural idea system, it is fungible between those systems unless there are cultural rules prohibiting it. Food is commonly fungible. In societies that have economic conventions, money is fungible although never universally. Money that you receive from your employer in the form of salary, handed over in the right ceremonies and duly documented, is yours. You have earned it. Earning it entitles you to spend it in any legal way you wish. However, money that you have obtained in ways that are disallowed and without proper ceremonies is stolen, and you are not allowed to keep or use it. Many other objects are treated similarly: fungible in defined ways but also limited in defined ways.

Rationality and Optimization

The possibility of moving resources between organizational contexts automatically generates the problem of having to ask which activities produce the best overall outcome in terms of our purposes. Given all the things I want to do, what combination allows me to do the most? This is the problem of general optimization. It is the same for the person wanting to do the most possible for himself alone as for the person wanting to do the most possible for others.

But while each cultural idea system and its organizational instantiations provide ways to compare the alternative courses to the goals defined within it, nothing within any of the systems provides a way to compare choices across them. So the question this presents is whether there is or can be any algorithm outside the systems.

Bounded Rationality

Economists now make a distinction between bounded rationality and unbounded rationality. This began with Herbert Simon (1957) and now has a substantial body of proponents. John Conlisk (1996) provided an important review, and Gigerenzer and Selten (2001) provided a coordinated set of essays by various contributors attempting to bring these developments together in a coherent theory. Anthropologists have also entered the discussion. Linda Garro, for example, discusses Simon's formulation among others in a review of descriptive decision theories that she tests against the problem of describing indigenous systems of medical diagnosis in a Mexican village. As Garro sees it, Simon defines bounded rationality by applying a "simplified model of the situation" but fails to recognize that such models are "culturally grounded" (Garro 1998, 324). Proponents of bounded rationality have not been responsive to this type of criticism; they seem not to recognize what it means. Perhaps I can clarify.

In a 1986 article, Simon paid more attention than he had in 1957 to the idea of the frame around bounded rationality. He recognized that it "must be comprehensive enough to encompass goals, the definition of the situation, and computational resources" (Simon 1986, S210). Moreover, he recognized that these components had to be determined empirically.

Logically, this might seem to call for connecting the idea of such a frame to organizations as I have been describing them, but this is not what Simon argued for. The main theme of the article was simply a call for more empirical methods generally, contrasting the empiricism of cognitive psychology with the postulational methods of neoclassical theory as represented in large part by Gary Becker. As the argument developed, Simon associated the more empirical methods with what he called a process conception of rationality and the neoclassical methods with a substantive conception. The distinction was evidently intended as a dichotomy, comparable to the distinction between a rationality of purpose and a rationality of process noted in chapter 1. Rationality must be one or the other. The argument then equated process with bounded rationality and equated substantive with the usual economic stipulation that the reasoning had to maximize a utility function. Plainly put, rationality is either unbounded or bounded by definition. The argument is not based on any evidence about how people actually think but only on what economists stipulate.

The obvious question, then, is where does the call for empiricism come into play? The answer is that it does so only for the very circumscribed problem of saying what the bounds of bounded rationality might be, and the sense that he gives to this problem is only psychological and not cultural:

> First, I would recommend that we stop debating whether a theory of substantive rationality and the assumption of utility maximization provide a suf-

ficient base for explaining and predicting economic behavior. The evidence is overwhelming that they do not.

We already have in psychology a substantial body of empirically tested theory about the processes people actually use to make boundedly rational, or "reasonable," decisions. This body of theory asserts that the processes are sensitive to the complexity of decision-making contexts and to learning processes as well.

The application of this procedural theory of rationality to economics requires extensive empirical research, much of it at micro-micro levels, to determine specifically how process is molded to context in actual economic environments and the consequences of this interaction for the economic outcomes of these processes. Economics without psychological and sociological research . . . is a one-bladed scissors. (Simon 1986, S224)

This kind of empiricism in arbitrarily isolated compartments is what Galileo's conception of the experimental method was intended to overthrow.

The review by Conlisk details the kind of psychological studies that Simon is referring to. Some have been conducted by psychologists, some by economists. The general pattern is to predict some optimal pattern of choices or behaviors on the basis of an unbounded economic algorithm and then compare the prediction either to some range of economic data from standard sources or the results in a psychological experiment, usually involving students on a university campus. Deviations from the prediction are common and are usually attributed to various kinds of psychological limitations or biases, such as misunderstanding statistical data, mistaking random data for patterned data and vice versa, failure to appreciate the law of large numbers, mistaking statistical probabilities, failures to recognize what is relevant and what is not, and so on (Conlisk 1996, 670).

All of these studies assume that economic rationality is the same as rationality in general. Their only question is the best way to characterize it: substantive or process, bounded or unbounded. They still want a culture-free or cross-culturally universal model of rationality and think that they can get it. In fact, the topic is not anywhere near this simple or this narrow. Simon's substantive rationality is just one instance of rationality as rule following, and his bounded rationality might be an instance of a rationality of purpose. But neither is the only example of each type.

The same applies to the arguments in Gigerenzer and Selten (2001), for whom unbounded rationality is not represented by Becker but by Leonard Savage's (1954) notion of subjective utility. I agree that Savage's algorithm was not empirically derived and is psychologically and computationally impossible for people to act on. The reasoning for it is hopelessly circular: whatever people pay or give up must be the equivalent of the subjective utility they obtain. But I do not agree that the alternative characterization of bounded rationality accounts for decision making as well as what I am describing. They describe unbounded algorithms as nonoptimizing and as fast and frugal. They also consider them to be something like a generalized aspect of human thought, as though when they get the list complete it will be equally applicable anywhere, depending only on the problem. While they recognize culture as relevant to context and conceptualization in a general way, they are not thinking in terms of finding and describing cultural ideas and algorithms and their uses.

And finally, the experimental studies by Henrich et al. (2001), noted in chapter 1, are problematic in the same way. Despite being conducted in a wide range of culturally alien communities, they firmly ignore the indigenous cultural idea systems and organizations of their experimental subjects. They therefore miss the possibility that their subjects' behaviors might be rational, or even optimal, in their own terms. On Kant's argument, rationality in the most fundamental sense is the self-consistent application of ends to means. As such, it must take many forms.

The Ethnographic Alternative

Most decision-making algorithms we encounter ethnographically are associated with technical idea systems: how to hunt, how to farm, how to make and use tools, how to navigate, how to prepare foods, how to build houses, how to make clothing, and so on. Some decision-making algorithms are part of or associated with social idea systems, as we have seen with the farm budget model and economic algorithms. Some are fast and frugal in the way that proponents of bounded rationality argue for, but others are complex and sophisticated. Many of them, of both types, are genuinely optimizing. Some indigenous models may aim at satisfying where this is good enough, but in many cases it is not. Finally, such algorithms are not part of a generalized pan-cultural or noncultural toolkit but rather are built into specific cultural systems and applied situationally.

Wherever formal systems are differentiated, there are logical inconsistencies or discordances between them. As we have shown, that is how the differentiation is done. It follows that whatever areas are brought under a community's limited number of common idea systems, other areas will be left in a limbo of undefinition between such systems. There are conventional ways to objectively compare one stock with another but not stocks with books. The Indian physical farm budget allows precise calculation of what to grow in order to best meet family needs for fuel, food, fodder, and funds, but no established cultural model provides a way to compare eating better with sending a child to school longer. Yet this is what real people in their real physical circumstances must decide.

The consequence is that when people need decision standards to apply across incompatible cultural idea systems, the only way they can develop them is to look to their personal circumstances. They must assign the decision to their underlying self. If there is no "what we do," they have to fall back on the personal "I." Only I as an individual can balance my obligations and opportunities as a husband, teacher, soldier, friend, citizen, officeholder, businessperson, creditor, debtor, employee, employer, writer, cousin, son, son-in-law, and so on. No one else has this precise configuration of pulls and pushes, and even if they did they would not be dealing with the same actual individuals. I can do it intuitively or emotionally, or I can invent an algorithm. If the latter, it will likely take the form of general statements of priorities such as "You cannot put a price on a daughter," "In the end what matters is to leave the world better than you found it," or "The first priority in the state is to have confidence in the ruler." It will not, however, be like the bounded rationality models of Gigerenzer and Selten, which are only computational techniques.

Although we live by trying to put ourselves in the place of others, in the end we know we cannot. We respond by doing the best we can. But this is neither a negation of culture nor an affirmation of hopeless isolation. We are not without cultural guidance in this process; this is how we experience the guidance. We are culturally compelled to use our cultural resources in a situated and individualistic way in order to meet our cultural obligations. This is the way culture works: through multiple relations and multiple choices forcing us to get a grip on ourselves, not as some sort of hidden puppeteer doing our thinking for us.

In short, although it is commonly assumed that subjective judgment and rational judgment are mutually exclusive, the most deeply subjective pursuit of personal purposes is not judgment without rule but rather a special kind of judgment with rules on top of rules in an inherently individualized configuration. It uses the established algorithms for rational calculation in whatever cultural systems are relevant and then applies an additional layer of considerations regarding how to balance them that individuals have to work out on their own.

A final observation is that while decisions or actions following subjective rules are separate from decisions or actions following objective rules in principle, for most people they are closely intertwined in practice. In practical action, we do not choose to make decisions exclusively either in terms of the objective standards of an organization or our personal complex of interests but rather shuttle back and forth between them. The question "If I accept this framework, what should I do?" alternates with "Since that is what I should do, should I accept this framework?" This is the nexus between the fact that groups are multiply organized and the dynamics of demographic and resource flows between them. Exactly how such considerations play out depends on the logic of the organizations concerned and on how that logic is applied by the group members.

Rationality and Resource Flows

When a person makes choices intended to achieve goals defined in terms of one or another of the organizations that person has a position in, the choice usually results in a movement of resources. Depending on the relationships between a person's organizational roles and the groups that the organizations pertain to, the flow may be within groups or between them.

The aggregate outcome of all such decisions is the ecological adaptation of a society. The adaptive problem for a society is to find a way to coordinate such decisions so as to preserve or enhance its resource base. This can be done by direct measures such as prohibiting or requiring certain allocations, by adjusting incentives, or by adjusting social or technological idea systems. It can also be done by evolutionary processes. Success is not automatic; failure is common.

Direct measures are obvious, and examples are numerous. A fundamental principle of Western law is that you cannot use your property in such a way as to deprive your neighbors of the use of theirs. We restrict the ways that people can acquire property with the aim of ensuring that the methods used are productive or at least not harmful. A university cannot dispose of hazardous chemicals by pouring them down the laboratory sinks. You cannot build a house in Euro-American cities without connecting it to sewer and water lines. Different areas of cities are zoned for different types of activities. Many destructive activities are simply outlawed, either formally or informally.

Adjusting incentives is much more complex and can occur in many ways, intended and unintended. The key theoretical point is that even though incentives are often framed in just one organizational context, their final effect varies from individual to individual depending in large part on the overall balance of relative attractions or threats they face in all of their other organizational frameworks.

As an example of the different ways that incentives can be adjusted, farmer cooperatives in India are a major source of development inputs for agriculture, but they have enjoyed very different degrees of success in different states. The cooperatives in Punjab state are the most successful in India. Those in Maharashtra are about average (Leaf 1998, 123–28). In Punjab until very recently the farmer cooperatives consistently grew and expanded their range of services. There are more cooperative members than farms, meaning that each farm family usually has several cooperative members. In Maharashtra the cooperatives have gone bankrupt periodically, serve only 21 percent of the farm households, provide their members only about one-third what the Punjab cooperatives do, and have not expanded the services they offer since their inception.

The reason for these differences is that in Punjab the rules of cooperative membership and the obligations of a person as a member of a farm family are mutually supportive and complementary, while in Maharashtra they are very often antagonistic. The Punjab cooperatives provide better than commercial credit rates while also providing material in kind and guaranteeing its quality. They allow any adult member of any household to be a member and have low penalties for late payment. Farm families can therefore use multiple memberships to enhance their overall cash flow by having each person borrow and then delay repayment over a season or two. Under these circumstances, it is in the interest of everyone in the household to get and maintain membership. At the same time, they all have incentives to repay and to see that each other repays. When they do, resource flows increase to the cooperative as well as to the household group.

In Maharashtra, on the other hand, cooperative interest rates are no better than market rates, cooperative procedures are time-consuming and cumbersome, cooperative membership is limited by rule to one person per household, each loan must be fully repaid before the next is taken, and cooperatives have no role in guaranteeing the quality of the inputs that farmers use the credit to obtain. It follows that it is much more likely that householders who are cooperative members will find the obligations of their cooperative membership to be in conflict with their demands in terms of their obligations in other household organizations and have to choose between them. Moreover, since the Maharashtra cooperatives have always been bailed out by the central government after they have gone into insolvency and have simply written off their uncollected debts, it is reasonable that when farmers sever their ties to cooperatives they will do so by not repaying outstanding loans. If they repay to the cooperative their household gains nothing, and it will also make no difference to the cooperative. If they put the money into educating a child, much will come back in many ways.

The basic problem in the two states is the same. The rationality is the same. The conclusion is different because the relative balance among the differing obligations is different. Nicholas Hopkins's (1987) meticulous study of the developmentally perverse effects of Egyptian pricing policies on the choices that Egyptian farmers make in their farm management strategies illustrates exactly the same situational logic.

By balancing the opportunities and obligations they have in the different organizations they take part in, people create an ongoing cycle of adaptive feedback in which cultural idea systems shape organizations, organizations shape resource flows, and the resource flows in turn come back to shape the spread and importance of the idea systems.

Rationality and Adaptation

The final question in this sequence is how does efficiency at the level of the decision-making organization result in efficiency at the level of the community of interacting organizations? This is the general form of Adam Smith's problem of the invisible hand. For example, as noted, studies of farm energy balances across the entire range of type of agricultural systems consistently show that all the different variations in any given niche arrived at in independent communities—such as independent Amazonian swidden farming systems or independent eighteenth-century English farms—perform very similarly and usually very well. How does this happen?

To answer the question, we need to connect two more processes to the preceding analysis of the development of rational thought and its relation to flows of resources. These are intergroup competition and imitation. When imitation is established as a recognized practice in a community, which it always seems to be, the logic of it in combination with competition is to turn the community into an effective real-time optimizing computer.

The Hill-Climbing Algorithm

The effect of imitation can be simulated in a multiagent model by the hill-climbing algorithm. In its narrowest mathematical sense, this involves only one decision. The actor compares his present elevation to the elevations of the adjacent actors. If any of them are higher, he moves to that location. Higher, for this purpose, can mean any continuous and transitive quantitative relation: more productive, more profitable, less travel time, less energy expended, and so on. As applied to the evolution of a farming system, each farmer would look at his neighbors and see if any were producing more of what he wanted. If they were, he would copy them. If every farmer in a group whose members were in a position to observe one another consistently did this, they would all settle on whatever combination of practices was most productive, whereby no further improvements were possible.

In this narrow sense, however, the hill-climbing model will only produce a local optimum and not necessarily a general optimum for two reasons. First, if we assume that the practices that are being developed and imitated are being generated randomly, it is quite possible that some better practice will simply not appear and hence not be imitated. Second, it will be local in the strictly geographical sense that the scope for imitation is only as wide as the area of contiguous farms, assuming that we do not set a search area for the actors in the model that is much wider than this.

What we actually see in farming communities is a three-pronged strategy: optimization, imitation, and extended search. Optimization is that each decision-making unit, usually a family group, tries to do the best they can with what they have, using an algorithm such as the physical farm budget. Imitation is that they also copy anything better from their neighbors. And extended search is that they are always alert to wider possibilities beyond what their neighbors do although they appreciate that adopting them from areas where conditions are different and less well known is riskier.

Suppose that there are a hundred farm households, perhaps twenty crops, and a thousand possible ways to combine them (in strict mathematical terms, the number of combinations would be many more, actually 2^{20}). Since there are one thousand combinations, each household has a one in one thousand chance of hitting upon the best combination in any given year. The average length of time for all households to hit their best combination would therefore be five hundred years. A normal reserve among traditional peasant households whose main subsistence crop is a durable grain seems to be two to four years. It follows that it would be a practical impossibility to arrive at a general optimization before all or almost all of the households died out.

However, if each household tries to do the best they can with what they have using an algorithm for planning such as that of the physical farm budget, watches to see what the other ninety-nine do, and selects their next cycle from what is best out of the whole community, then what you have is a hundred trials in the first year from which the community will eliminate, say, ninety and leave ten that are clearly superior. Since each option eliminated also eliminates a path to the next most likely variations on it, this reduces the total number of likely paths to optimal outcomes more or less proportionally. It is less risky to stay with what works but improve upon it than to leap to a variation on something that did not work well or something completely untried. So if each crop pattern that could be tried in the first year would lead to four or five variations likely to be better in the next year, by eliminating ninety in the first year you eliminate something like ninety times five for the second and leave something like ten times five. For the next round, the obvious course of action is for each family to select again from the ten best, according to their individual circumstances. This will once again give a hundred variants but in a much narrower range of ratios of gain to effort. With this procedure, it is not difficult to see that even if individual households cannot calculate optimal dispositions in a very accurate way, the community will probably have a viable system within two cycles and within a very few years will settle on a range of combinations that are genuinely optimal. After that, the same process would continue to keep the system stable. This is an enormously powerful adaptive mechanism.

Lansing and Kremer (1993) tested this kind of reasoning process in their article on Balinese water temples although in a different way. The article was framed as a choice between two kinds of agent-based simulations. One was a natural selection model. In this model the agents are programmed to respond only to their environments, not to each other. What happened in succeeding generations (iterations) depended only on which agents adapted and which failed. This is the counterpart to farm families seeking crop patterns in isolation. This was the model that Lansing and Kremer rejected. The second model was based on coadaptation in which each agent compared his own adaptation to that of his neighbors and adopted theirs if it was better. This was the model they chose, and that led to the establishment of a local optimum *subak* size and matched the actual size of the areas associated with the traditional water temples. This was the size that repeated runs of the model consistently settled on. The number of cycles required to reach them varied from eight to thirty-five, representing eight to thirty-five years.

Lansing and Kremer did not actually run both models and explicitly compare the two kinds of simulations. Rather, they accepted an earlier critique of natural selection models by Eric Alden Smith (1984) and were concerned only with demonstrating that coadaptation was an alternative. But the reason for not setting up both models was not only that Smith's argument was so convincing. It was also clear to them from the mathematics of the model that natural selection was "a process that would take a very long time, even on a computer" (Lansing and Kremer 1993, 111).

Yet the coadaptation model does not represent the entire adaptive process. It represents the way superior practices spread but not how they originate. A complete predictive simulation of peasant adaptation would involve the farm budget model as an algorithm for farm-level optimization plus the hill-climbing model for coadaptation. I have not tried to construct this as a multiagent model, but my spreadsheet-based projection of the likelihood of adopting sunflower for the whole irrigation command incorporated the same ideas. The aggregated prediction assumed that what was optimal for each would be quickly adopted by all, that the village would act like a single farm.

The analysis has important implications for what often strikes observers as the force of tradition. When a community includes imitation in its adaptive toolkit, optimization becomes closely tied to standardization. Both are accomplished at the same time and by the same process. Such a process necessarily involves a tradeoff between the few things that have been tried and the larger range of possibilities that has not been tried. However, so long as each community can see that all other standardizations in view are not demonstrably better, they will stay with what they have. In hill-climbing terms, if you are at a local maximum and all other local maxima are about the same, you are better off staying where you are than going through a valley to get someplace else that in the end will not be any better.

In a comparative study of swidden farming covering more than thirty different communities in six major language groups scattered across the Amazon basin, Stephen Beckerman (1987) found that the farming systems varied in detail for every group. Crops differed, crop mixtures differed, ecologies differed, and how the work was done differed. Yet in terms of caloric efficiency—caloric input for caloric output—all the systems of the different ethnic groups came out in a narrow range of from 1:20 to 1:52, and all but two were between 1:20 and 1:30 (Beckerman 1987, 84). This is a very consistent kind of finding in studies of agricultural energy budgets generally, and the only way to explain it is by the combination of rational action and imitation together, not just one or the other.

The hill-climbing algorithm with local optimization and extended search is by no means limited to optimizing farming systems. If any algorithm is universal in human adaptation in the way the proponents of bounded rationality want to suggest, this is probably it.

Multiagent Models of Multiple Adaptive Strategies

For a pluralistic theory of rational decision making, one of the most useful features of multiagent models is that they do not require a single objective function, meaning a single parameter to be maximized or minimized. Agents can be readily programmed to make decisions on the basis of several quite different goals while drawing on a fixed pool of resources. The program can then cycle through all of the decisions for each of the agents in as many iterations as the programmer desires and can simulate the way the decisions change the conditions for other agents and for the original agent's own subsequent decisions. Such a system can then optimize even though there is no overall optimizing function or it could collapse or do whatever else its component decisions lead to just as real communities do.

To set up an agent-based model that recognizes multiple idea systems in practice it is not necessary to recognize multiple idea systems theoretically. It is sufficient to recognize multiple adaptive goals with their respective culturally defined means-ends relationships. Cathy Small's (1999) TongaSim, as noted in chapter 3, is such a model.

Small's interest was to simulate a problem in Tongan ethnohistory concerning the relationship between stratification and warfare on the one hand and the status of women on the other. According to some, when society is simple and kinship-based and warfare is infrequent or uncommon, inequality is low or rare. As a lineage or clan type society moves toward chiefdoms and as organized warfare increases, gender inequality increases. The problem posed by Tongan society was that while it did indeed show a movement over time toward the formation of increasingly differentiated chiefdoms and while warfare did increase, gender inequality did not. Women had high social rank as far back as history ran, and this did not change.

In Tongan society rank is inherited; everyone is ranked, and rank is important. Lineages are divided into chiefly lines and commoners, and chiefly lines are ranked in relation to each other. Within families, siblings are ranked by birth order, and sisters rank above brothers. The superiority of a sister over her brother extends to her children over his children. Marriage is also based on rank. The proper and expected pattern is that chiefly women marry into a more highly ranked chiefly lineage than their own. Marriage entails economic support. When a woman from one chiefly lineage marries a chief of a higher lineage, that chiefly lineage becomes *fahu* to her brother's lineage, and her brother is obligated to provide it with economic support on the principle that the brother should support his sister and her children. The rank of women thus reinforced the general system of rank among chiefly families.

The question, then, was whether warfare would disturb this. On the assumption that both the general theory and the ethnohistorical accounts were right,

Small hypothesized the following scenario: "The prerogatives of women in Tonga were problematic for increasing stratification fueled by military conquest. However, because the emergent military powers simply married into old powers and appropriated traditional rank through kinship, women's prerogatives—part of the older base of power—were not challenged directly and so were not events that showed up in historical accounts" (1999, para. 1.2).

The problem was that if this hypothesis was true, none of the existing evidence would show it. The ethnohistorical accounts would be exactly the same whether the status of women became problematic or not. This was why a simulation was required to resolve the question.

The agents in her model are chiefly lines, each with its own base of land, population, wealth, and rank. The model as a whole has an incest rule controlling how close a marriageable person can be, a rate of population increase, a maximum density, and a maximum population. All are closely based on the ethnography.

Agent decision rules concern inheritance, marriage, and warfare. All are relevant to the overall cultural ecological adaptation, but each is separate from the others. The inheritance rule is that the chief will pass on the chiefship to a son or brother, depending on primogeniture and rank, although other conditions could enter for specific lineages. The line will split when the population reaches half the carrying capacity of the land (defined in the model as a set population density), and the younger brother of the chief will leave with his close kin to settle new land.

The first rule for marriage is that everyone marries, including all chiefs. Chiefs' marriage choices depend on the situation of the lineage; they will marry for wealth or alliance, whichever they most need. The wife-giving lineage would give wealth to the wife-receiving lineage, as per the *fahu* custom. The model as run for the print article assumed that each marriage would result in four children. Other fertility rates can be specified in the downloaded model.

The way that Small constructed the program implies that the marriage strategy and the warfare strategy are in ethnographic fact defined in two distinct idea systems. The decision to engage in warfare is based on population growth and competition for land. The decision model calculates the amount of land in relation to population, wealth, power as measured by number of kin, a measure of loyalty, and a measure of leadership, all compared to similar measures of other groups in the vicinity. The decision to marry is based on considerations of rank and wealth, represented by the *fahu* custom, and marriages according to rule have proper *fahu* relations. The overall model calculates the results of changes in each person's status on the basis of his own status and the status of his wife (or wives) and wife's or wives' lineage and what wealth the wife's or wives' lineages can provide. Warfare is a toggle. That is, it can be turned on or off. If it is off, the agents do not consider it.

Thus the marriage idea system is logically separate from the warfare idea system, although the two decisions can interact. Marriage strategies *must* take into consideration relative rank and wealth and *may* take into account population, power, and land shortage. Warfare decisions *must* take into account population, power, and land and *may* take into account relative rank. If it had not been possible to separate the rules for marriage from the rules for warfare (and make warfare a toggle), this would have argued that marriage and warfare were defined in a single idea system.

Each iteration of the model is a generation. The calculations for the article were based on twenty-one generations, although a user can set other values. For each generation, the program output indicates the action of each chiefly lineage.

The crucial question for Small was whether running the simulation with warfare "on" would increase the number of marriages following inverse *fahu* in which a male from a lower line marries a female from a higher line, which under normal circumstances would reverse rather than reinforce the power structure. The answer was that it did. With warfare "off" incidences of reverse *fahu* were 4.6 percent of all marriages over all twenty-one generations. With warfare "on" they were 12.2 percent. Moreover, when warfare was "on" warfare did not occur until the eleventh generation. Up to that time, land was still available to be filled in by splitting off. In consequence the rates of inverse *fahu* were the same as for no warfare. Once warfare began, however, the percentages of inverse *fahu* increased very dramatically. Figure 20 gives the results. The line with the square data points is warfare "on." The line with diamond data points is warfare "off."

The reasons for the decisions emerged from a closer examination of the (simulated) circumstances under which they were made, the considerations of advantage of the bride-giving and bride-receiving lineages. The usual situation

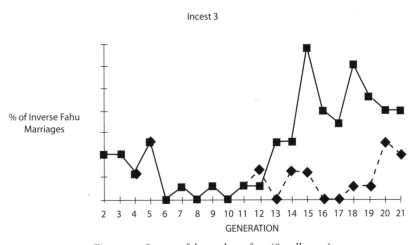

Figure 20. Inverse *fahu* and warfare (Small 1999)

is that such marriages occur when a low-ranking but labor-rich and land-poor lineage has acquired more land by warfare and a high-ranking lineage is in need of wealth or protection. The high-ranking lineage may not be able to provide much wealth by *fahu* to the low-ranking (bride-receiving) lineage, but what the low-ranking lineage does get is a higher status because the children will take the rank of the mother. This will bring more wealth in the future as other lineages send brides to it. There is therefore no political need to suppress the traditionally high status of women because the rising powerful lines simply appropriate their status through marriage and incorporate that status in their own lines. For example, in one case the threat faced by the high-ranking lineage was from a low-ranking but more powerful lineage immediately adjacent to it. The high-ranking lineage agreed to the marriage as their best option to retain their land.

From Small's point of view, the simulation confirmed her hypotheses and demonstrated the ability of simulations to resolve factual distinctions that more conventional ways of mobilizing the ethnographic and ethnohistorical data could not. From my point of view, the main point is more general. It is that the analysis shows quite plainly the difference between the aggregate outcome of adaptive decisions based on just one set of ideas (the marriage strategy) and decisions based on several distinct sets of ideas (marriage strategy plus warfare strategy) that interact by bearing upon the same set of people and resources. Agent-based models have a distinctive ability to simulate this type of pluralistic, interactive decision process.

Conclusion

Rationality is socially constructed, and social evolution is driven by instrumentally rational choices and purposes, massively and at many levels. But rationality is not something we have; it is something we do when we are compelled to. The capacity is universal as are the cultural tools for it, but its production is occasional. Just as our natural environment poses challenges that we must rise to, so does our social environment. The conflicting demands of multiple organizations challenge every one of us to develop an individual self-conception that will allow us to consolidate our responses into a discipline of personal rationality. Of course, we do not develop these individual self-conceptions and strategies alone; we also learn from others. The lessons are not standardized in the way the basic cultural idea systems are or our inherited technological toolkit is. The understandings we arrive at remain inherently relativistic and situational for us—subjective rather than objective—in ways that the social ideas and technologies do not. But the challenge to develop them, each of us for ourselves, is our ultimate adaptive challenge and drives all larger adjustments.

CHAPTER 9

Conclusion

My complete analysis is schematized in figure 21. This is a representation of what people do, not something they are supposed to be in. Creating an organization and a sense of being in it in an organized situation is a central part of the process around which is created the further sense of an organizational context, a community, and an ecological adaptation. This is a description of the way communities use and sustain their cultural idea systems and the organizations based on them.

The model is iterative, cyclical, and recursive. It is iterative in the sense that it applies at all levels of communicative and organizational scale, not just one or a few. It therefore also represents what has been shown about the way these levels are interrelated: they are homologous in structure, as represented by the basic cycle of communication.

It is cyclical in that it says that at all these different levels the process of organization involves a specific recurrent feedback loop: cultural information sources provide ideas used in shaping interactions. Interactions, through organization

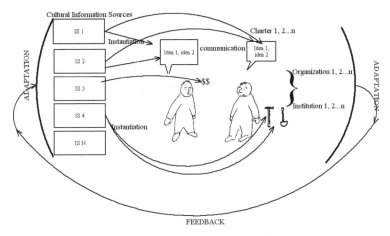

Figure 21. The social process

and adaptation, in turn instantiate, promulgate, stabilize, and sanction the cultural information sources. Accordingly, the two arcs at either end of the model represent the same phenomenon, the cultural-ecological adaptation in which the entire cultural system is set and that it embodies.

It is recursive in the sense that the levels both replicate each other and interact. Smaller patterns are consciously taken up into large patterns just in the way, for example, noun phrases are knowingly taken up into sentences, sentences into arguments, and arguments into agreements. Social actors know that the small can affect the large and vice versa. They conduct themselves with that in view and also create specific organizations to manage these relationships.

Cultural Information Sources

The blocks on the left side of the model designated IS1 to ISn are the cultural information sources, arranged in order of increasing information potential (decreasing order). These run from the highly ordered and abstract-seeming sources whose elements only appear as ideas to the much more concrete-seeming technical information sources whose elements often appear as physical toolkits and parts of cultural ecologies. The boundary around each indicates the fact that they are separated from one another semantically and formally, as has been described. For individuals in organizations together, the sources would also include their common knowledge of the charters and their uses, but these would be subordinate to, or extensions of, the main idea systems that the organizations draw their ideas from.

Cultural information sources are differentially distributed across populations. In every community some are held by substantially everyone while some are held by only a few. When we think of a large-scale society in the sense of Great Britain or America, the number of cultural information sources from IS1 to ISn in concurrent use somewhere or another in the population is enormous. But the number shared by substantially everyone is very low, perhaps just one or two (the governmental idea system and the economic idea system). Both of these observations are involved in the sense that such societies are specialized or highly differentiated. By contrast, in societies that we think of as small scale, such as an English, Navajo, or South Asian village, the total number of information sources from 1 to n in use somewhere or another is much smaller, but the proportion of these shared by substantially everyone is much larger, both relatively and absolutely. Thus, such communities seem more homogenous.

However, while the total number of major information sources in general consensus differs in communities on these different levels of scale, the number in use for each individual generally does not. We cannot go from speaking of complex versus simple societies to complex versus simple people. For adult individuals, the number of information sources held in mind and used regularly seems to be more or less constant at something like five to eight, depending on the range of activities the person habitually engages in and, doubtless, something about the person's intellectual capacity. These always run across the same range of formal types. There are a few, perhaps two to four, low information sources and most often a smaller number of high information sources. Of course there are different levels of mastery; some people know a great deal about a few things, and others know a little about many things.

When the assumptions of cultural information sources are so thoroughly established as to acquire the status of deeply ingrained habit rather than conscious belief, the relationship between a wide-scale pattern and its more localized instances becomes that between canons of taste in Bourdieu's (1979) sense and instances of displays of taste. The boundaries of the sources and the distributions of their users define the contexts within which those canons apply. There are standard American ways to dress for a formal occasion, and there are some distinctive regional ways. People can recognize them without necessarily being able to articulate them. They simply know when something is wrong and will be able to say what is better or right. But the underlying ideas can still be elicited with appropriate methods.

Instantiation

In the communicative process represented in the central section of figure 21, symbolic media are used to evoke the ideas of the information sources in order to create agreements interactively. The relation between the message sources and organizations involves two distinct steps, as the model indicates. One is the process of using the basic information system to construct organizational charters. The second is going from organizational charters to organizations and institutions (in the sense of groups with multiple organizations). Both must be constructed by communicative interaction among the people who will be bound together by its outcome. The relation between constructing charters and constructing organizations is logically linear but practically cyclical. Whatever is proposed is inevitably altered in the process of acceptance and is constantly subject to adjustment in use. In order to be a relationship about something, such interaction must relate the ideas from one system of relational ideas (IS1 or IS2 in the model) to at least one set of technical ideas (ISn in the model) and their associated objects (such as a rake and a shovel).

People who form organizations do not, as a rule, want that organization to be recognized only by those who make up its membership. They also want it to be recognized by those outside of the organization. To provide for this, they utilize social charters that are already established in consensus and modify them rather than trying to invent wholly new ones. These take three main forms: relational models to be acted out (ceremonies), verbal models (authoritative stereotyped descriptions, spoken or written), and symbolic models (such as the statue of blind justice as a model of how courts should act). Of these, by far the most widespread is ceremonies.

Ceremonies take the ideas out of the abstract systems of definitions that are current as cultural information sources and instantiate them in scripts for enactment in daily behavior. Of course, the ceremony is also a message source of a certain kind. In terms of the way it is constructed, it is related to the primary message source in a manner very much like the relationship between an established mathematical proof and the basic ideas of mathematics that the proof draws upon.

Contexts appear to participants as the manifestations of organizations in behavior. Invoking a context (or creating a context by invoking an organization) allows participants to engage in activities in title of their organized relationships. They can then "turn off" the organization (disinvoke it) and do something else (change the context). Later they can reinvoke the organization (return to that context) while acting as though the separate appearances were all continuous with one another and there is no need to take into account other intervening activities that the individuals concerned may have participated in. It is a wonderful device, essential to the development of any sort of social complexity, and there is no human community where we do not find it. The separate segments of a complex ceremony such as a wedding define separate contexts in the ordinary activity that the household group engages in; people move from context to context in exactly the same way they move from ceremonial segment to ceremonial segment, adopting its distinctive language, assumptions, and canons of appropriate behavior.

Although isolated analyses of instantiations of general cultural ideas such as a religious system or political system are as old as literature itself, their precise and careful study in the terms presented here has been greatly aided in recent years by the possibility of creating computerized simulations of a wide variety of complex transformations that very few people can consistently conceptualize without such aids. These analyses demonstrate that the relationships between ideas and their uses in creating organized behavior can be characterized as a deontic mapping, a mathematical instantiation of ideas selected from the information sources according to a deontic logic, even though exactly what that logic is still needs to be worked out.

Communication

Communication is represented in the model by the interaction between the two individuals. We can speak of communication in either a strong or a weak sense. In the weak sense, it means that someone spoke and someone else understood the words. In the strong sense, it means that someone spoke and someone else understood the person. They understood what the other person was trying to say, what they were intending. It is communication in this latter sense that leads to establishing relationships.

The same point about differing levels of scale that applies to the previous aspects of the model applies again here. The individuals of the diagram may be individual persons, organizations, national governments, or even international bodies or associations speaking through their representatives. The process is the same, and the constraints are the same. Individuals must use idea systems that define relations that may be established among individuals, groups must use idea systems that pertain to groups, and nations must use idea systems that define relations among nations. Diplomacy, at every level, is the art of using the appropriate idea systems for the group in question in ways that can be reliably understood by those you are interacting with in order to make agreements of mutual interest that will be adhered to.

Organization

When two or more individuals or groups, by means of communication, establish mutual adjustments of behavior, they have created an organization. While it is conceivable that a specific set of communications between individuals, if restricted enough, might involve one and only one cultural information system and frame one and only one organization, actual organized groups are almost always more complex and pluralistic in a particular way that follows a very specific logic. One set of ideas drawn from one information system generally brings them together and provides their main formal or proper (or otherwise to-be-recognized-by-all) organization, but other sets will always frame additional systems of relationships thought of as in some way within or behind or possibly even subversive to this dominant organization. A household's proper organization may be based on kinship, but underlying organizations will be economic, perhaps political, religious, and so on. A business's proper organization will be managerial, but underlying organizations will be economic, kinship, and so on.

Finally, at what seems to be the most encompassing level, whenever any group uses cultural idea systems to create mutual expectations among themselves, in the same process they necessarily establish that these relations are relations of a kind, that their own creation is not unique. I cannot build my family without saying it is a family; I cannot form my law firm without saying it is a law firm. And as my family and your family and all other families consist of people doing what we all mutually assert to be the same thing, we necessarily also assert the existence of a larger process that we all participate in.

Adaptation

Efficiency at the level of the individual productive organizations is provided for through rational choice, competition, and imitation. All of these, in different ways, are rooted in the same fundamental facts of multiple cultural information sources and their application in the creation of multiple organizations. Competition is established by the use of the common idea systems to create a multiplicity of groups of the same sort. The most direct competitors of a group are almost always other groups of the same kind because they need the same resources. But it is these same competitors whom they are most likely to learn from.

Individual rational choice is provided for by multiple means-ends relations in the several idea systems coupled with the fact that no single idea system excludes or dominates all others. Individuals must therefore find their own ways to combine them in order to make the best use of their fungible resources. The result is a system whose participants are compelled to recognize that they are much more likely to succeed by working with the accepted ideas and technologies than trying to ignore them. Imitation is learning from the experience of others trying to solve the same problems.

Culture is not the antithesis of rational foresight and choice but instead is its embodiment. The consequence is the universal sense of the force of tradition, represented in the diagram by the feedback arrow from the adaptive outcome back to the cultural idea systems, and again exists at every level of organizational scale.

But if people are rational and their immediate productive contexts are at least similarly efficient, how can societies as wholes (mainly in the sense of nation-states) be so obviously different in their degrees of success? The answer appears to lie in the importance of organizational support for trust. Individuals may be instrumentally rational and individual organizations may be efficient, but if those organizations cannot cooperate for mutual advantage, the efficiency cannot be multiplied. Freedom without a framework to ensure trust is insecurity. It is only with the ability to trust one another that freedom allows organizations to find ever more ways to expand their reach and aggregate their efficiencies, forming far more flexible, complex, and precisely directed patterns than any central authority could ever possibly design or direct.

Theory and Policy

We are entering an era of open economies, global communication, and greatly increased physical access to one another. There is an urgent need for a deeper system of globalized law and globalized patterns of social relations. This will require a vast expansion and deepening of popular government, and governmental and international bodies almost everywhere are working to bring this about. The lesson of history is that this effort will require the support of a vigorous and free social science that is capable of crossing national boundaries and restraining the ideological and purely personal predilections of those who practice it. Pragmatic theory has had great successes in the past. It forms the mainstream of Anglo-American common law legal theory as its Kantian counterpart forms the mainstream of Continental civil law jurisprudence. It is the basis of the increasing worldwide realization that rule of law fundamentally depends on recognition of individual human rights and is the surest path to sustainable material progress. It was crucial to articulating the strategy of American public education in the twentieth century and was the basis of the New Deal and the postwar recovery programs in Europe and Japan and hence ultimately of the European Union (EU) as we now see it forming (Leaf 1998, 5ff.).[1] But as important as the kinds of organizations involved in these developments are, there are many additional kinds, and almost all of them pose some kind of serious problem somewhere.

Colonial and communist governments were designed to be controlled from above and suppress initiatives from below. The main technique was to limit organizational options. Since most former colonial countries opted for some form of dirigiste socialistic central planning immediately after independence, this built-in unresponsiveness was not initially recognized as an impediment to development. Rather, it was often argued that it should be enhanced: state control over organizational activity should be increased, not reduced.

Central planning has been abandoned and the Soviet Union has collapsed, but the contest between authoritarian and pluralist assumptions continues in the competition between the EU and the former Soviet Union. The EU has moved to the forefront of a worldwide push for greater democratization and protection of human rights, exemplified by the criteria for joining the EU itself. The former Soviet Union has been more responsive to the demands of the World Bank and International Monetary Fund, caring little about pluralism and human rights and focusing on the economy alone. The result is a large-scale natural experiment, and the EU is clearly winning. It has more growth, smoother growth, better quality of life, and a list of countries waiting to get in. The Commonwealth of Independent States has irregular growth, instability, poorer quality of life, and countries trying to get out.

Two recent groups of studies make clear why. They are not anthropological, but they are empirical in the present sense. *The Market Meets Its Match: Restructuring the Economies of Eastern Europe* (Amsden, Kochanowicz, and Taylor 1994) describes the failures of the post-Soviet transition from the point of view of what the neoliberal policies left out. In New Deal terms, it is an anatomy of market failure and also of the failure of International Monetary Fund policies to prevent it. The essays edited by Peter Murrell (2001) under the title of *Assessing the Value of Law in Transition Economies* do it by describing the success of legal institution-building where it has occurred. The grounding is a mixture of institutional economics and the same pragmatic-Kantian jurisprudential perspective that I have incorporated. Organizations involve systems of incentives and succeed or fail depending on how those incentives are aligned in relation to their purposes. The studies focus on incentives over a wide range of levels of analysis, from the effect of different types of legal recourse on the rate at which orders are filled in purchasing departments through the success of foreign firms in Russian courts up to a compelling analysis by Leonid Polishchuk (2001) of the cycle of perverse incentives that led the eighty-nine governments of the Commonwealth of Independent States to block central constitutional reforms that would allow the central Duma to provide them with effective economic coordination.

Taken together, the collections show the same thing that I would argue on more general grounds. First, the market cannot do it because the market in the sense imagined does not exist; markets must be constructed, and in modern states this takes legislation backed by effective, independent courts. Second and more fundamentally, the market cannot do it because no one type of organization can do it. Only pluralism can and only if it is made effective by intelligent public action. Third, as the Murrell studies especially make clear, effective public action involves the constructive balancing of incentives, just in the way that is made clear in the line of jurisprudential studies that the theory here incorporates.

When law does grow as Kant imagined and embodies the expansion of freedom, we invariably find that one of the principal manifestations of this freedom is that it supports and expands the capacity of individuals to form ever more kinds of organizations. It follows that to expand law in other places with the same effect we have to know what organizations will be wanted and needed there. This theory does not provide a list of such organizations. It explains why no such list can be provided, why the organizational forms and their interrelations must be developed in situ.

In the end, what is at stake is human survival itself. The challenge cannot be met by imposition. It must be found by engagement. We must engage the interests and efforts of those concerned in such a way that they make the kind of self-sustaining, pervasive, and constructive organizational changes that societal success requires, and this can only be done by assuring a fair deal, or reciprocity.

There are social scientists who argue that scientific theories can be true without necessarily being useful. Perhaps this is so in the abstract, but social theory really is needed, and there is no large-scale or decisive way to test such theory except in living communities. So we have two options: test theories by applying them in ways intended to lead to improvement, or test them in ways not intended to lead to improvement. The latter makes neither intellectual nor moral sense, especially since in the case of the present theory a test would necessarily involve the informed and reasoned cooperation of the intended beneficiaries, just as the Marshall Plan and New Deal did. The failure of policies grounded in positivist and Marxist social theory was both theoretical and practical. The results were not as predicted and also were not good. Policies grounded in the assumptions of the present theory have succeeded in the same two senses. Their predictions held up, and the results were good. The problem, intellectually, has been that these assumptions have not been articulated in a single coherent theory. Now we have one.

Radical Empiricism

Physical science could not advance until it shed the idea that physical nature was only an imperfect manifestation of something more perfect that lay behind it, that could only be revealed to our minds directly rather than through experience. Why do we cling to such ideas in social science? Society is not some organic, cognitive, economic, or philosophical unity beyond observable social behavior, manifested only obscurely through it. It is a presumption that we generate in organizing our social interactions, and the way we do so is palpably observable if only we attend to it.

We normally speak as though society surrounds us and we move through it. We speak as though organizations encompass us and we have positions or relations within them. We speak as though our relationships are enduring while our behaviors are ephemeral. We speak this way because we know we must; it is required to maintain the documentary method. Anything else would invite confusion and alienation. In fact, however, in each case if we step back and observe what is stable and what is ephemeral, what is directly present and what is imputed, it is the other way around. Our ideas of society are far less clear and firm than our immediate purposes in invoking them, our organizations are only as firm and definite as our abilities to create an ongoing consensus in their name, and our putatively firm and enduring relations and values are talking points for forming the behaviors we place under their aegis.

Radical empiricism is empiricism that lets experience speak for itself by letting it be itself. It is easy to say that you are doing this but not easy to be sure. No formula can be applied as a guarantee. All formulas are suspect except that, in general, descriptions should avoid being self-contradictory, the description should recognize the interaction between observer and observed, and there should be no point in the chain of reasoning from observation to explanation where descriptions knowingly or intentionally leave the world of experience.

I think I have described the complete array of separate but interrelated empirical problems into which the analysis of human social organization naturally divides itself. Nothing is offered as a matter of faith or dogma either at the beginning of the argument or at any point in it, and no description is self-contradictory or unclear in what it applies to. We have gone from the most evident minutia of daily behavior to the formal requirements of consciousness and communication, from cultural idea systems to their organizational uses and adaptive consequences, and back to the maintenance of the idea systems. But science is always a conversation, never a discourse. Now we can see how the conversation proceeds.

NOTES

Introduction

1. Generally, I will use the term "community" to designate the physical people who live and work together in an area in an ecological sense. I will use the term "society" for the community and its organizations and ideas in a more social sense but without implying any particular type or degree of unity or cohesiveness beyond self-recognition.

2. For an early attempt by a prominent physicist to explain how theory explains, see Bridgman (1936).

3. Reichenbach and Hempel identified themselves with the Berlin school of logical empiricism, which can also be properly called neopositivism. This school also includes Nicholas Rescher and Wesley Salmon. There are significant differences between the Berlin school and the Vienna Circle. Most of the founding figures in the Vienna Circle were trained in philosophy; those of the Berlin school were trained in science. While both groups sought to integrate science by making it into a monolithic mathematico-deductive system, the Vienna Circle arguments depended on a dogmatic philosophical sense of what scientific reasoning had to involve, grounded in the analytic-synthetic dichotomy (cf. Carnap 1937, 1967). The Berlin school focused on formalizing especially important physical theories and, in Rescher's view, "were mainly concerned for the systematic regimentation of scientific procedure through the use of mathematics (especially probability theory)" (Rescher, personal communication, email of September 6, 2006). In their impact on the social sciences, however, the similarities between the two groups have been more important than their differences. They still agreed in seeing scientific reasoning only in terms of what they take as its formal properties rather than seeing how it emerges from the constraints of experimental practices and results, and they still see science as a matter of imposing such formalizations rather than finding them, as deductive, arbitrary, and top-down. Rescher has recently provided a concise person-by-person review of the major figures on his Web site at the University of Pittsburgh (Rescher 2006).

Popper's position (2002) is yet another variation on the same themes. Imagining, like Mill, that all scientific reasoning must be reducible to Aristotelian logic, he argues that since it is impossible for particular evidence to confirm a general premise, all that science can actually seek is falsification, as though there were no fundamental difference between, for example, the empirical firmness of the theory that allows us to build atomic weapons and the claim that human beings must be the product of the intervention of extraterrestrials.

4. The antiscience arguments have made much of Kuhn's ambiguities to interpret him as supporting their criticisms. Kuznar (1997, 52–58) provides a cogent explanation of what is wrong with this interpretation of Kuhn.

Chapter 2

1. For a wide-ranging account of the importance of Herder as a pathway for Kant's influence in subsequent developments in the social sciences, including anthropology, see Zammito (2002). Zammito takes "anthropology" in the same broad sense that Kant did but also connects it to the development of anthropology in a more disciplinary sense (see also Leaf 1979, 80–82).

2. The phrase invokes the language of Sextus Empiricus's *Against the Dogmatists*. Many similar allusions recur throughout his corpus. He knew the skeptical criticisms that Hume was building upon and did not reject them. Kant's criticism of Hume was only that he ended his criticism within this familiar ground before putting it into a general and constructive form.

3. Page numbers for the *Prolegomena* refer to the original pagination as given in Beck's Library of the Liberal Arts edition, 1950.

4. For a thorough and clear analysis of the grounding of Kant's philosophy of science in the history of science, see Brittan (1978).

5. The title is also translated as *The Fundamental Principles of the Metaphysics of Morals*.

6. The German title is *Metaphysische Anfangsgrunde der Rechtslehre,* which is Part I of the *Metaphysics of Morals (Metaphysik der Sitten).*

7. This is also why it is not quite accurate for Stephen Levinson and Penelope Brown to characterize Kant as saying that space is a "subjective framework we impose on the objective world" (Levinson and Brown 1994, 4) or to force his argument into the frame of trying to decide whether spatial categories come from culture or nature. Levinson and Brown are absolutely right to describe Kant's claims as empirical philosophy, and Kant certainly shared their interest in the cultural basis of spatial orientations, but the thrust of his analysis was that such problems cannot be resolved in terms of such dualistic dichotomies as ideal versus material (culture vs. nature) or subjective versus objective. Nor is it a matter of Kant changing his mind. Although Levinson and Brown focus on a pre-*Critique* paper of 1768, they quote a passage (1994, 6) that is almost identical to the one in the *Prolegomena* quoted here. For a clear contemporary discussion of the relation between the *Critiques* and Kant's earlier views in philosophical terms, see Murphy (1994, 1–10).

8. See Brittan (1978, 68ff.).

9. J. H. Bernard provides a list of Kant's key terms in the introduction to his translation of the *Critique of Judgment* (Bernard 1974, xxxvi).

10. For a more expanded description, see Jones's chapter 2 on Kant's theory of knowledge (1975, 14–68).

11. A linking concept, the statement in a logical syllogism that connects premise to conclusion.

12. The translation has to be watched carefully. Hegel's term was *Geist,* whose associations are very close to the French *esprit* but different from the English "mind." The term "mind" suggests rational faculties largely to the exclusion of character or motivation. *Geist* and *esprit* suggest all three at once.

Chapter 3

1. English and Punjabi can be diagrammed in two dimensions (although one could argue for three to take into account relations by marriage, which require overlays because

they cannot be laid into the two-dimensional chart without confusing it). Navajo, which requires us to think of kinship relations in terms of positions of the relatives in their respective clans, might be considered a system in three dimensions. Exactly how many dimensions are possible is an empirical question, although more than four (three plus time) seems unlikely. The same applies to representations of other kinds of relations. Although people clearly represent their social ideas most often in two or three dimensions, there are no upper limits in mathematics, so anything is logically possible.

Chapter 4

1. As Saxe (1983, 136) notes, Chomsky's view can also be described as Levi-Strauss's.
2. Capitalization indicates that the consonant is retroflex, meaning that the sound is made with the underedge of the tip of the tongue touching the palate.
3. In Roman law, the term "leges" had a similar sense and is from the term for leather thongs, which were used to bind the fasces, the symbols of magisterial power.

Chapter 6

1. Starring Skip Homeier and directed by Joseph Kane. When it appeared on television in 1959 (where I saw it), the television critic for the *Los Angeles Times* described it as "humdrum." Between 1934 and 1975, Kane directed more than a hundred Western potboilers of this sort.
2. The spreadsheet can be downloaded from http://www.mathematicalanthropology .org/?PG=TOC.
3. Maharashtra allocates canal water only against applications. The irrigation department advertises the crops and areas that farmers may irrigate. Others will not be sanctioned. For this season at this part of the command, there was a two-acre limit on new sugarcane planting and a five-acre limit on new planning plus ratoon (which is the stubble from the previous year allowed to regrow). Sunflower was being encouraged; I don't know if there was a limit.
4. His budget is published in Leaf (1998, 75).
5. All the distribution channels are unlined, and the ground is often very porous.
6. Of course it is possible to try to limit members' ability to leave by social compulsion, but the effect will necessarily be to remove an important mechanism for promoting productive efficiency and societal adaptation.
7. If the number of negotiators is N, the number of bilateral negotiations is $(N^2-N)/2$.

Chapter 7

1. Historically and conventionally, this is explicitly described as an adaptation of the Hindu ritual circumambulation of the sacred fire, so Sikhs could have a ritual of their own and would not need to use the Hindu ritual. That is, it is a matter of convenience and convention, not a sacrament in a Christian sense.
2. Odd numbers are auspicious because imbalance suggests an ongoing interaction. Even numbers are inauspicious because they suggest stasis.
3. For example, Sikhs generally do not shave their beards, but Brahmins do. Brahmins in wedding parties also are usually identifiable by a slightly different way of tying their

turbans. The Brahmin turbans are generally white, while the Sikhs of different castes are more likely to wear colored turbans.

Chapter 9

1. For an excellent and relatively compact review of the increasing importance of human rights in modern systems of law, see Paul Gordon Lauren's *The Evolution of International Human Rights* (2003).

BIBLIOGRAPHY

American Bar Association. 1983. *The Model Rules of Professional Conduct.* Chicago: American Bar Association.

Amsden, Alice H., Jacek Kochanowicz, and Lance Taylor. 1994. *The Market Meets Its Match: Restructuring of the Economies of Eastern Europe.* Cambridge: Harvard University Press.

Axtell, R. L., J. M. Epstein, J. S. Dean, G. J. Gumerman, A. C. Swedlund, J. Harburger, S. Chakravarty, R. Hammond, J. Parker, and M. Parker. 1999. "Population Growth and Collapse in a Multiagent Model of the Kayenta Anasazi in Long House Valley." *Proceedings of the National Academy of Sciences* 99(3): 7275–79.

Bailey, F. G. 1960. *Tribe, Caste, and Nation.* Manchester, UK: Manchester University Press.

———. 1969. *Stratagems and Spoils: A Social Anthropology of Politics.* Oxford, UK: Basil Blackwell.

———. 1988. *Humbuggery and Manipulation.* Ithaca, N.Y.: Cornell University Press.

———. 1997. *A Witch-Hunt in an Indian Village or, the Triumph of Morality.* Delhi: Oxford University Press.

Barth, Fredrik. 1959. "Segmentary Opposition and the Theory of Games: A Study of Pathan Organization." *Journal of the Royal Anthropological Institute of Great Britain and Ireland* 89: 5–21.

Barlett, Peggy, ed. 1980. *Agricultural Decision Making: Anthropological Contributions to Rural Development.* New York: Academic Press.

Bates, Daniel G. 2001. *Human Adaptive Strategies.* Needham Heights, Mass.: Allyn and Bacon.

Bateson, Gregory. 1958. *Naven.* Stanford, Calif.: Stanford University Press.

Bayless-Smith, T. P. 1982. *The Ecology of Agricultural Systems.* Cambridge: Cambridge University Press.

Beckerman, Stephen. 1987. "Swidden in Amazonia and the Amazon Rim." In *Comparative Farming Systems,* edited by B. L. Turner and Stephen B. Brush, 55–87. New York and London: Guilford.

Bernard, J. H. 1974. *Kant: Critique of Judgement.* New York: Hafner Library of Classics. First published in 1951.

Bharwani, Sukaina. 2006. "Understanding Complex Behavior and Decision Making Using Ethnographic Knowledge." *Social Science Computer Review* 24: 78–105.

Bharwani, Sukaina, Michael Fischer, and Nick Ryan. 2002. "Modeling Adaptive Dynamics and Social Knowledge." *Cybernetics and Systems, Austrian Society for Cybernetics Studies* 1: 377–82.

Biersack, Aletta. 1999. "From the New Ecology to the New Ecologies." *American Anthropologist* 100(1): 5–18.

Boas, Franz. 1940. *Race, Language, and Culture.* New York: Free Press.

Bohannan, Laura. 1952. "A Genealogical Charter." *Africa* 22: 301–5.

Bohannan, Paul. 1957. *Justice and Judgment among the Tiv.* London: Oxford University Press.

———. 1968. "Law and Legal Institutions." In *International Encyclopedia of the Social Sciences,* 8:73–78. New York: Macmillan.

Boissevain, Jeremy. 1966. "Factions, Parties and Politics in a Maltese Village." *American Anthropologist* 66(6): 1275–87.

Boring, Edwin G. 1950. *A History of Experimental Psychology.* New York: Appleton-Century-Crofts.

Boserup, Ester. 1965. *The Conditions for Agricultural Growth.* London: Allen and Unwin.

———. 1981. *Population and Technological Change: A Study of Long-Term Trends.* Chicago: University of Chicago Press.

Boster, James, and Roy D'Andrade. 1989. "Natural and Human Sources of Cross-Cultural Agreement in Ornithological Classification." *American Anthropologist* 91(1): 132–42.

Bourdieu, Pierre. 1979. *La Distinction: Critique Sociale du Jugement.* Paris: les Editions de Minuit.

Bridgman, P. W. 1936. *The Nature of Physical Theory.* New York: Dover.

Brittan, Gordon G., Jr. 1978. *Kant's Theory of Science.* Princeton, N.J.: Princeton University Press.

Burnyeat, Myles, ed. 1983. *The Skeptical Tradition.* Berkeley, Los Angeles, and London: University of California Press.

Carnap, Rudolf. 1937. *The Logical Syntax of Language.* New York: Humanities Press. Original German edition published in 1934.

———. 1967. *The Logical Structure of the World.* Translated by Rolf A. George. Berkeley and Los Angeles: University of California Press. Original German edition published in 1928.

Cernea, Michael, ed. 1991. *Putting People First: Sociological Variables in Rural Development.* 2nd ed. New York: Oxford University Press.

Chambers, Robert. 1983. *Rural Development: Putting the Last First.* New York: Wiley.

Chibnick, Michael. 2005. "Experimental Economics: A Critical Assessment." *American Ethnologist* 32(2): 198–209.

Clifford, James. 1982. *Person and Myth: Maurice Leenhardt in the Melanesian World.* Berkeley: University of California Press.

———. 1988. *The Predicament of Culture: Twentieth-Century Ethnography, Literature, and Art.* Cambridge: Harvard University Press.

Clifford, James, and George Marcus. 1986. *Writing Culture: The Poetics and Politics of Ethnography.* Berkeley: University of California Press.

Comaroff, Jean, and John Comaroff. 1991. *Of Revelation and Revolution: Christianity, Colonialism and Consciousness in South Africa,* Vol. 1. Chicago and London: University of Chicago Press.

Comte, Auguste. 1851. *The Positive Philosophy of Auguste Comte.* Translated by Harriet Martineau. Undated edition, ca. 1853. Original French edition of first volume, 1851. New York: Peter Eckler.

———. 1854. *The Catechism of Positivism.* London: Savill and Edwards.

Conlisk, John. 1996. "Why Bounded Rationality." *Journal of Economic Literature* 334 (June): 669–700.

D'Andrade, Roy. 1995. *The Development of Cognitive Anthropology*. Cambridge: Cambridge University Press.

D'Andrade, Roy G., and Claudia Strauss. 1992. *Human Motives and Cultural Models*. New York: Cambridge University Press.

Dewey, John. 1929. *The Quest for Certainty: A Study of the Relation of Knowledge and Action*. New York: Minton, Balch, and Company.

Dominguez, Virginia R. 1990. "Representing Value and the Value of Representation: A Different Look at Money." *Cultural Anthropology* 5(1): 16–44.

Dulles, Allen. 1993. *The Marshall Plan*. Edited and with an Introduction by Michael Wala. Providence, Oxford, UK: Berg.

Dumont, Louis. 1970. *Homo Hierarchicus*. Chicago: University of Chicago Press.

Durkheim, Emile. 1915. *The Elementary Forms of the Religious Life*. London: Allen and Unwin. First French edition 1912.

Dworkin, Ronald. 1986. *Law's Empire*. Cambridge, Mass.: Belknap.

Ehrlich, Eugen. 1975. *Fundamental Principles of the Sociology of Law*. New York: Arno. First published 1913. Reprint of the 1936 Harvard University Press edition, translated by Walter L. Moll with an Introduction by Roscoe Pound.

Elkind, David. 1961. "Children's Conceptions of Brother and Sister: Piaget Replication Study V." *Journal of Genetic Psychology* 99: 269–76.

Epstein, T. S. 1967. *Economic Development and Social Change in South India*. Manchester, UK: Manchester University Press. First published in 1962.

Evans-Pritchard, E. E. 1967. *The Nuer*. Oxford: Clarendon. Originally published in 1940.

Feinberg, Richard. 2001. "Introduction: Schneider's Cultural Analysis of Kinship and Its Implications for Anthropological Relativism." In *The Cultural Analysis of Kinship: The Legacy of David M. Schneider*, edited by Richard Feinberg and Martin Ottenheimer, 1–32. Urbana: University of Illinois Press.

Feinberg, Richard, and Martin Ottenheimer. 2001. *The Cultural Analysis of Kinship: The Legacy of David M. Schneider*. Urbana: University of Illinois Press.

Firth, Raymond. 1949. "Authority and Public Opinion in Tikopia." In *Social Structure: Studies Presented to A. R. Radcliffe-Brown*, edited by Meyer Fortes, 168–88. Oxford: Oxford University Press.

Fischer, Michael. 2002. "Integrating Anthropological Approaches to the Study of Culture: The 'Hard' and the 'Soft' Cybernetics and Systems." In *Proceedings of the Sixteenth European Meeting on Cybernetics and Systems Research*, Vol. 1, edited by Robert Trappl, 367–72. Vienna: Austrian Society for Cybernetic Studies.

Fogelin, Robert J. 1985. *Hume's Skepticism in the Treatise on Human Nature*. London, Boston, Melbourne, and Henley: Routledge and Kegan Paul.

Fox, Robin. 1967. *Kinship and Marriage: An Anthropological Perspective*. Middlesex, UK: Penguin.

Galilei, Galileo. 1953. *Dialogue concerning the Two Chief World Systems*. Translated by Stillman Drake. Berkeley and Los Angeles: University of California Press.

Galison, Peter. 1997. *Image and Logic: A Material Culture of Physics*. Chicago: University of Chicago Press.

Garfinkel, Harold. 1967. *Studies in Ethnomethodology*. Englewood Cliffs, N.J.: Prentice Hall.

———. 2002. *Ethnomethodology's Program*. Edited and introduced by Anne Warfield Rawls. Lanham, Md.: Rowman and Littlefield.

Garro, Linda C. 1998. "On the Rationality of Decision-Making Studies, Part 1, Decision Models of Treatment Choice." *Medical Anthropology Quarterly* 12(3): 319–40.

Gatewood, John B. 1994. "Personal Knowledge and Collective Representations." Paper presented in the panel Intracultural Variation and Cultural Models. Annual Meeting of the American Anthropological Association, Atlanta, Georgia. Revised version available at http://www.lehigh.edu/%7Ejbg1/persknow.htm.

———. 2001. "Active Cognition in Bartending." Paper presented in the panel Cultural Idea-Systems: Logical Structures and the Logic of Instantiation. Annual Meetings of the American Anthropological Association, Washington, D.C.

Geertz, Clifford. 1960. *The Religion of Java*. Glencoe, Ill.: Free Press.

———. 1964. "Ideology as a Cultural System." In *Ideology and Discontent,* edited by D. Apter, 47–56. Glencoe, Ill.: Free Press.

———. 1966. "Religion as a Cultural System." In *Anthropological Approaches to the Study of Religion,* edited by Michael Banton, 1–46. London: Tavistock.

———. 1973. *The Interpretation of Cultures*. New York: Basic Books.

Gigerenzer, Gerd, and Reinhard Selten. 2001. *Bounded Rationality: The Adaptive Toolbox*. Cambridge, Mass.: MIT Press.

Gintis, Herbert. 2000. *Game Theory Evolving*. Princeton, N.J.: Princeton University Press.

Goethe, Johann Wolfgang von. 1950. *Faust by Goethe*. Translated by R. Jarrell. New York: Modern Library.

Goffman, Erving. 1959. *The Presentation of Self in Everyday Life*. Garden City, N.Y.: Doubleday Anchor.

Goodman, Russell B. 1995. *Pragmatism: A Contemporary Reader*. London: Routledge.

Goold, G. P., ed. 1976. *Sextus Empiricus*. 4 vols. English translation by R. G. Bury. 1933; reprint Cambridge: Harvard University Press.

Gregor, Mary J. 1974. *Immanuel Kant: Anthropology from a Pragmatic Point of View*. The Hague: Martinus Nijhoff.

Greif, Avner. 1998. "Historical and Comparative Institutional Analysis." *American Economic Review* 88(2): 80–84.

Gross, Paul R., and Norman Levitt. 1994. *Higher Superstition*. Baltimore and London: Johns Hopkins University Press.

Habermas, Jürgen. 1996. *Postmetaphysical Thinking*. Translated by William Mark Hohengarten. Cambridge and London: MIT Press.

Hacking, Ian. 1999. *The Social Construction of What?* Cambridge: Harvard University Press.

Haviland, Susan, and Eve Clark. 1974. "'This Man's Father Is My Father's Son': A Study of the Acquisition of English Kin Terms." *Journal of Child Language* 1: 23–47.

Hawking, Stephen. 1988. *A Brief History of Time: From the Big Bang to Black Holes*. Toronto: Bantam.

Henrich, Joseph, Robert Boyd, Sam Bowles, Colin Camerer, Herbert Gintis, Richard McElreath, and Ernst Fehr. 2001. "In Search of Homo Economicus: Experiments in 15 Small-Scale Societies." *American Economic Review* 91(2): 73–79.

Henrich, Joseph, Robert Boyd, Samuel Bowles, Colin Camerer, Ernst Fehr, and Herbert Gintis, eds. 2004. *Foundations of Human Sociality: Economic Experiments and Ethnographic Evidence from Fifteen Small-Scale Societies*. New York: Oxford University Press.

Holland, Dorothy, and Naomi Quinn, eds. 1987. *Cultural Models in Language and Thought.* Cambridge and New York: Cambridge University Press.

Hollinger, Robert, and David Depew, eds. 1995. *Pragmatism: From Progressivism to Postmodernism.* Westport and London: Praeger.

Holmes, Oliver Wendell, Jr. 1923. *The Common Law.* Boston: Little, Brown. First published in 1881.

Holy, Ladislav, and Milan Stuchlik. 1981. *The Structure of Folk Models.* ASA Monograph No. 20. London: Academic Press.

Hopkins, Nicholas S. 1987. *Agrarian Transformation in Egypt.* Cairo: American University Press.

Hopper, W. David. 1965. "Allocative Efficiency in Traditional Indian Agriculture." *Journal of Farm Economics* 47: 611–29.

Hume, David. 1748. *An Inquiry concerning Human Understanding, with a Supplement: An Abstract of a Treatise on Human Nature.* Edited with an introduction by Charles W. Hendel. Indianapolis and New York: Bobbs-Merrill.

Hutton, J. H. 1946. *Caste in India.* Cambridge: Cambridge University Press.

Izmerlian, Harry. 1979. *The Politics of Passion: Structure and Strategy in Sikh Society.* Columbia, Mo.: South Asia Books.

James, William. 1904. "A World of Pure Experience." *Journal of Philosophy, Psychology and Scientific Methods* 1(20): 533–43.

Jhering, Rudolph von. 1913. *Law as a Means to an End.* Translated by Isaac Husik from the fourth German edition of *Der Zweck im Recht.* Boston: Boston Book Company. Vol. 1 first published in 1877; vol. 2 first published in 1883.

———. 1915. *The Struggle for Law.* 2nd ed., with an Introduction by Albert Kocourek. Translated by John Lalor from the fifth German edition of *Kampf ums Recht.* First published in 1872. Chicago: Callaghan.

Joas, Hans. 1993. *Pragmatism and Social Theory.* Chicago: University of Chicago Press.

Johnson, C. David, Timothy A. Kohler, and Jason Cowan. 2005. "Modeling Historical Ecology, Thinking about Contemporary Systems." *American Anthropologist* 107(1): 96–107.

Jones, W. T. 1975. *Kant and the Nineteenth Century.* 2nd ed., revised. First published in 1952. San Diego: Harcourt Brace Jovanovich.

Kant, Immanuel. 1781. *Critique of Pure Reason.* Translated and edited by Paul Guyer and Allen W. Wood. Cambridge and New York: Cambridge University Press, 1998.

———. 1783. *Prolegomena to Any Future Metaphysics.* Edited and with an Introduction by Lewis White Beck. New York: Bobbs-Merrill, 1950.

———. 1784. *Idea for a Universal History from a Cosmopolitan Point of View.* Translated by Lewis White Beck. From Immanuel Kant, "On History." Indianapolis and New York: Bobbs-Merrill, 1963.

———. 1785. *Groundwork of the Metaphysic of Morals.* Translated by H. J. Patton, 1948. Third edition published in 1956. Harper and Row: Harper Torchbooks.

———. 1788. *Critique of Practical Reason.* Translated by Lewis White Beck. Indianapolis and New York: Bobbs-Merrill, 1956.

———. 1790. *Critique of Judgment.* Translated by Werner F. Pluhar. Indianapolis: Hackett, 1987.

———. 1795. *Perpetual Peace.* Translated with an Introduction by Lewis White Beck. Indianapolis and New York: Bobbs-Merrill, 1957.

———. 1796. *Kant's Philosophy of Law (Metaphysische Anfangsgrunde der Rechtslehre*; Part I of *Metaphysik der Sitten)*. Translated by W. B. Hastie, 1887. Edinburgh: T. and T. Clark. Available from the Online Library of Liberty at http://oll.libertyfund.org/Home3/Book.php.

———. 1797. *Anthropology from a Pragmatic Point of View*. Translated by Mary J. Gregor. The Hague: Martinus Nijhoff, 1974.

Korsgaard, Christine M. 1996. *The Sources of Normativity*. Cambridge: Cambridge University Press.

Kottak, Conrad P. 1999a. "The New Ecological Anthropology." *American Anthropologist* 101(1): 23–35.

———. 1999b. *Assault on Paradise: Social Change in a Brazilian Village*. 3rd ed. New York: McGraw Hill.

Kuhn, Thomas S. 1973. "The Structure of Scientific Revolutions." *The International Encyclopedia of Unified Science* 2(2). First published 1962; second enlarged ed. published in 1970; reprinted in 1973. Chicago: University of Chicago Press.

Kuznar, Lawrence. 1997. *Reclaiming a Scientific Anthropology*. Walnut Creek, Calif.: AltaMira.

Kuznar, Lawrence, and Robert Sedlmeyer. 2005. "Collective Violence in Darfur: An Agent-Based Model of Pastoral Nomad/Sedentary Farmer Interaction." *Mathematical Anthropology and Cultural Theory: An International Journal* 1(4). http://www.mathematicalanthropology.org/pdf/KuznarSedlmeyer1005.pdf.

Langsdorf, Lenore, and Andrew R. Smith, eds. 1995. *Recovering Pragmatism's Voice*. Albany: State University of New York Press.

Lansing, John Stephen. 1991. *Priests and Programmers: Technologies of Power in the Engineered Landscape of Bali*. Princeton, N.J.: Princeton University Press.

Lansing, John Stephen, and James N. Kremer. 1993. "Emergent Properties of Balinese Water Temple Networks: Coadaptation on a Rugged Fitness Landscape." *American Anthropologist*, n.s., 95(1): 97–114.

Lauren, Paul Gordon. 2003. *The Evolution of International Human Rights*. 2nd ed. Pittsburgh: University of Pennsylvania Press.

Leach, E. R. 1951. "The Structural Implications of Matrilateral Cross-Cousin Marriage." *Journal of the Royal Anthropological Institute of Great Britain and Ireland* 81: 23–55.

———. 1954. *Political Systems of Highland Burma*. London: G. Bell.

Leaf, Murray J. 1971. "The Panjabi Kinship Terminology as a Semantic System." *American Anthropologist* 73(3): 545–54.

———. 1972. *Information and Behavior in a Sikh Village*. Berkeley and Los Angeles: University of California Press.

———. 1974. "Sikh Marriage Rituals." In *Frontiers of Anthropology*, edited by Murray J. Leaf, with Bernard G. Campbell, Constance Cronin, George DeVos, William Longacre, Marlys McClaran, Fred T. Plog, Jack H. Prost, and Roy Wagner, 123–62. New York: Van Nostrand.

———. 1979. *Man, Mind, and Science: A History of Anthropology*. New York: Columbia University Press.

———. 1984. *Song of Hope: The Green Revolution in a Sikh Village*. New Brunswick, N.J.: Rutgers University Press.

———. 1998. *Pragmatism and Development*. Westport and London: Bergin and Garvey.

———. 2000. "The Physical Farm Budget: An Indigenous Optimizing Algorithm." *Mathematical Anthropology and Cultural Theory* 1(1). http://www.mathematicalanthropology.org/pdf/MACTLEAF1100.PDF.

———. 2001. "Schneider's Idealism, Relativism, and the Confusion of Kinship." In *The Cultural Analysis of Kinship: The Legacy of David M. Schneider,* edited by Richard Feinberg and Martin Ottenheimer, 60–77. Urbana: University of Illinois Press.

———. 2005. "The Message Is the Medium: Language, Culture and Informatics." *Cybernetics and Systems: An International Journal* 36(8): 903–17.

———. 2006. "Experimental Analysis of Kinship Terminologies." *Ethnology* 45: 305–30.

Lett, James. 1997. *Science, Reason, and Anthropology.* Lanham, Md.: Rowman and Littlefield.

Levinson, Stephen C., and Penelope Brown. 1994. "Immanuel Kant among the Tenejapans: Anthropology as Empirical Philosophy." *Ethos* 22(1): 3–41.

Levi-Strauss, Claude. 1949. *Elementary Structures of Kinship.* Edited by J. H. Bell and J. R. Sturmer. Translation 1969 by Rodney Needham. Oxford, UK: Alden and Mowbray.

———. 1955. "The Structural Study of Myth." *American Journal of Folklore* 68: 270.

———. 1962. *Totemism.* Boston: Beacon.

Lowie, Robert H. 1937. *The History of Ethnological Theory.* New York: Holt, Rinehart, and Winston.

Luong, Hy Van. 1986. "Language, Cognition, and Ontogenetic Development: A Reexamination of Piaget's Premises." *Ethos* 14(1): 7–46.

Lyon, Stephen M. 2002. "Modeling Competing Contextual Rules: Conflict Resolution in Punjab, Pakistan." In *Cybernetics and Systems,* Vol. 1, edited by Robert Trappl, 383–88. Proceedings of the Sixteenth European Meeting on Cybernetics and Systems Research. Vienna: Austrian Society for Cybernetic Studies.

Malinowski, Bronislaw. 1922. *Argonauts of the Western Pacific: An Account of Native Enterprise and Adventure in the Archipelagoes of Melanesian New Guinea.* First published London: Studies in Economics and Political Science. Reprint 1961, New York: Dutton.

———. 1926. *Crime and Custom in Savage Society.* Paterson, N.J.: Littlefield, Adams.

Manners, Robert A. 1980. "Man, Mind and Science: A History of Anthropology." Book review. *American Ethnologist* 7(2): 378–80.

Marcus, George E., and Michael M. J. Fischer. 1999. *Anthropology as Cultural Critique.* 2nd ed. Chicago: University of Chicago Press.

McGowan, Margaret M. 1974. *Montaigne's Deceits: The Art of Persuasion in the Essais.* London: University of London Press.

McKinley, Robert. 2001. "The Philosophy of Kinship: A Reply to Schneider's Critique of the Study of Kinship." In *The Cultural Analysis of Kinship: The Legacy of David M. Schneider,* edited by Richard Feinberg and Martin Ottenheimer, 131–67. Urbana: University of Illinois Press.

McLennan, John F. 1865. *Primitive Marriage.* Edinburgh: Black.

McMullin, Ernan, ed. 1967. *Galileo: Man of Science.* New York: Basic Books.

———. 1994. "A System of Pragmatic Idealism, Vol. 1, Human Knowledge in Idealistic Perspective—Book Reviews." *Mind* 103(410): 219–22.

Mead, George Herbert. 1913. "The Social Self." *Journal of Philosophy, Psychology and Scientific Methods* 10: 374–80.

——. 1934. *Mind, Self, and Society*. Chicago: University of Chicago Press.

Medin, Douglas L., Elizabeth B. Lynch, John D. Coley, and Scott Atran. 1997. "Categorization and Reasoning among Tree Experts: Do All Roads Lead to Rome?" *Cognitive Psychology* 32: 49–96.

Meltzer, Bernard N., John W. Petras, and Larry T. Reynolds. 1974. *Symbolic Interactionism: Genesis, Varieties and Criticism*. Monographs in Social Theory. London and Boston: Routledge and Kegan Paul.

Mill, John Stuart. 1891. *August Comte and Positivism*. 4th ed. London: Kegan Paul, Trench, Trubner. First published 1865.

——. 1950. *Philosophy of Scientific Method, Containing the Text of a System of Logic*. Edited with an Introduction by Ernest Nagel. New York: Haffner. First published 1843.

Moody, James, and Douglas R. White. 2003. "Social Cohesion and Imbeddedness: A Hierarchical Concept of Social Groups." *American Sociological Review* 68(1): 1–25.

Moore, Sally Falk, and Barbara B. Meyerhoff, eds. 1977. *Secular Rituals*. Assen, Netherlands: Van Gorcum.

Montagu, Ashley. 1946. *Man's Most Dangerous Myth: The Fallacy of Race*. 2nd ed. New York: Columbia University Press.

Morales, Alfonso, ed. 2003. *Renascent Pragmatism*. Burlington, Vt.: Ashgate.

Murphy, Jeffrie G. 1994. *Kant: The Philosophy of Right*. Macon, Ga.: Mercer University Press.

Murrell, Peter. 2001. *Assessing the Value of Law in Transition Economies*. Ann Arbor: University of Michigan Press.

Neale, Walter C. 1958. "The Limitations of Indian Village Survey Data." *Journal of Asian Studies* 17 (May): 383–402.

——. 1959. "Economic Accounting and Family Farming in India." *Economic Development and Cultural Change* 7 (April): 286–301.

——. 1976. *Monies in Societies*. San Francisco: Chandler and Sharp.

Nolan, Justin M. 2002. "Wild Plant Classification in Little Dixie: Variation in a Regional Culture." *Journal of Ecological Anthropology* 6(1): 69–81.

Occhipinti, S., and M. Siegal. 1996. "Cultural Evolution and Divergent Rationalities in Human Reasoning." *Ethos: Journal of Psychological Anthropology* 24: 510–26.

O'Meara, J. Tim. 1989. "Anthropology as Empirical Science." *American Anthropologist* 91(2): 354–69.

Ostrom, Elinor, Larry Shroeder, and Susan Wynne. 1993. *Institutional Incentives and Sustainable Development: Infrastructure Policies in Perspective*. Boulder, Colo.: Westview.

Parkin, Robert. 1997. *Kinship: An Introduction to the Basic Concepts*. Oxford, UK: Blackwell.

Parsons, Talcott. 1951. *The Social System*. Glencoe, Ill.: Free Press.

Parsons, Talcott, and Edward Shils. 1951. *Toward a General Theory of Action*. Cambridge: Harvard University Press.

Pertierra, Raul. 1988. *Religion, Politics, and Rationality in a Philippine Community*. Honolulu: University of Hawaii Press.

Piaget, Jean. 1953. *Logic and Psychology*. Translated from the French by W. Mays and F. Whitehead. Manchester, UK: Manchester University Press.

——. 1962. *Play, Dreams and Imitation in Childhood*. New York: Norton.

————. 1970. *Genetic Epistemology.* New York and London: Columbia University Press.

————. 1976 [1928]. *Judgment and Reasoning in the Child.* Translated by M. Warden. Totowa, N.J.: Littlefield and Adams.

Piaget, Jean, and Bärbel Inhelder. 1964. *The Early Growth of Logic in the Child.* London and New York: Routledge and Kegan Paul.

Polishchuk, Leonid. 2001. "Legal Initiative in Russian Regions: Determinants and Effects." In *The Value of Law in Transition Economies,* edited by Peter Murrell, 330–68. Ann Arbor: University of Michigan Press.

Popper, Karl. 2002. *The Logic of Scientific Discovery.* First English edition, 1959. London: Routledge.

Pound, Roscoe. 1943. "A Survey of Social Interests." *Harvard Law Review* 57: 1–39.

Price-Williams, Douglass, Ormond Hammond, Ceel Edgerton, and Michael Walker. 1977. "Kinship Concepts among Rural Hawaiian Children." In *Piagetian Psychology: Cross Cultural Contributions,* edited by P. Dasen, 296–334. New York: Gardener.

Radcliffe-Brown, A. R. 1952. *Structure and Function in Primitive Society.* Glencoe, Ill.: Free Press.

Rappaport, Roy A. 1971. "Ritual, Sanctity, and Cybernetics." *American Anthropologist* 73(1): 98–112.

————. 1974. *Pigs for the Ancestors: Ritual in the Ecology of a New Guinea People.* New Haven, Conn.: Yale University Press.

————. 1984. *Pigs for the Ancestors.* 2nd ed. New Haven, Conn.: Yale University Press.

Read, Dwight W. 1974. "Kinship Algebra: A Mathematical Study of Kinship Structure." In *Genealogical Mathematics,* edited by Paul Ballonoff, 135–61. The Hague: Mouton.

————. 1984. "An Algebraic Account of the American Kinship Terminology." *Current Anthropology* 25(4): 417–49.

————. 2002. "Mathematical Modeling Issues in Analytical Representations of Human Societies." In *Cybernetics and Systems,* Vol. 1, edited by Robert Trappl, 408–10. Vienna: Austrian Society for Cybernetic Studies.

Read, Dwight, and C. Behrens. 1990. "KAES: An Expert System for the Algebraic Analysis of Kinship Terminologies." *Journal of Quantitative Anthropology* 2: 353–93.

Rescher, Nicholas. 1958. "On Prediction and Explanation." *British Journal for the Philosophy of Science* 8(32): 281–90.

————. 1962. "The Revolt against Process." *Journal of Philosophy* 15: 410–17.

————. 1976. "Peirce and the Economy of Research." *Philosophy of Science* 43(1): 71–98.

————. 1991. *A System of Pragmatic Idealism,* Vol. 1, *Human Knowledge in Idealistic Perspective.* Princeton, N.J.: Princeton University Press.

————. 1993. *A System of Pragmatic Idealism,* Vol. 2, *The Validity of Values.* Princeton, N.J.: Princeton University Press.

————. 1994. *A System of Pragmatic Idealism,* Vol. 3, *Metaphilosophical Inquiries.* Princeton, N.J.: Princeton University Press.

————. 2006. *The Berlin School of Logical Empiricism and Its Legacy.* July 6. http://www .pitt.edu/~Pittcntr/About/The_Berlin_School.pdf.

Rice, G. Elizabeth. 1980. "On Cultural Schemata." *American Ethnologist* 7(1): 152–71.

Rorty, Richard. 1979. *Philosophy and the Mirror of Nature.* Princeton, N.J.: Princeton University Press.

————. 1982. *Consequences of Pragmatism.* Minneapolis: University of Minnesota Press.

———. 1992. *The Linguistic Turn: Essays in Philosophical Method.* Chicago: University of Chicago Press.

Rosaldo, Renato. 1989. *Culture and Truth: The Remaking of Social Analysis.* Boston: Beacon.

Roscoe, Paul B. 1995. "The Perils of 'Positivism' in Anthropology." *American Anthropologist,* n.s., 97(3): 492–504.

Rosenthal, Sandra B., Carl R. Hausman, and Douglas R. Anderson. 1999. *Classical American Pragmatism: Its Contemporary Vitality.* Urbana: University of Illinois Press.

Russell, Bertrand. 1972. *A History of Western Philosophy.* New York: Touchstone Books. First published 1945.

Sahlins, Marshall. 1976. *Culture and Practical Reason.* Chicago: University of Chicago Press.

Savage, Leonard J. 1954. *The Foundation of Statistics.* New York: Wiley.

Saxe, Geoffrey. 1983. "Piaget and Anthropology." *American Anthropologist,* n.s., 85(1): 136–43.

Schneider, David M. 1965. "Some Muddles in the Models." In *The Relevance of Models for Social Anthropology,* edited by Michael Banton, 25–85. Association for Social Anthropologists Monographs No. 1. New York: Taplinger.

———. 1968. *American Kinship: A Cultural Account.* Englewood Cliffs, N.J.: Prentice Hall.

———. 1987. *A Critique of the Study of Kinship.* Ann Arbor: University of Michigan Press.

———. 1995. *Schneider on Schneider: The Conversion of the Jews and Other Anthropological Stories.* As told to Richard Handler. Durham, N.C., and London: Duke University Press.

Schultz, Theodore. 1964. *Transforming Traditional Agriculture.* Berkeley and Los Angeles: University of California Press.

Schusky, Ernest L. 1989. *Culture and Agriculture: An Ecological Introduction to Traditional and Modern Farming Systems.* New York, Westport, and London: Bergin and Garvey.

Settle, Thomas B. 1967. "Galileo's Use of Experiment as a Tool of Investigation." In *Galileo: Man of Science,* edited by E. McMullin, 315–37. 1988, reprint of 1967 Basic Books edition. Princeton Junction, N.J.: Scholar's Bookshelf.

Shannon, C. E., and Warren Weaver. 1963. *The Mathematical Theory of Communication.* Urbana: University of Illinois Press.

Shapin, Steven, and Simon Schaffer. 1985. *Leviathan and the Air-Pump: Hobbes, Boyle, and the Experimental Life.* Princeton, N.J.: Princeton University Press.

Silverstein, Michael, and Greg Urban, eds. 1996. *Natural Histories of Discourse.* Chicago: University of Chicago Press.

Simon, Herbert A. 1957. *Models of Man.* New York: Wiley.

———. 1986. "Rationality in Psychology and Economics." *The Journal of Business: Part 2, The Behavioral Foundations of Economic Theory* 59(4): S209–S224.

Singer, Andre, and Stephen Lansing. 1998. *The Goddess and the Computer.* Watertown, Mass.: Documentary Educational Resources.

Small, Cathy. 1999. "Finding an Invisible History: A Computer Simulation Experiment (in Virtual Polynesia)." *Journal of Artificial Societies and Social Simulation* 2(3). http://www.soc.surrey.ac.uk/JASSS/2/3/6.html.

Small, Cathy, Virginia Blankenship, and Ronald Whale. 1997. "A Computer Simulation Approach to Ethnographic Analysis." *Field Methods* 9(3): 1–8.

Smith, David A., and Douglas R. White. 1992. "Structure and Dynamics of the Global Economy: Network Analysis of International Trade, 1965–1980." *Social Forces* 70(4): 857–93.

Smith, Eric A. 1984. "Anthropology, Evolutionary Theory and the Explanatory Limits of the Ecosystem Concept." In *The Ecosystem Concept in Anthropology*, edited by Emilio Moran, 51–86. AAAS Selected Symposium 92. Boulder, Colo.: Westview.

Spencer, Herbert. 1880. *First Principles*. 4th ed. New York: H. M. Caldwell. First published 1862.

Srinivas, M. N. 1976. *The Remembered Village*. Berkeley and Los Angeles: University of California Press.

Switzer, Les. 1998. "Christianity, Colonialism and the Postmodern Project in South Africa: The Comaroffs Revisited." *Canadian Journal of African Studies* 32(1): 181 96.

Tambiah, S. 1973. "The Meaning and Form of Magical Acts." In *Modes of Thought*, edited by R. Horton and R. Finnegan, 199–299. London: Faber.

Tax, Sol. 1963. *Penny Capitalism: A Guatemalan Indian Economy*. Chicago: University of Chicago Press. First published 1953.

Timberlake, Lloyd. 1985. *Africa in Crisis*. London: Earthscan.

Turnbull, Colin. 1972. *The Mountain People*. New York: Simon and Schuster.

Turner, B. L., and Stephen B. Brush. 1987. *Comparative Farming Systems*. New York and London: Guilford.

Turner, Victor. 1967. *The Forest of Symbols*. Ithaca, N.Y.: Cornell University Press.

———. 1969. *The Ritual Process*. Chicago: Aldine.

Tylor, Edward B. 1889. *Primitive Culture*. New York: Henry Holt. First published 1871.

Vatuk, Sylvia. 1972. "Kinship Terminology in Northern India." *American Anthropologist* 74(3) (June): 791–93.

Wagner, Roy. 1974. "Are There Social Groups in the New Guinea Highlands?" In *Frontiers of Anthropology*, edited by Murray J. Leaf, with Bernard G. Campbell, Constance Cronin, George DeVos, William Longacre, Marlys McClaran, Fred T. Plog, Jack H. Prost, and Roy Wagner, 95–122. New York: Van Nostrand.

Wallace, Anthony F. C., and John Atkins. 1960. "The Meaning of Kinship Terms." *American Anthropologist* 62: 58–80.

Warren, D. Michael, and Peter Blunt. 1996. *Indigenous Organizations and Development*. IT Studies in Indigenous Knowledge and Development. London: Intermediate Technology Publications.

Warren, D. Michael, L. Jan Slikkerveer, and David Brokensha. 1995. *The Cultural Dimension of Development*. IT Studies in Indigenous Knowledge and Development. London: Intermediate Technology Publications.

Wax, Murray. 1997. "On Negating Positivism: An Anthropological Dialectic." *American Anthropologist* 99(1): 17–23.

White, Douglas. 1999. "Controlled Simulation of Marriage Systems." *Journal of Artificial Societies and Social Simulation* 2(3). http://www.soc.surrey.ac.uk/JASSS/2/3/5.html.

White, Douglas, and Ulla Johansen. 2004. *Network Analysis and Ethnographic Problems: Process Models of a Turkish Clan*. Lanham, Md.: Lexington Books.

Windelband, Wilhelm. 1901. *A History of Philosophy*. 2 vols. 1958, reprint of 1901 edition. New York: Harper Torchebooks.

Wiser, William H., and Charlotte Wiser. 1960. *Behind Mud Walls*. Berkeley: University of California Press.

Wittgenstein, Ludwig. 1953. *Philosophical Investigations*. New York: Macmillan.

Zammito, John H. 2002. *Kant, Herder & the Birth of Anthropology*. Chicago and London: University of Chicago Press.

INDEX

Against the Dogmatists (Sextus Empiricus), 9, 222n2

Agricultural Decision Making: Anthropological Contributions to Rural Development (Bartlett), 36

agriculture, 35, 36, 74; applications of the farming model, 157–58, 160, 162; Balinese rice farmers, 137–39; crop variation issues, 155–57, 158, 160, 162; efficiency and intensification measures of, 37; farm communities and the hill-climbing algorithm, 204–6; farm cooperatives, 202–3; the four "F's" of farm requirements (food, fodder, fuel, funds), 153–55; Indian farmers' conceptualization of labor rates, 118–21; irrigation issues, 76, 157–58; peasant farming and farm budget models, 150, 153–57, 158, 160, 162; pesticide use, 156–57

"Algebraic Account of the American Kinship Terminology, An" (Read), 72

analytic systems, 12–13

anthropology, 37, 222n1; cognitive, 71, 83; as comparative sociology, 4; as cultural critique, 30; current topics of, 30; journals associated with, 71; mathematical, 70, 71; positivism in, 1–2, 3; scientific anthropologists, 65. *See also* participant observation

Anthropology from a Pragmatic Point of View (Kant), 43, 46, 51–52, 53

Amsden et. al., 217.

appearance/reality dichotomy, 2

Aristotle, 10. *See also* logic, syllogistic (Aristotelian)

Assessing the Value of Law in Transition Economies (Murrell), 217

Atkins, John, 104

authoritarianism, 56, 57

"Authority and Public Opinion in Tikopia" (Firth), 83

Bacon, Francis, 8

Bailey, F. G., 87, 89, 126; later monographs of, 84

Ballonoff, Paul, 71

Barth, Fredrik, 84, 87, 89, 128

baseball, 74, 75

Bastian, Adolph, 40

Bates, Daniel, 37, 164

Bateson, Gregory, 84

Becker, Gary, 198, 199

Beckerman, Stephen, 206

Behrens, Clifford, 72

Bennardo, Giovanni, 71

Berlin school, see *logical empiricism*

Bernard, Russ, 65

Biersack, Aletta, 35

Blankenship, Virginia, 79

Blunt, Peter, 89

Boas, Franz, 3, 26

Bohannan, Laura, 83

Bohannan, Paul, 83

Boissevain, Jeremy, 129

Boserup, Ester, 36–37; efficiency measure of, 37; intensification measure of, 37

boundary conditions, 88

Bourdieu, Pierre, 213

Boyle, Robert, 8, 9

Brahmins, 188, 223–24n3

Brief History of Time, A (Hawking), 7

Brittan, Gordon G., Jr., 57

Brokensha, David, 89

Brown, Penelope, 222n7

Burnyeat, Myles, 8

Carnap, Rudolf, 39, 65

Casablanca (1942), 145

Catholicism, medieval, 2

causality, historical, 1

ceremonies, 82, 84, 85, 126, 149, 177–78, 214; authoritative, 176; trade, 113. *See also* wedding ceremonies, of the Sikh religion

chess, 75

Chibnick, Michael, 26

Chomsky, Noam, 110

Clifford, James, 5–6, 176

cognitive complexity, 106–7

"Collective Violence in Darfur: An Agent-Based Model of Pastoral Nomad/Sedentary Farmer Interaction" (Kuznar and Sedlmeyer), 78
Commonwealth of Independent States, 217, 218
communication theory, *see* information theory
communities, 16, 38, 113, 164–65, 195, 221n1; factional activity in, 124–29; farming, 204–6; organization of, 16; and social charters, 149–50
computers, 68
Comte, Auguste, 2, 3, 30
conceptual development, 107–8; and de-centering, 108
Conlisk, John, 198, 199
Consequences of Pragmatism (Rorty), 40, 60–61
"Copernican Revolution, The" (Dewey), 62–63
Copernicus, 62–63
Critique of Judgment (Kant), 42
Critique of Practical Reason (Kant), 42, 43
Critique of Pure Reason (Kant), 42, 43, 49
Critique of the Study of Kinship (Schneider), 29–30
Cultural Analysis of Kinship: The Legacy of David M. Schneider (Feinberg and Ottenheimer), 32
"cultural description," 6
"Cultural Idea Systems: Logical Structures and the Logic of Instantiation" (Read and Leaf), 80
cultural information sources, 212–13
cultural systems, 70–71
culture, 3, 201, 216; European cultural ideas concerning, 29–30; and structure, 27; as superorganic, 3. *See also* ecology, cultural
Culture and Practical Reason (Sahlins), 33
cybernetics, 33–34

D'Andrade, Roy, 104; on "emic" analysis, 104
Darwin, Charles, 40
databases, ethnographic, 68–70
decision algorithms: decision-making, 200–201; hill-climbing, 204–6; indigenous, 26
DeMaille, Raymond, 32
Depew, David, 39, 40
Descartes, René, 58, 59, 61
determinism, 40, 87; contemporary arguments for, 33–35; social, 2, 3
Dewey, John, 40, 58; on the development of pragmatism, 62–63; on the Kantian method

of analysis, 61–62; on Kant's idealism, 62; on Kant's "knowing mind," 62, 63
Dialogue concerning the Two Chief World Systems (Galileo), 9
diffusionism, 3
dogmatism, 58
Durkheim, Emile, 3, 84; and social facts, 28–29
Dworkin, Ronald, 55

ecology, cultural, 33–38, 135, 195
Economic Development and Social Change in South India (Epstein), 38
economics, 28, 116–18; economic adjustments, 118; ethnographic treatment of, 35–36; of Indian farmers, 118–21, 124; indigenous economic models, 121, 124. *See also* economics, experimental; money
economics, experimental, 23–26; and the Nash equilibrium, 25, 26
egoism, 52, 56; aesthetic, 52; logical, 52; moral, 52–53
Ehrlich, Eugen, 18, 19, 129
"Emergent Properties of Balinese Water Temple Networks: Coadaptation on a Rugged Fitness Landscape" (Lansing), 76
empiricism, 4, 7–11, 198–99; empirical theory defined, 7, 221n2; radical, 1, 10, 219. *See also* formalism, empirical; Kant, Immanuel, empiricism of; logical empiricists/logical empiricism
energy budgets, 37
Epstein, T. S., 87, 89
ethnology, scientific, 3, 4, 11, 13, 56; ethnographic databases, 68–70; experimental design in, 22
ethnomethodology, 21
European Union (EU), 217
Evans-Pritchard, E. E., 29
experiment/experimentation, 8
experimentalism/experimentalists, 4, 6, 7–11, 24–25
experimental method, and observation, 8–9

factions (in South Asia, India), 124–29, 187; celebration of, 128; factional power as hidden/secret, 126; formal algebra of, 127–28; function of, 127; logic by which factions are instantiated, 128; public moralizing over, 128; in small communities, 129
farming/farmers. *See* agriculture
Faust (Goethe), 55–56
Fechner, Gustav, 40
Feinberg, Richard, 71

Ferguson, Adam, 40
Fichte, Johann Gottlieb, 56
fieldwork, 5–6
films: as replacement for epic poetry, 147–48; specific film genres as vehicles for organizational ideas, 148–49; Westerns, 148
"Finding an Invisible History: A Computer Simulation Experiment (in Virtual Polynesia)" (Small), 77
Firth, Raymond, 38, 83
Fischer, Michael M., 30, 71, 72, 96, 140, 141
Fogelson, Raymond, 32
folk models, 82, 83, 84, 85, 149, 189
formalism, empirical, 11–14
Foundations of Human Sociality: Economic Experiments and Ethnographic Evidence from Fifteen Small-Scale Societies (Henrich et al.), 26
"four-square gospel" of the societal whole, 30–31
Freud, Sigmund, 30

Galileo: arguments for the Copernican system, 9; and the law of acceleration, 8–9
Galileo: Man of Science (McMullin), 8
Galison, Peter, 8, 10, 11, 134
Garfinkel, Harold, 21, 84
Gatewood, John, 162–63
Geertz, Clifford, 29
"Genealogical Charter, A" (L. Bohannan), 83
Genealogical Mathematics (ed. Ballonoff), 72
geometry: Euclidean, 12, 13; Kant's view of, 44–45
gestures, 17
Gigerenzer, Gerd, 198, 199, 201
Gladwin, Christina, 36
God, 56, 57, 180
Goddess and the Computer, The (1998), 135, 136–39
Gödel, Kurt, 11
Goethe, Johann Wolfgang von, 40, 55
Goffman, Erving, 21, 84, 176
Goodenough, Ward, 32
Greechie, Richard, 71
Greif, Avner, 24, 26
Groundwork of the Metaphysics of Morals (Kant), 43, 49
groups, 175–76; creation of, 177; difference of from organizations, 15–16

Habermas, Jürgen, 57
Hacking, Ian, 40, 176
Handler, Harry, 30
Harvey, William, 9

Hawking, Stephen, 7
Hegel, G. W. F.; interpretation of Kant, 56–57; phenomenology of ("phenomenology of mind"), 57, 222n12
Heidegger, Martin, 58
Heinrich, Joseph, 200
Heisenberg's uncertainty principle, 63–64
Helmholtz, Wilhelm von, 17, 40
Hempel, Karl, 7, 8, 39, 221n3
Henrich, Joseph, 24
Herder, Gottfried, 40, 222n1
History of Ethnological Theory, The (Lowie), 3
Hobbes, Thomas, 8, 51
Hollinger, Robert, 39
Hooke, Robert, 9
Hopi people, 164
Humboldt, Alexander von, 40
Humboldt, Wilhelm, 40
Hume, David, 10, 40; critique of Locke's materialistic theory of perception, 42; Kant's criticism of, 42, 222n2
Hunters, The (1958), 135–36

idea systems, cultural, 11–12, 19, 70, 74–75, 77, 78, 140; formal properties of, 85–86; general considerations of, 83–85; modeling of, 80–81; observation and elicitation of, 87–89; synthetic a priori, 13–14; two types of, 19
idea systems, social, 19–21, 74, 75, 82–83, 89, 126, 133; association of ideas and beliefs, 22–23; difference of from technical idea systems, 135; and the differentiation of situations, 21–22; and organizational charters, 145–46; types of, 89. *See also* kinship; management/managerial control
idea systems, technical, 19, 21, 74, 89, 134, 200; in bartending, 163; difference of from social idea systems, 135; observation of, 134–39; semantic properties of, 135; and social scale, 139
Idea for a Universal History from a Cosmopolitan Point of View (Kant), 55
idealism, 35, 56; "pragmatic idealism," 39
ideologies, 7, 12
Ik people (northern Kenya), 19
Iliad (Homer), and organizational charters, 146–47
Image and Logic (Galison), 8, 10
India, 112, 114, 118–21; factions and factional activity in, 124–29. *See also* Maharashtra state; Punjab state
Information and Behavior in a Sikh Village: Social Organization Reconsidered (Leaf), 38, 86, 87–88

information theory, 131–33, 140

Inhelder, Bärbel, 107

instantiation, 75, 141, 172, 213–14; analysis of, 80–81, 141–42

institutions, 27–32, 175–76, 193–94; as established process, 27–28; four functional subsystems of, 31; metacultural idea of, 31–32; as a specific kind of supraorganization, 28. *See also* legal profession, as an institution/organization

International Monetary Fund, 217

interpretivism, 43

James, William, 4, 10

Jhering, Rudolph von, 18, 19, 40

Joas, Hans, 39

Johansen, Ulla, 173

Jones, W. T., 43, 57

Justice and Judgment among the Tiv (P. Bohannan), 83

Kalahari Bushmen, 135–36

Kane, Joseph, 223n1

Kant, Immanuel, 13, 40, 57–58, 177, 200; analytical writings of, 42–43; anthropological writings of, 43; on the capacity for judgment, 51; on the categorical imperative, 49, 50; conception of the a priori, 50, 56; critical (synthetic) writings of, 42; criticism of Hume, 42, 222n2; on defects of judgment, 54; on duty and reason, 49; on egoism, 52–53; empiricism of, 40–56 *passim*; on geometry, 44–45; on knowledge and experience, 47–48; and the "knowing mind," 62, 63; on law and freedom, 54–55; on law and reason, 49; on learning from others, 46; on madness, 54; on moral judgments, 49, 53–54; on noumena, 46, 47, 48, 65; on objective and subjective judgments, 44, 45–46, 48; on perception, 46, 47; on phenomena, 46–47; and positivism, 61; on the relations of means to an end, 50–51; on transcendental objects and *überschwänglich*, 47, 65; on the universal, 49–50

Kant and the Nineteenth Century (Jones), 43

kinship, 20, 27, 28, 30, 90, 168, 173; as a distinct cultural/organizational system, 32; kinship positions in Punjab, 111–12; kinship terminologies, 71–72, 107–8; and the organizational fundamentals of self-construction, 110–11; as a philosophy, 73–74; recruitment rules in kinship systems, 90–91; rules of incest, 105; rules of inheritance, 105–6, 111; sexual intercourse as central symbol of, 29; and socialization, 106–11; Vietnamese

kinship ideas, 108–10. *See also* kinship maps; management/managerial control

Kinship Algebra Expert System (KAES), 72–73, 96–100, 170

"Kinship Algebra: A Mathematical Study of Kinship Structure" (Read), 72

kinship maps, 90–104 *passim*; and Cayley tables, 101–2; and componential analysis, 103–4; core positions of, 91–92; design of, 107; and elicitation, 91, 92; for English, 91–92, 93–95, 97–99, 104; and the KAES computer program, 96–100; for Punjab, 91–92, 93, 95, 96, 99, 102, 104; and sibling structure, 101–2; and spatial imagery, 91

knowledge, 62; active, 163; and experience, 47–48; as the mirror of nature, 59, 60

Korsgaard, Christine, 49

Kremer, James N., 76, 77; on agent-based simulations, 205–6

Kroeber, Alfred, 3

Kronenfeld, David, 71

Kuhn, Thomas, 1, 221n4

Kuznar, Lawrence, 65, 78

Lansing, Stephen, 71, 74, 76, 77, 135, 136, 138; on agent-based simulations, 205–6

law/jurisprudence, 40, 49; 18; common law legal theory, 216–17; and freedom, 54–55; and property, 202; sociology of, 18. *See also* legal profession, as an institution/organization

Laws of Manu, The, 112

Leach, E. R., 84; on the indigenous models of society, 86–87

Leaf, Murray J., 5, 38, 80, 86, 87–88, 91; diagrammatic analysis of Punjabi and English by, 72, 222–23n1; note taking practice of, 125–26; work on factional activity in South Asia, 124–26; work of on the Irrigation and Water Management Project, 119–20, 151, 153–57, 158, 160, 162. *See also* kinship maps; Sidhpur Kalan, research on conflicts in

Leenhardt, Maurice, 6

Lees, Susan, 37

legal profession, as an institution/organization, 190–93; ceremonies of lawyers other than trials, 191; rights and duties of members of legal organizations, 191–92; trials as legal ceremonies, 191

Lehman, Kris, 71

Leviathan and the Air-Pump (Shapin and Schaffer), 8

Levinson, Stephen, 222n7

Levi-Strauss, Claude, 29, 35, 84

Lévy-Bruhl, Lucien, 4, 6

liberalism, political, 55
Locke, John, 42, 58, 59, 65; on perception, 43–44
logic, 10; deontic, 140; of an idea system, 12; in the sciences, 10; syllogistic (Aristotelian), 10, 221n3
logical empiricists/logical empiricism, 63–64, 221n3
logical positivists/logical positivism, 4, 8, 12, 39; aim of, 10–11; relation to Berlin school, 221n3
Lowie, Robert, 3
Luong, Hy Van, 108–9

Mach, Ernst, 3
Machiguenga people, 24
Maharashtra state: farm cooperatives in, 202–3; Maharashtra Irrigation Department, 157–58, 223n3
Malinowski, Bronislaw, 3, 4–5, 38
Man, Mind, and Science (Leaf), 6
management/managerial control, 113–16; computer simulations of management decision making, 116; distinctiveness of management ideas, 113–14; in India, 114–15; in South Asia compared to the West, 115–16
Manners, Robert, 6–7
Marcus, George, 30, 176
Market Meets Its Match, The: Restructuring the Economies of Eastern Europe (Amsden, Kochanowicz, and Taylor), 217
Marshall, John, 135–36
Marshall Plan, 40, 218
Marx, Karl, 2
Marxism, 33, 43, 218
materialism, 35
mathematics, 214; monetary, 117–18; systems of, 12, 14, 74. *See also* geometry
Matrix, The (1999), 149
Mauss, Marcel, 4, 6, 84
McKinley, Robert, 32, 71, 73–74
McLennan, J. F., 189
McMullin, Ernan, 8, 39
Mead, George Herbert, 16–17, 27–28, 54, 63
"Meaning and Form of Magical Acts, The" (Tambiah), 84
metaphysics, 2; positivistic rejection of, 13
Metaphysics of Morals (Kant), 43
Meur, Gesele de, 71
Meyerhoff, Barbara B., 84
Mill, John Stuart, 2, 10, 12, 30, 64; on essential and nonessential propositions, 12–13
Mind, Self, and Society (Mead), 17, 27–28
Model Rules of Professional Conduct (American Bar Association), 192

models: agent-based, 67–68, 205–6; agent and system, 74–80; generative system, 70–74; multiagent, 67, 78, 204; multiagent models of adaptive strategies, 207–10; network, 75
money, 19; as culturally defined, 116–17; economic conceptions of, 117; maintenance of its value, 117; monetary mathematics, 117–18; objectivization of, 67; production of, 117
Monies in Societies (Neale), 116–17
Montague, Susan, 32
Montesquieu, 41–42
Moore, Sally Falk, 84
Morales, Alfonso, 40
Murrell, Peter, 217, 218
myth, and movies, 145–50

Navaho people, 20, 114, 142; language of, 222–23n1
Neale, Walter, 116–17, 121
neo-Kantianism, 56, 58, 59, 61
network analysis, 79–80, 172–73
Network Analysis and Ethnographic Problems: Process Models of a Turkish Nomad Clan (White and Johansen), 173
networks, 80, 167–73; definition of, 167; formation of, 167–68
New Deal, the, 40, 217, 218
New Guinea, 21

objectivity, 2, 3, 4, 6, 7, 41
objectivization, 41; of money, 67
Occhipinti, S., 23
Odyssey (Homer), and organizational charters, 146–47
O'Meara, J., 65
Oppenheimer, Martin, 71
organizations, 4, 16–19, 20, 22, 35, 75, 81, 111, 141–43, 195; charters of, 143–45, 176–77, 213–14; charters of and myth, 145–50; creation/formation of, 13, 74–75, 83–84, 211, 215; difference of from groups, 15–16; difference of from networks, 80; economic, 117; and incentive systems, 217–18; and member benefits, 18–19; multiple, 215–16; and the "mutual adjustment of behavior," 16–18, 21, 28; organizational goal and individual agendas, 22; productive and regulatory purposes of, 142–43; purposes of, 19, 142; role of sanctions in, 18; and shared cultural information (idea) systems, 11–12, 13, 19–21; translocal, 129–30. *See also* legal profession; as an institution/organization; networks; organizations, productive; organizations, regulatory; rationality, individual

organizations, productive, 150, 166, 173–74; and applications of the farming model, 157–58, 160, 162; bartending, 162–63; peasant farming, 150, 153–57

organizations, regulatory, 163–64; courts as a subset of, 164; and the formal problem of occupational choice, 164–66; and the necessity of collective expression, 166–67

Organon (Aristotle), 10

Pajek software, 79; Pajek analysis of *meli* (marriage support group) relations, 168–69

Parsons, Talcott, 30–31

participant observation, 4–7

Penny Capitalism (Tax), 35

Perpetual Peace (Kant), 55

Pertierra, Raul, 129

Philosophy of Law, The (Kant), 43, 51

Philosophy and the Mirror of Nature (Rorty), 58–59

Piaget, Jean, 106, 107, 110

Pigs for the Ancestors (Rappaport), 33, 35

Plato, 58, 61

pluralism, 42, 217, 218

poetry, epic, 146; film in America as replacement for, 147–50

Polishchuk, Leonid, 218

Political Systems of Highland Burma (Leach), 86

Popper, Karl, 7, 8, 65, 87, 221n3

positivism, 1–2, 31, 33, 43, 65; academic proponents and apologists of, 3–4; and culture, 3; and Kant, 61; neopositivism, 221n3; as a philosophical movement, 2; positivistic tradition and social facts, 29; and social science, 4

postmodernism, 4, 29, 43; postmodernist constructionism, 40; postmodernist constructivism, 71

pragmatism, 6, 10, 59–61, 64, 216; classical, 39–40; as empirical philosophy, 61; four complementary bodies of scholarship concerning, 40; renewed interest in, 39–40

Pragmatism: From Progressivism to Postmodernism (Hollinger and Depew), 39

Priestley, Joseph, 64

Priests and Programmers (Lansing), 76

Primitive Culture (Tylor), 3

Prolegomena to Any Future Metaphysics (Kant), 43

psychology: cognitive, 198; developmental, 106; evolutionary, 24, 26; experimental, 4; functional, 4. See also *Volkerpsychologie*

Punjab state, 5, 111–13, 142; caste concepts in, 112–13; farm cooperatives in, 202–3; marriage rules, 112; property rights in, 112. See also kinship maps, for Punjab

purpose: in idea systems, 142; in organizations, 19, 142; productive and regulatory, 142–43

Quest for Certainty, The (Dewey), 61

Quételet, Adolphe, 75

Quine, W. V. O., 39, 60

Radcliffe-Brown, Alfred, 4, 29

Rappaport, Roy, 33–35, 84; on pig demography, 34–35

rationality, 26, 210; of process, 23; of purpose, 23; situational nature of, 24. See also rationality, and adaptation; rationality, individual

rationality, and adaptation, 203–4; and the hill-climbing algorithm, 204–6

rationality, individual, 195, 216; bounded rationality, 198–200; formation of, 195–96; formation of the self, 196; and optimization, 197; and our physical bodies, 197; and resource flows, 201–3. See also rationality, and adaptation

Read, Dwight, 32, 71, 72, 80, 96, 97, 103, 141

realism, 65

reality, social construction of, 1, 45

reciprocity, in the logic of social relations, 41–42

Reclaiming a Scientific Anthropology (Kuznar), 65

reflexivity, 41

Reichenbach, Hans, 7, 39, 221n3

relativism, 6

Renascent Pragmatism (Morales), 40

Rescher, Nicholas, 39, 221n3

Ritual Process, The (Turner), 84

"Ritual, Sanctity, and Cybernetics" (Rappaport), 33–34

Rorty, Richard, 40, 61, 64; on the correspondence theory of truth, 58; dualism of, 58; and Kant, 58–61; on Philosophy, 58–59; on pragmatism, 59–61

Rosaldo, Renato, 6–7

Roscoe, Paul B., 1–2, 3, 65

Russell, Bertrand, 10, 11; on Kant's politics, 57–58

Sahlins, Marshall, 33; assertion that cultures were self-determining, 35

St. Simon, Claude Henri, 2

Salmon, Wesley, 7, 221n3
Savage, Leonard, 199
Savigny, Carl von, 40
Schlick, Moritz, 65
Schneider, David, 5, 27; on kinship relations, 29; neopositivism of, 31; rejection of empiricism, 29–30; turn of to postmodernism, 29
Schultz, Theodore, 35
science: development of, 4; empirical, 55; ethnography of, 7–8; history of, 7–8; as the imposition of subjectivity, 3; physical, 7, 12, 219; physics, 1; social and behavioral, 9–10
Science of Right (Kant), 43
Secular Rituals (Moore and Meyerhoff), 84
Sedlmeyer, Robert, 78
self, the: self-definition, 27–28; social construction of, 17
Sellars, Wilfrid, 60
Selten, Reinhard, 198, 199, 201
Sextus Empiricus, 9, 222n2
sexuality, 21
Shane (1953), 148
Shannon, C. E., 131, 132
Sidhpur Kalan, research on conflicts in, 170–72
Siegel, M., 23
Sikhism, 180, 223–24n3. *See also* wedding ceremonies, of the Sikh religion
Silverstein, Michael, 130
Simmel, Georg, 4
Simon, Herbert, 198
Singer, Andre, 135, 136, 138
Singh, Bachan, 171, 172
Singh, Dial, 171
Singh, Kaka, 171
Singh, Kalkatta, 171
Singh, Mahinder, 171
Singh, Mehima, 171
Singh, Naranjan, 125
Singh, Rachan, 171
Singh Sarpanch, Ujagar, 171, 172
Singh, Sher, 171
Skeptical Tradition, The (Burnyeat), 8
skepticism, 7–11, 39, 40; as a "formal science," 9
Small, Cathy, 77, 78, 79, 207–8, 210
Smith, Adam, 24, 40, 67
Smith, Eric Alden, 206
social Darwinism, 3, 33
social facts, 28–29
social patterns, and individual decisions, 67
social process, model of, 211–12; representation of communication in, 214–15

social relations, 5, 79, 172; globalized patterns of, 216; performative, 19; reciprocal logic of, 41–42
social theory, 1, 29, 30, 40, 68, 218; Marxist, 218
society, 28, 219; civil, 54; indigenous models of, 86–87; as inherently monolithic, 84, 86; as a whole, 32
Society for Economic Anthropology, 36
sociology, 2, 3; French 3–4; of law, 18. *See also* anthropology, as comparative sociology
Socrates, 58
Soviet Union, 217–18
Spencer, Herbert, 2, 3, 33
Spirit of the Laws, The (Montesquieu), 41
Star Wars (1977), 149
"Structural Implications of Matrilateral Cross-Cousin Marriage" (Leach), 84
structuralism, 35
Structure of Folk Models, The (Holy and Stuchlik), 83
subaks, 76–77
subjective/objective dichotomies, 2
subjectivity, 4, 6; "metabiological" intersubjectivity, 57; and order, 2. *See also* science, as the imposition of subjectivity
substantivist/formalist controversy, 36
Swat Pathan factionalism, 84, 87
symbols, 17

Tambiah, Stanley, 19, 84
Tax, Sol, 35, 119
technology/technologies: causes of technological development, 36–37; effect of population increases on, 37; factors determining effectiveness of, 36–37; indigenous, 35, 36; logic of, 72; traditional/primitive systems of, 37–38
theory/fact disparity, 87
"Theory of Real-Life Choice, A" (Gladwin), 36
Thomas, W. I., 21
Thunder Over Arizona (1956), 145, 147–48, 223n1
Tonga: marriage and the *fahu* custom in, 208–10; social ranking in, 207
TongaSim, 77, 207
Tonnies, Ferdinand, 29
Tractatus (Wittgenstein), 10–11
Transforming Traditional Agriculture (Schultz), 35
Tribe, Caste, and Nation (Bailey), 87
Trobriand Islanders, systems of trade of, 113
Tsembaga Maring people (Papua), 33; and the *kaiko* ceremony, 33, 34

244

Index

Turing, Alan, 80
Turnbull, Colin, 19
Turner, Victor, 84, 178
Tylor, Edward, 3

Urban, Greg, 130

Vatuk, Sylvia, 72
Vienna Circle, 3, 221n3
Vlado, Andrej, 79
Volkerpsychologie, 4, 40

Wagner, Roy, 21
Wallace, Anthony, 104
Warren, Michael, 90
Watson, Patty Jo, 65
Wax, Murray, 1
Weaver, Warren, 131, 132
Weber, Max, 3, 4, 29
wedding ceremonies, of the Sikh religion, 177,
    178–82, 184–90, 223nn1–2; and the "Asa
    di War" ("Song of Hope") prayer, 180; cir-
cumambulation of the Guru Granth Sahib,
182; drinking associated with, 179–80;
and factionalism, 187; and gift giving
(*kaTH*), 182, 184–85, 189–90; indispensable
ceremony (*anand*) of, 180; instruction as
integral to the ceremony, 180–81; minor
ceremonies associated with, 178–79; role of
the Barber caste member in, 179, 180, 185;
role of the *brāt* (wedding party) in, 187–89;
role of the Guru Granth Sahib in, 180, 181;
women's ceremonies in, 185–86
Whale, Ronald, 79
White, Douglas, 71, 79, 167, 172–73
Whitehead, Alfred North, 10, 11
Windelband, Wilhelm, 56
Wissler, Clark, 3
Wittgenstein, Ludwig, 10–11, 58
World Bank, 217
Wundt, Wilhelm, 4, 17, 40

Zammito, John H., 222n1
Zimmer-Tomaloshi, Laura, 32

MURRAY J. LEAF is Professor of Anthropology and Political Economy, University of Texas at Dallas; Speaker of the Faculty, University of Texas at Dallas; Member, University of Texas System Faculty Advisory Council; and Member, Editorial Board of Mathematical Anthropology and Cultural Theory. He teaches undergraduate courses on comparative religion, law and society, cultural ecology, and South Asia. Graduate courses include ethics and socioeconomic development. He holds a BA in philosophy from Reed College and a PhD in social anthropology from the University of Chicago. He has served as the Senior Social Scientist on USAID-sponsored development projects in India and Bangladesh and as a consultant for the United Nations Centre for Regional Development in Nagoya, Japan. His monographs include *Information and Behavior in a Sikh Village: Social Organization Reconsidered* (University of California Press, 1972), *Man, Mind, and Science: A History of Anthropology* (Columbia University Press, 1979), *Song of Hope* (Rutgers University Press, 1984), and *Pragmatism and Development* (Bergin and Garvey, 1998). His articles cover a wide range of topics including the meaning of marriage ceremonies, the language issue in South Asia, household economics, the relationship between irrigation and social organization, law and legal decision making, the Sikh religion, the relationship between government centralization and the causes of violent secessionist movements, the green revolution, and the evolution of agricultural systems.

The University of Illinois Press
is a founding member of the
Association of American University Presses.

Composed in 10.5/13 Adobe Minion
with Adobe Minion display
by BookComp, Inc.
Manufactured by Thomson-Shore, Inc.

University of Illinois Press
1325 South Oak Street
Champaign, IL 61820-6903
www.press.uillinois.edu